A Collection of Lo

by Ken Howe

as featured in

Teddington TW11

TW Magazines

Acknowledgements

The author wishes to acknowledge the help and kind assistance of friends and colleagues of The Teddington Society History Group, especially Paddy Ching, Dick & Gillie Hughes, the Borough of Twickenham Local History Society, John Sheaf, Mike Cherry and Ed Harris in particular, and the London Borough of Richmond Local Studies Library. And lastly his two lovely editors, Dawn Stoddart and Christiane Ella, without whose kind guidance and assistance this book would would not have happened.

First published 2020 by TW Magazines
www.twmagazines.co.uk

British Library Cataloguing in Publication Data. A catalogue record for this book is available from the British Library.

Printed in the UK.

ISBN 978-1-5272-7235-4

A Collection of Local History Articles

Publisher & Editor: Christiane Ella, TW Magazines
Author: Ken Howe
Designer: David J. Scawn, PDS Print
Editorial Support: Mary Bennett & Christina Haindl @ The Word Sanctum, Teddington copywriters supporting local business. www.thewordsanctum.co.uk; Instagram @thewordsanctum.
Marketing & Distribution: Teddington Together; www.teddingtontogether.org

Publishing information
Printed in the UK by PDS Print; www.pdsprint.co.uk

Distribution requests
Please send all enquiries to Ken Howe, howe64@btinternet.com or call 020 8943 1513. We love to work with independent bookshops and local sellers.

Sponsored by PDS Print, UK Book Binders, and Premier Paper Group

Contents

Foreword

Our little corner of south west London marks the end of the tidal Thames and is blessed with a rich and fascinating history. For many years I've been lucky enough to call the area home, and in 2018, after taking over as editor and publisher of TW Magazines, I was introduced to local historian and author Ken Howe. Since 2012, Ken's painstaking research and dedication has brought the Teddington of old to life in a series of articles published in the magazine. This book is the culmination of his work.

Ken is a much respected and well-known figure in the local area, and a resounding voice of authority. A lifelong resident of Teddington, his research into the area began in earnest in 1985, since which time he has published numerous articles, papers and books on Teddington's history.

Readers of the magazine will be familiar with Ken's trademark wit and warmth, and his ability to educate and entertain through his writing. *A Collection of Local History Articles* takes us on a revealing journey back in time, where we learn not only about the history of Teddington but also the stories of those who once called it home.

I'm thrilled to have played a part in bringing Ken's work to a wider audience and hope you enjoy stepping back in time to Teddington's past as much as I have.

Christiane Ella
Editor & Publisher
TW Magazines

Introduction

It was in the late summer of 2012 when Dawn Stoddart, the-then editor of TW Magazines, contacted me. The magazine had started in September 2010 and had included some local history articles that had gone down well with the readers. Dawn was looking for a regular columnist and someone had suggested my name.

I had been interested in history since childhood and started to take it seriously when I became too old to be knocked around the park every Saturday playing rugby. I had joined the History Group of The Teddington Society and the Borough of Twickenham Local History Society where I met many interesting and learned colleagues. This led to long hours in the Local Studies Library, first at Twickenham and latterly Richmond, digging into old files and books to research some aspects of Teddington History.

My pet subject was the Bronze Age Barrow in Sandy Lane, which I started in 1985 and led to my paper being published in 2005. As regular readers of the magazine will know, we now have an illustrated plaque at the site of the Barrow to tell all and sundry what it was.

I started writing Teddington history with friends of The Teddington Society and published *"Teddington Past and Present"* in 1994. The following year I wrote *"Hampton and Teddington Past"* with my friend John Sheaf and since then several picture books have been published. My last major work was *"Edwardian Teddington"* where I edited the journal of a lifelong Teddington lady.

Dawn and I met over a coffee or two and hit it off, with the result that I started my history column in October 2012 with issue No. 26. I said at that time that I intended to bring up some interesting facts and stories about Teddington people and places and I hope, eight years on, that I have achieved this.

As I've told many people, it is not difficult to challenge something that has been put into print...the difficulty lies in putting the facts into print in the first place.

I have met many wonderful people in the course of writing my articles, all of whom have contributed something towards the quality and continuity of my work. I'm stopped in pubs, shops, restaurants, the street, at bus stops and even on a hospital trolley when I was being wheeled into a clinic for a nasty procedure (thank you, Chris Jarvis). Thank you all. I love meeting and talking to you and acting on what you have to tell me.

When Christiane Ella took over TW Magazines from Dawn I was ready to quietly retire, but Christiane enjoyed the articles and hence they continue to roll.

Many readers wanted to know how to access old articles, right back to the beginning, for their collections. Well here we are – thanks to Christiane – the complete set. Thank you all and keep the stories coming.

Ken Howe,
September 2020

The Bronze Age Barrow

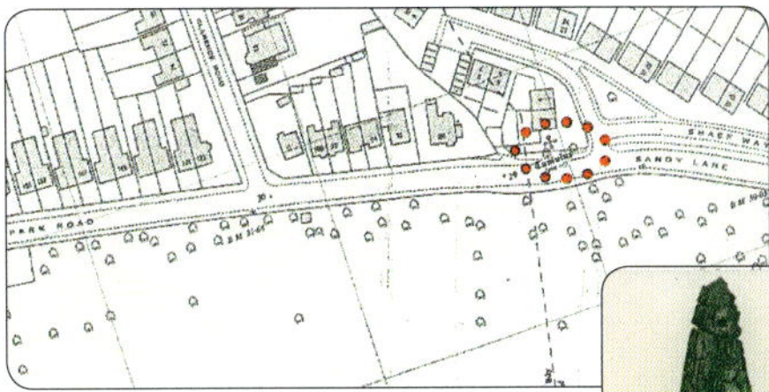

ONE OF THE MOST AMAZING features of Teddington History is that we have or probably more correctly, had a Bronze Age barrow in the town. One of only three in the Greater London area, out of about 40,000 in the country.

Our barrow stood at Sandy Lane, about 350 yards from the Teddington gate to Bushy Park. At its peak, it was 12'3" high and 96' in diameter; it must have been an imposing landmark for miles around. The earliest record I have discovered of this is in Charles Bridgeman's map of the Bushy Park estate of 1730. It is shown as a tumulus at the side of the main road to Kingston. It was known as Barrow Hill and was in Barrow Field. Various local rumours arose about it and some claimed it to be a mass grave for victims of the Great Plague. This so disconcerted William IV, then Duke of Clarence and living in Bushy Park, that he blocked all attempts to investigate it.

The barrow withstood the enclosure of Bushy Park in Wolsey's day, although it may have lost its southern tip in road widening, and also the Teddington Enclosure Act of 1800 when all of the common land was apportioned amongst the existing landowners. Fifty-eight acres of copyhold land granted to Thomas Davis Esq included the barrow. It was suggested that Field Lane which turns south from the High Street, was the pathway to the barrow from the old town centre.

It is not clear what resurrected interest in the barrow; maybe rumours that the new railway was to cut through it, or perhaps the new national pastime of archaeology found its way to Teddington. The Surrey Archaeological Society was formed in 1853 and they sought permission from the landowner to excavate the barrow. On their first anniversary – 30th June 1854 – 150 members and visitors held their first AGM, lunched at the Griffin in the marketplace and then set off across Kingston Bridge for their first ever 'dig' at the site.

They quickly found evidence of treasure hunters and other signs that the barrow had been disturbed but they pressed on to the very centre of the mound and were rewarded to find a pile of burnt bones on which had been placed a fine bronze dagger. On the floor of the grave were several fragments of charcoal and pieces of worked flint. A second day's digging revealed a second cremation only four feet below the apex and later, the bones of a third burial, an adult buried superficially were found.

As archaeology was in its infancy at that time, there was no plan or sketch of the site ever made and the interesting finds seem to have been dispersed amongst the members nearest to the diggers. The following year the London and Middlesex Archaeological Society was formed and all finds were handed over to them. At their second AGM, their President Rev Thomas Hugo exhibited the dagger and a flint from the barrow. In 1860 it was reported that the dagger had 'suffered considerably from incautious handling' and would not be shown again. Indeed there is no record of it ever being seen again!

The barrow itself has come to a sorry end. As housing and road widening have moved in, an electricity sub-station has been installed on what remains of this once impressive site.

I have spent many years following clues to the whereabouts of the finds from the barrow but have only succeeded in tracing some of the flints that were discovered. An array of very interesting people have come to light in the course of my enquiries and these would provide the basis for a Victorian mystery drama themselves. Anyone wishing to known a little of this saga should obtain *The Bronze Age Barrow at Teddington* by me, available at Waterstones price £3.

Borough Plans

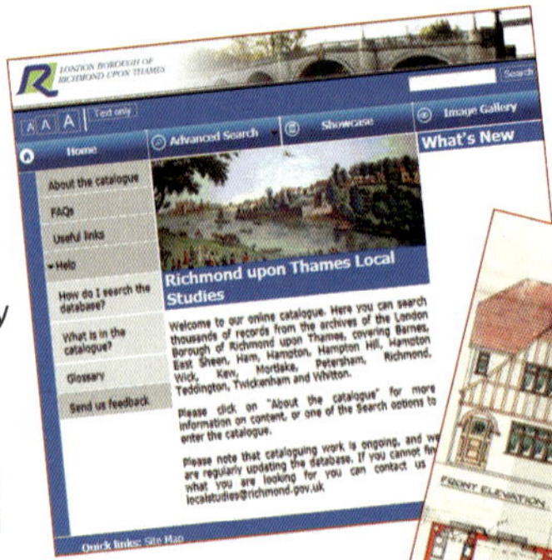

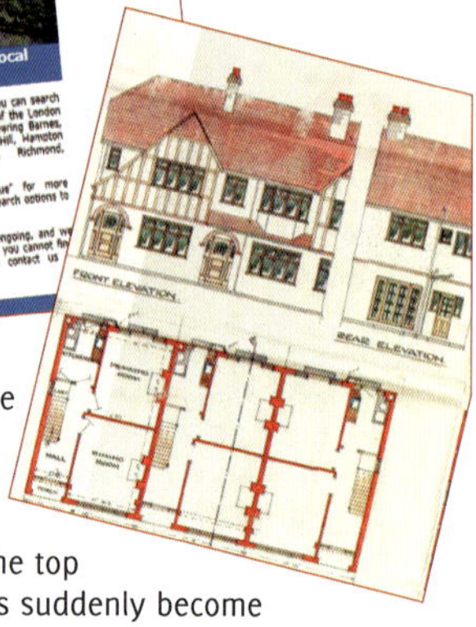

WHILST REVIEWING VARIOUS buildings owned by the Council, attention was given to a rather miserable and near-derelict hut in a remote part of the Borough looking ready for demolition. A cursory look inside revealed that it was crammed with over 160 cranes of paper. A closer inspection revealed these papers to be building plans; in fact the plan for every building in the Borough whether newly built, altered or extended for the approximate period of 1870–1960. Quite how they got there has been lost in the mists of time but the pressing question was what to do with them.

A councillor asked our local studies librarian, Jane Baxter, if they were of any use or value. Seeing their potential, Jane quickly laid claim to them and set about devising a way of bringing the plans to the public without commanding an enormous amount of space. A scheme was put together to put in a Heritage Lottery Fund grant to digitise the plans and create a website, matching the Heritage monies with labour from a volunteer force. A team of 40 volunteers set about sifting through the weather stained boxes.

Some of the plans were completely ruined but there was sufficient of every type of building to enable us to capture the designs of the past decades. The majority of the plans related to the building of private dwellings but also included were all manner of commercial buildings, shops, office blocks, public houses, factories, restaurants and even a theatre (which was never built) as well as all alterations and extensions.

The grant was awarded and 18 months of hard and diligent work paid off to create a unique record of the buildings in the Borough since 1870/80. Because of the sheer mass of documents available, it was not possible to select every record for digitisation and some painful decisions were made as to what should be copied and what should be left out. The result is a marvellous collection of plans easily available on the web. I have discovered my house, so it can't be that difficult.

To access the site, type in **www.calmview.eu/Richmond/calmview.** Insert Teddington in the search box at the top right and 2,432 records suddenly become available, 1,377 of which will be building plans. Alternatively you may enter the name of the road you are seeking and then scroll down alphabetically until you find your record. The degree of information given will depend entirely on the level that was logged onto the catalogue initially. For example some plans may be accompanied by photographs.

Once the individual street plans are shown, you will see that each plan will have a PLA prefix eg PLA/01565. This should show the date of the application, the name of the road, the local authority involved, the type of planning (new build etc), the name of the architect and/or the builder and a thumbnail sketch of the actual building plan. Click on the plan and this will bring up a full screen copy of the plan.

To demonstrate the good work that has been done, an exhibition has been arranged to run concurrently at Richmond Museum from 2nd December 2012 to March 2013 and Orleans House Gallery again from 2nd December to February 2013. Entitled *The Building of a Borough* it will show many framed plans, some for air raid shelters and for the re-building after the war. Admission is free and a comprehensive free catalogue is also provided.

The Kensits at Teddington

IN 1884 THE VERY AMBITIOUS Rev Francis Leith Boyd came to Teddington at the invitation of the Earl of Bradford. He had heard of the rapid expansion of the village from 1,183 people in 1861 to 6,599 in 1881 and saw that St Mary's Church, already extended on two sides, was not going to be big enough to support what was still a growing population.

He set about a massive fund raising campaign and the new church of St Alban's began to take shape. Although it was not yet completed, a service of dedication took place on 8th July 1889. Such was the power of Boyd's oratory that the new church was packed to bursting on Sundays with people coming from miles around to listen to him; so much so that the Surrey Comet reported that it was impossible to close the doors for the numbers inside and trying to get inside.

With such solid support, Boyd decided to extend things and introduced founder's day – the feast of St Alban – on 17th June each year. I am not sure when these festivals commenced, the first report occurs in 1907.

But first a word about the Kensits or to give them their full title – the Kensit Wickliffe Preachers. This was an extremist group of the Protestant Truth Society, founded by John Kensit, to make sure that the Anglican Church remained Protestant and did not slip back to Roman Catholicism. They objected to the high church rituals and the wearing of vestments and urged a return to plain ceremonies.

Teddington had long held high church tendencies; indeed Boyd's predecessor Rev Daniel Trinder caused such a rift with his congregation for his 'popish' habits that a section of them had broken away to form the Free Church of Christ in 1864.

The idea of the festival was for communion to be celebrated at the church and then a procession led by the cross bearer with two red cassocked and white surpliced acolytes bearing lighted candles on either side, then Rev Boyd and the other alter boys carrying various banners, the choir again in full clerical dress, a local

St Alban's Church, now the Landmark Arts Centre

John Kensit, founder of the Protestant Truth Society

band, various church guilds etc, to march from the church to the foot of the railway bridge, turning at the council offices at Elmfield House and returning to the church.

Such high church activity was anathema to the Kensits, who, by now, had gained support from several quarters, and they were determined to voice their opinion at the procession. As soon as it started from the Church, a group of five Kensits appeared, raising banners and chanting cries of 'No Popery' along the route of the procession. All went well until on the return leg, the priest and church officials having gone back into the Church, some members of the public made a rush for the Kensits.

The Thames Valley Times tells us that *'The gentleman holding a single banner lost his silk hat, and the larger banner was pulled down. For a time there was AN UGLY RUSH but the Police appeared, and dealing diplomatically with the situation, saved further trouble, although several names and addresses were taken.'*

The following year, everyone knew what to expect, *the Richmond & Twickenham Times* reported that *'disorderly scenes were fully anticipated and about 50 policemen were called into service.'* Once again *the Thames Valley Times* had a banner headline of 'RELIGIOUS RIOT' and described *'free fights in various parts of the streets; on all sides black eyes were received and given; women in their excitement pulled off each other's hats and dragged off tufts of hair, and blood was brought on several instances...'*

What had happened was that there was a much bigger crowd than the previous year and shop keepers were decorating their shops with national emblems and bunting. A dozen members of the Thames Valley branch of the Kensits had arrived with a few more from Thornton Heath with some rolled up banners and they attracted a good deal of attention as they took up their position on the corner of Kingston Lane, close to the Church. The vicar came out and surveyed the crowd in the High Street and a short while later, it was announced that the procession was to be postponed, on account of the weather.

This coincided with the Kensits starting to unfurl their banners, thus clearly identifying themselves and the surrounding crowd blamed them for the cancellation of the parade. *The Richmond & Twickenham Times* tells the story:
'No sooner was it known that the procession had been postponed then the crowd made a rush for Kingston Lane. The holder on unfurling his banner was immediately attacked, and before the Police had time to be transferred from the corner of Langham Road, where they were stationed, he had received three blows to the face, two of them badly cutting him. A strong muscular man, on receiving the third blow, struck his assailant full in the face which settled this part of the disturbance.

The Police who displayed considerable tact throughout and only interfered where necessary, then acted as a bodyguard and at their suggestion, escorted the Kensit Crusaders to the railway station. Assailed on either side, banners were wrenched one after the other from the crusaders and trampled into the ground, the sticks being broken in pieces. Threats were freely used and the Kensit party were told that if they ventured so near the Church again, they would be taken to the Thames and given a ducking. The train removing them steamed out at about 11.30am and the crowd slowly dispersed.'

The procession resumed on the following Sunday and this time it was completely under the control of the Police. They allowed the Kensits to join the front of the procession from their point of assembly on the corner of Kingston Lane, with their banners erect. They were followed by a contingent of mounted policemen who ensured that a brisk pace was maintained. Then came the Church party, the Sunday school children, the choir, church workers, the banners and lastly, the Ham and Petersham Brass Band. All went well until the Triangle at Elmfield House; the Kensits turned and were face to face with the Church procession 'and in the centre of a huge crowd who cheered lustily and hissed alternately, the noise created quite drowning the music from the band, the choristers and school children.' A strong police presence prevented any outbreaks of violence.

One might have expected 1909 to continue in the vein of previous years but the event passed off without even a mention in the two local papers. The only evidence that it took place was from a series of photographs by local photographer, Richard Young. Again no reports appeared for 1910, 1911 and 1912. 1913 produced a brief six line article of the occasion and 1914 was similar. The Festival was still observed during the war years although any photographs of those times show a much diminished crowd and a distinct shortage of manpower.

Obviously the war years changed many things in this country and the Festival seems to have fizzled out shortly afterwards. The Protestant Truth Society still exists today but the Kensit Preachers also seem to have died out.

What would 21st Century Teddington make of such goings-on ?

Rev Robert Feron, Vicar of Teddington

VIEWERS OF THE TV series *The Tudors* will know the story of Henry VIII's divorce from Katherine of Aragon and subsequent marriage to Anne Boleyn. The 1530s were turbulent years with most of the population still in favour of Queen Katherine and supporters of the 'Old' religion. Henry charged his Lord Chancellor, Thomas Cromwell, to seek out any dissenters to his new rules and punish them accordingly. Surprisingly, one son of Teddington was caught up in this act of insurrection and was connected to the conspiracy happening at Syon House at the time.

Syon House had become a hotbed of treasonable gossip:
• Cromwell's spies reported in 1534 that 'a fellow of Bristol' had several conversations at Syon about the King's marriage 'and other behaviours of his bodily lust.'
• Richard Reynolds, the confessor at Syon, repeated a conversation with a porter, who claimed that 'our sovereign lord has a company of maidens over one of the chambers at Farnham (Castle) while he was staying there with the old Bishop of Winchester.'
• Thomas Moody, a priest had written to Robert Feron (or Fern), a young priest of Teddington, that Henry had meddled with Anne's sister.
• John Haile, the vicar of Isleworth said the King's life was 'more foul and more stinking than a sow wallowing and defiling herself in any filthy place. For however great he is, he is fully given to his foul pleasure of the flesh ... Look how many matrons be in court or given to marriage – these almost all he has violated, so often neglecting his duty to his wife and offending the sacrament of matrimony. Now he has taken to this matron Anne, not only to the highest shame and undoing of himself but also of all this realm.'

Cromwell acted swiftly and Reynolds, Haile and Feron and the Priors of three Carthusian Houses found themselves in the Tower, under arrest. A special commission was set up to hear two clear and separate indictments. The first against Reynolds and the priors for simply rejecting the

ABOVE: Syon House
RIGHT: Henry VIII's enforcer, Thomas Cromwell

Act of Supremacy, passed on 18th November 1534. Haile and Feron were charged with offences committed between 2nd–20th May that year, six months before that Act became law but were held in violation of the Act for the Establishment of the King's Succession. Both Haile and Feron pleaded Not Guilty originally but changed their plea to Guilty after being remanded.

All six were found guilty of high treason and sentenced to the traitor's death of hanging, drawing and quartering. On 4th May 1535, Reynolds, Haile and the priors were dragged on sheep hurdles from the Tower of London to Tyburn. There they were hanged until half dead, cut down, castrated and their vital organs ripped from their bodies and burnt. Finally their corpses were beheaded and quartered. The scaffold was like a gigantic gory butcher's block. Reynolds' head was stuck on a pike above the gatehouse of Syon Abbey as a warning of Henry's vengeance towards all transgressors against his laws and policies.

But what of Teddington's Robert Feron? Somewhere along the line, he received a pardon. It was officially stated that this was on account of 'his youth' but this would appear to have been a euphemism for turning King's evidence.

We know Feron returned to Teddington as his name appears on the list of incumbents from 1535 to 1554. However his name does not appear in any other form of documentation, although if his evidence had sent five people to the gallows, it should not be surprising that he would want to keep a low profile.

The Coming of the Railway

TEDDINGTON IN THE EIGHTEENTH century was a very different place to the Teddington we see today and very little change took place in the first half of the nineteenth century. A census of 1801 shows a small agricultural village with a population of 699 people living in 123 houses.

By 1841 the census required more detailed information and this shows 1,199 people living in 215 houses. Discounting wives, children and about 150 domestic servants, there were 570 others who consisted of 50 gardeners, 10 farmers and 78 agricultural labourers, 12 working on the river, 35 in the building trades and 40 shopkeepers. The only trade noted was candle making in Fry's Lane (now Waldegrave Road) which employed 15 people. There was little change by 1851; in fact the population had dropped to 1,146 people in 212 houses.

In the meantime, the Richmond Railway Bill received the royal ascent on 21st July 1845 and the London & South Western Railway line opened at Richmond Station a year later. It was estimated that this would carry 767,104 passengers per annum. Enquiries had been made to take the line to Kingston but because of their very financially viable coaching interests, they rejected the proposals and the line went to Surbiton instead.

The Lord of Teddington manor, Thomas Woodrouffe Smith, had died in 1812 and the manor had been administered in trust on behalf of his two daughters. Ann who married John Barton but died without producing an heir and Maria who married George Head Head and also died without offspring. John Barton was a trustee of the manor but George Head Head was not. John Barton remarried and went on to have six children. After some lengthy negotiations, the Barton family came to own all of the manor lands. John Barton died in 1852 and on his advice the estate was broken up and put up for sale in small building plots, although this did not take place until 1862.

A young classics master had moved into Hampton Wick in 1854, having accepted a teaching position at Wellesley House School, Twickenham. He was Richard Doddridge Blackmore and in 1857, he inherited a legacy which enabled him to fulfil an early ambition to become 'a gardener and horticulturist' and he purchased land for a market garden in Teddington.

Just when the railway was first mentioned as being of interest to Teddington cannot be pinpointed. In many ways the village blundered along in its own sweet way, almost oblivious to the outside world. In October 1851, Joseph Reed, grocer and overseer of the poor gave a talk to the Mutual Instruction Society in which he said of Teddington 'The salubrious air, the purity of its waters, and the general moral tone and habits of the people, are advantages that are not to be found in many if any other villages in the kingdom.' This was rather fanciful and it is highly probable that the air was anything but salubrious. The drainage ditch in the High Street pioneered by Rev Stephen Hales one hundred years earlier, had become clogged 'and been allowed to become a stagnant and putrid open ditch' and was the cause of a running battle between the Vestry and the Metropolitan Commissioners of Sewers.

The proposal was for the railway to be continued from Twickenham, through to Teddington and stopping at Kingston. The Railway set about buying up land on which to lay the track. They purchased a narrow strip of land from the Barton Trustees which included the village pond and the Cricket Club.

The pond was filled in and this conveniently ended squabbles over the village drain. The Cricket Club was given notice to quit and latterly platforms were built on the site of the wicket. Fortunately royalty came to their rescue and granted them facilities in Bushy Park where they still are today.

A further Act of Parliament was enacted giving the green light for an extension of the line from Twickenham to Kingston via Teddington. There were protests from Kingston but the councillors having recognised the lost opportunity of 1845, were not going to make the same mistake again. An amendment to the bill introduced a further station at Hampton Wick.

In the centre of the village, one of the oldest inns had been following the progress of the railway with interest. The Duke of Clarence Arms decided to upgrade its premises to be able to offer something more beneficial to the modern rail traveller. It closed its doors, demolished the old inn and rebuilt on the same site The Clarence Hotel which opened on 1st July 1863.

One would have thought that Blackmore would have welcomed the coming of the railway as a quick way of getting his produce into the London markets but perhaps because he was forced to sell some land to the London & South Western, he fell out with them and carried a running grudge for many years. However he did force them to build the pedestrian footbridge to the south of the station.

Work on the track of the railway must have been a massive undertaking and must have started no later than June 1861 as the plan required a road bridge to be constructed over the railway line at the High Street. Hundreds of tons of sand and gravel were dug out of ground off Sandy Lane. So much so that when the construction was completed, it was possible to reform the village pond from the hole in the ground.

The bridge building was far more onerous than the laying of the track and took two years, during which time the village was literally cut in half with access being gained from one side to the other only by the crossing at Shacklegate Junction to the north or by the level crossing at the gasworks to the south. When opened the road to the west was named Broad Street and the road to the east retained the name High Street, a lasting division to the once simple track going through the centre of the village.

The great day came – 1st July 1863 – the new length of track was opened with new stations Teddington, Hampton Wick and Kingston also opened that same day.

The immediate consequences of the rail were growth. The Clarence Hotel had opened and The Adelaide Inn followed suit shortly afterwards. The Railway Refreshment Rooms (later The Railway Hotel) came slightly later in 1869. The 1871 census shows 4,063 people in 788 houses, 1881 shows 6,599 in 1,216 houses, 1891 shows 10,052 in 1,935 houses and by 1901 we had 14,038 in 2,756 houses. The coming of the railway had turned the village into a town.

The Maypole Murder of 1710

THE FESTIVAL OF MAYDAY has been celebrated in Northern Europe for centuries. No one seems to know quite where it came from but all agree that it involves the erection of a maypole, decorating it with coloured stings or ropes and dancing around it in a fashion that interweaves the strings.

In England it was banned by Henry VIII and reinstated by Queen Mary. It was again banned by Cromwell and the Commonwealth but bounced back under the Restoration. Teddington was no different from any other village and had its maypole roughly opposite Queen Elizabeth's Hunting Box, a lodge sometimes used by Queen Elizabeth when hunting in Bushy and Home Parks, at the junction of High Street and what was to become Udney Park Road.

An 18th Century Maypole Celebration

Queen Elizabeth's Hunting Box

It became the fashion for villages to send parties to neighbouring villages for the purpose of stealing each other's maypoles. Something like this was about to happen on the night of 18th May 1710 when a gang of Twickenham lads arrived to seize the Teddington maypole when they met a crowd of Teddington youths determined to retain it. In the melee that ensued a Teddington boy, John Roust, was struck on the head with a wooden staff and rendered unconscious. The attackers dispersed without their souvenir.

The senior resident of Teddington at that time was Sir Charles Duncombe, an ex MP, retired Sheriff of the City of London and Lord Mayor of London in 1708. He was also a goldsmith and banker of some renown and said to be the richest man in England. When he heard of this incident, he was incandescent with rage and ordered the arrest of the perpetrators.

Thus "William Cripp, Benjamin Goodwin, and James Rabb of the Parish of Twittenham were all three indicted for the Murder of John Roust by giving him one mortal Wound with a wooden Staff upon the Head, on 18th May last, of which he languished till 9th June following and then dy'd." Sir Charles directed the jury at the Coroner's Inquest at Teddington to find them "Guilty" and from there, they were bound over to Newgate Jail for trial at the Old Bailey.

The tale is well told by Lady Isabella Wentworth, who spent her summers on Twickenham's riverside at her son Lord Raby's house, recorded the local gossip about the event in her letters. She had a rather eccentric way of spelling as she wrote to her correspondent :
"Most of the young men of this town are in Newgate. It seems its a custom in thees country towns for the young men to steel the Maypoale

from one to the other, soe all the young men of Twitnam went to Whitton and they it seems had notice of it, soe was upon thear gard and fought for it. It was in the dark, and they had not been known only one of them to save himself told the rest, and one of the Whitten men is dead and another very ill, but he its thought will recover. Sir Charls Duncome livs at Whitten, soe he must be for his own towns men. One of thees poore wretchis was brought home hear last night dead of the small pox, ..., he is much lamented."

Unfortunately her letter was not dated but the Old Bailey Sessions were held on 6th 7th 8th and 9th September 1710. It was reported "It appeared that the Deceas'd came by his death in a Fray, ... But their appearing no positive Evidence against any of the Prisoners, the Jury acquitted them."

Lady Wentworth was forced to amend her letter and correct some of the details : "I told you a great lye in a former letter, that thear was a great many of the young men of this town in Newgate, but thear was but twoe, most of the rest run away; one of those twoe dyed thear, and yesterday the other was quitted, which was your poor glazier's son, whoe is grown very poor, being laime this great while." This still greatly contradicts the Old Bailey indictment but gives the only information of the death of one of the accused prisoners, unfortunately without naming him.

She goes on "Its said Sir Charles Dunckom made the jury at Tedinton bring it in murder, but the jury at London brought it chanc medly. Al this town hate Dunckom and Secretary Johnson, (James Johnson - Secretary of State built and lived at Orleans House, Twickenham) for he said he would have them all hanged ... P.S. Just now I hear Dunckom is soe much concerned for the death of that poor good young man that dyed in Newgate, that he has been a friend to this and bayled him his own self."

Such a course of action seems very out of character for Sir Charles but he was a very

Sir Charles Dunkom

political animal and may well have reacted to the adverse opinion given to him, arising out of his earlier actions. He died the following year and no further reference seems to have been made to this incident.

What we do know is that John Roust died from his injuries, that Cripp, Goodwin and Babb were charged and acquitted and that Sir Charles Duncombe made himself very unpopular with the populace of Twickenham. One or more of the prisoners may have caught smallpox in Newgate and one seems to have died whilst imprisoned there.

Many years later, the maypole was found rotting away in a churchyard against a fence. A sad end to the whole affair.

Ref.

Old Bailey Proceedings Online
Twickenham Society in Queen Anne's Reign from the Letters of Isabella Wentworth by D H Simpson (BOTLHS no. 35) 1976

James Messenger: Bargemaster and Boatbuilder

IT IS EASY TO IMAGINE that any town on a river would have a long tradition of boat building in some form or another. And so I thought that Teddington would be no exception but that was not quite true.

Boatbuilding seems to have started here with a man named James Arthur Messenger. He was born in Twickenham in 1826, the son of James and Sarah Messenger. James Senior worked on the river at Twickenham, probably as a fisherman and the two had six children including James Arthur. James Senior died and the family move off the radar for a few years and later re-emerged in the 1841 Census at Water Lane Teddington. Sarah has remarried to John Francis, fisherman. James Arthur then became apprenticed to John Francis on 14th October 1841 as a waterman. His apprenticeship ended in 1848 and he was 'freed' on 7th November. Almost the first thing he did in his independent state was to marry a seamstress, Charlotte Sarah Johnson in that same year.

By 1851 he is described as a waterman, someone who carries people by water, living at 20 Water Lane with his wife Charlotte, daughter Emily aged 2 and son William aged 5 months. Also living in the house are his stepfather John Francis aged 66, His mother Sarah aged 70, Samuel Kemp 36 a fisherman and James Brown an apprentice aged 16. A trade directory of 1853 lists him as 'Boatbuilder and Waterman at the Lock'. A few years later he took part in the World Sculling Championships and on 20th November 1854, he beat Tom Cole, the reigning champion to take the title which he held for three years.

The 1861 census saw him now living at 31 Water Lane with Charlotte, Emily now 12, William now 10, James A Jnr aged 8, Charles aged 6, Walter aged 4, Wilhelmina aged 1 and an apprentice Henry Harris aged 20. He is described as a Boatbuilder and Waterman employing 4 men and 3 boys. Sarah had died in 1853 and John, his stepfather, in 1856 in Kingston Workhouse. At some point around this time, he must have been made a Queen's an honour which is only bestowed on the most accomplished watermen for 1862; he was appointed Royal Bargemaster, a rank he held until his death.

James Arthur Messenger

By 1868 his advertisements were describing him as 'Barge Master By Appointment To Her Majesty'. They also noted that he had a second boatyard in Kingston and went on to say 'J.A.M. begs to state that he builds Rowing Boats of every description, Eight and Four-Oared Cutters, Pair-Oared, Sculling, Single Streaks, Canoes, Gigs, and every kind of Boats on the shortist notice, and on reasonable charges.' That same year, he purchased two lots of the old Maude Cottage Estate in Stanley Road for £146.00.

Business was good and obviously Messenger's boats were successful and by 1871 he and his family are in 38 Ferry Road (Water Lane had been renamed). There are James and Charlotte, Emily 22, now in the business as an assistant, William 20, James A Jnr 18, Charles 16, all boatbuilders, Wilhelmina 11, Gertrude 7 and Fanny 5, all at school, Frederick Wooldridge 19, his nephew and a waterman and a domestic servant, Caroline Hallett. He is noted as Boatbuilder and Waterman employing about 30 men.

At this stage in his career, his reputation as a builder of one-off custom made boats was growing and very soon a further commission to add to his fame was about to take place. Dr David Livingstone's body had been returned from Africa for burial in Westminster Abbey in April 1874. Henry Morton Stanley had led the pallbearers and shortly after, was summoned to the office of The Daily Telegraph's

The Queen's Watermen

Edwin Arnold. Interest in Africa was running high after Livingstone's funeral and it was decided in conjunction with the New York Herald to fund a further expedition to finish the work started by Livingstone and both papers wanted Stanley to lead it. Stanley readily agreed and the start date was set for 17th July 1874.

Stanley had designed a boat to be portable and capable of easy inland transit to the African Lakes. The boat which was to be built of Spanish cedar, was in five separate sections, each of which was eight feet long and each section was in two halves to be carried by porters. When assembled, the boat would be 40 feet long with a six feet beam and 30 inches deep. She was to be named Lady Alice after Stanley's fiancée, Alice Pike. The search for a boat builder to carry this assignment was on. Quite what happened next is unclear but in later years the owner of the Telegraph recounted :
'At that time I had a small Country house at Twickenham, and in river matters relied upon the well-known firm of Messengers.'

Stanley wrote to Messenger and met him for lunch at The Anglers Hotel. Messenger was pleased to take on the commission and agreed to the building, testing and shipping before the expedition date. In his next set of advertisements, he would go on describe his achievements thus :
'Builder of the five-section Boat 'Lady Alice,' the Livingstone Expedition Boat; Builder of the 'Nautilus' Canoe belonging to W A Baden Powell Esq, ... Builder the five-section twin-screw Steam Launch 'Daisy' for the Church Missionary Society etc.' He had also established another yard at Raven's Ait, Surbiton.

1881, James Arthur is taking something of a back seat and his son William Arthur is running the business with his nephew Frederick Wooldridge. Two other sons, Walter and Herbert are

Lady Alice

also in the business but James Jnr and Charles have both moved on. James Snr is now described solely as Bargemaster. William is doing well and is also a Queen's Waterman and deputy bargemaster, giving swimming lessons to members of the royal family.

At some point between the 1881 and 1891 censuses, something went wrong and the business empire fell apart. The Kingston and Surbiton yards were either sold or closed. The royal barge which was housed in Messenger's Boathouse and 'was jealously guarded by him' was moved to the Kensington Museum (it now sits in the National Maritime Museum at Greenwich). William is still boat building along with two sons, nephew Frederick is a waterman and James has moved to High Street and is still Bargemaster.

Disaster struck in 1892 when his daughter Emily died in the January and his wife, Charlotte, died in the June. This must have put a strain on James and the fire seems to have gone out of his advertisements. More bad luck was to follow in November 1899 when William, aged only 48, died suddenly. Both the Queen and Princess Beatrice sent wreaths to his funeral. This was a blow from which James never fully recovered. Already William had been carrying out some of his duties as Royal Bargemaster and these were now taken on by a grandson. James moved into William's widow's house where he too died in June 1901.

The Messenger Empire had dispersed as quickly as it had grown.

Robbery on The Thames

STROLLING ALONG THE TOWPATH on an afternoon, the River Thames is usually the very idyll of peace and tranquillity. With the sun streaming down and a gentle breeze blowing, it is hard to consider violent acts having any connection with the Thames. Yet such things did occur and fortunately we have the records to back them up.

The first lock was opened on 20th June 1811. It was 150 feet long, 20 feet wide and originally had circular gates. The lock keeper was Richard Savory and he was paid 36s out of which he had to find coals, candles and other necessaries.

On the morning of 28th March 1818 Richard Savory had risen early and was working in his office when he heard a man's voice calling to say that a barge was heading for the lock. When he opened the door, he was overpowered by three men: 'I was thrown with violence over a chair and came rolling to ye ground and then I felt one of them cover my head with a sack and press it so close down that I really began to fear they meant to suffocate me. I heard the third man opening desks and cupboards and he called out to the men that held me – If the Old Bugger won't be quiet, stick it into him!'

The robbers escaped with 'about 11 or 12 single pound notes and full six pounds silver and ye most part small silver and four or five shillings in copper.' Savory said 'I do indeed much fear that this is only ye beginning, for whichever lock receives much value it will be a temptation to such villains to make an attempt at ye end of ye week.'

These words were to prove quite prophetic and on 20th April 1828, thieves struck again. *The Morning Chronicle* carried the story: 'They broke open the house by means of a large iron crow bar; and having gained an entrance, they entered the bedroom of the lock keeper with their faces disguised with black crepe. One of them presented a pistol at the head of the old man (Richard Savory), and desired him to be quiet or he would blow his brains out.' They made off with money and as much other property as they could carry.

A few days later, a man was walking in Kingston and noticed a child playing with a medallion, which rolled into a ditch. On retrieving it for the child, he noticed an inscription giving Mr Savory's name, address and date of birth but it was not until a week later that he read a report of the burglary and recognised Savory's name. He contacted the Police at Kingston and this led to the arrest of Charles Kite aged 25, William Wheatley aged 29, George King aged 23 and the leader William Young.

Young decided to turn King's evidence and shopped the other three. In the course of the trial it came to light that Young was not a stranger to giving King's evidence, having done so once before in which he testified against his brother or brother-in-law, thus sentencing him to death. Kite, Wheatley and King were all found guilty and sentenced to death. On 20th April 1929 they were hanged at Horsemonger Lane Prison to the delight of a huge crowd which extended in all directions as far as the eye could reach.

Two years later, William Young was indicted for breaking and entering the house of Robert Gordon at Harmondsworth on 12th May and stealing a side of bacon, a jacket and several items. Young defended himself stating that the King's pardon absolved him of all crimes and that there was no evidence against him despite the stolen bacon being found under his bed and being arrested wearing the stolen jacket. Young's luck had now run out. He was found guilty, sentenced to death and hanged.

What of Richard Savory? He was granted an assistant (his son) and a blunderbuss with a bayonet for future protection.

What's in a Name?

– TEDDINGTON, TUDINTUN, TOTTYNGTUN OR TODYGTON ?

'Twenty bridges from Tower to Kew
(Twenty bridges or twenty two)
Wanted to know what the River knew
For they were young and the Thames was old
And this is the tale that the River told:

"I walk my beat before London Town,
Five hours up and seven down,
Up I go till I end my run
At Tide-end-town which is Teddington."

LITTLE DID RUDYARD KIPLING know the problems he would set for local Teddington historians when he penned these now famous words in 1911. Although to be fair to him, he was not the first to make Tide-end-town out of Teddington.

The Rev Daniel Lysons discussed the etymology in his *Environs of London* in 1795 and came to the conclusion that it must have come from the Saxon 'Tyd-end-ton'. The only problem with this is that this appears to be a form of spelling that does not appear ever have been used.

S C Hall also supported this explanation in his *Book of the Thames* in 1859.

James Thorne looked at the issue in 1876 in his *Handbook to the Environs of London* and in quoting the now popular legend, also noted that this explanation is the 'one adopted by the Emperor, Napoleon III in his *CESAR*.' However in later years, he dismissed the tide-end theory because of so many variations in the spelling.

In 1909, Kenneth Ingram produced *A Short History of the Parish of Teddington*, reciting the Napoleon

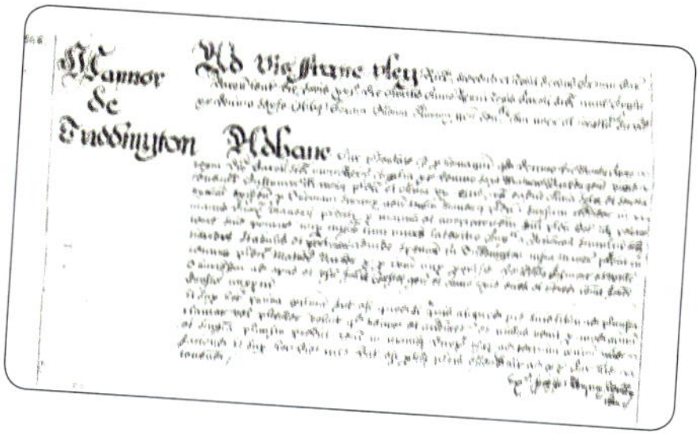

connection stating that Napoleon III favoured the view that 'TED' meant 'TIDE'.

Two years later, Kipling wrote *The River's Tale* as a commission for C R I Fletcher's *A History of England* (1911) and there it was in print for all to see.

Going back to Lysons, he definitely hedged his bets when he produced two early spellings – 'Todynton' and 'Totyngton' which he attempted to break down into their component parts:
'TOD' or 'TOT' or 'TOTE' – which is not defined
'YN' or 'YNG' – a meadow
'TON' – an enclosure.

Writing in parish magazine in 1875, Rev Daniel Trinder followed this theme and produced some early spellings of his own, namely 'Tuddington', 'Todyngton' and 'Totyngton' and produced the following interpretation:-
'TUDD' or 'TOD' or 'TOT' – a small grove
'ING' or 'YNG' – a meadow or pasture
'TON' – an enclosure or town.

Edward Walford, writing his *Greater London* in 1883 (later reproduced as *Village London* in 1985), generally supported the Trinder theory but threw some doubt on 'TOT' which he claimed meant 'lofty beacon'.

1914 saw a fresh approach on the origin of the name when Sir Montague Sharpe, writing in *The Antiquities of Middlesex* suggested that it was a corruption of 'TOTHILLTOWN' as there had been a Roman 'botontinus' or 'tothill' (an artificial mound probably used as a look-out post) almost opposite the Teddington entrance to Bushy Park.

Local librarian, C S Johnson lectured on the history of Teddington in 1937 and he again cited the Trinder theory, making special emphasis on Teddington Grove, suggesting that this may have been the 'TOT' part of the Saxon name.

More recently when E G Woodward penned 'Teddington Town and All About It Up to 1956', he introduced an additional meaning of 'TOT' as being 'a small tribe' as well as 'a grove'. Unfortunately Mr Woodward did not reveal his sources for this.

Confused or what? Just what is the true origin of the name 'TEDDINGTON'? It is true to say that until the half lock was built at Richmond in 1861, Teddington did mark the end of tidal waters but it must also be borne in mind that the first lock was not constructed here until 1811.

There was a 'Tothill' at the entrance to Bushy Park. It was described as being the size of a haystack and it was dismantled in 1808, we think for roadworks. This may well have been the Bronze Age Barrow excavated in 1854 and subsequently largely removed for road widening. There is a strong possibility that both features were one and the same.

I did come across the will of Aelfflaed, a Saxon ealdorman in 968 AD in which the spelling 'Tudincgatun' is used.

A trip to the Muniments Room at Westminster Abbey revealed the earliest written sources of 'Teddington', going back to pre-conquest times when Teddington was a manor of Westminster Abbey. On examining the documents here, I encountered thirty five different spellings of 'Teddington' from 969 AD to 1736 AD. Where do I go from here?

To arrive at the most probable explanation, it is necessary to refer to the English Placename Society. They have selected as the earliest spelling in common usage – 'TUDINTUN' (969 AD) and have translated this as follows :
'TUD(A) – the name of an Anglo Saxon leader
'IN(G)' – the people of
'TUN' – enclosure/village/farm.

Hence : the village of Tuda's people.
The only Tuda mentioned in the Anglo Saxon Chronicle was the Bishop of Lindisfarne and died of a plague in 664 AD so it seems unlikely that he was the same Tuda of Teddington but given the close proximity to Kingston where six Saxon kings were crowned, it is not impossible.

Having cleared up that little conundrum, I was sitting back thinking of the uniqueness of Teddington when I discovered that there was also a Teddington in Gloucestershire. This is a very small hamlet close to Tewkesbury which is very much a rural community. It was in the county of Worcestershire until boundary changes moved it to Gloucester. It has an unusual five directional finger post called the 'Teddington Hands' which also gives its name to the village pub.

I smugly thought 'another town of Tuda's people' and was immediately smacked down by *The Place Names of Gloucestershire* which states that their Teddington is from 'Teoda', which may be a hypocoristic form of the name 'Teodbald' in the nearby Tibblestone. Over the years, there are many other spellings and the earliest seems to be 780 AD when Offa, King of Mercia gave the village to a monastery at Bredon, now long gone.

It seems strange to me that two places of the same name and originating at about the same time can have such different explanations as to the formation of that name but I am sure similar anomalies must exist in other parts of the country.

The Wilkinson Letters

IN THE EARLY 1970s, Chris and Monica Read decided to find an alternative use for the coal shed in their house at 55 Elmfield Avenue, Teddington. It was then that they came across a folio book of copy letters on a shelf. A quick look at these showed several pages of figure work with various estimates and accounts. Thinking that they must have belonged to the previous owner, Chris' father, Sam Read who was a local builder, the book was put aside. The Reads retired to Devon in 1985 taking all of their possessions, including the book with them. On Chris' death in 2001, Monica returned to Teddington and 'rediscovered' the book. Finding difficulty in reading the script, she passed it to her sister Noeleen Kerry, who she knew was interested in 'that sort of thing' and thus commenced an interesting few years of research

It transpired that the letters were hand written copies of letters written between December 1823 and September 1825 by London lawyer, Mr John Wilkinson of Smith, Lake and Wilkinson of Lincoln's Inn, either to or concerning the affairs of Viscount Lord Courtenay of Powderham Castle who later succeeded to the title of ninth Earl of Devon. Lord Courtenay had fled England in 1811 to avoid charges of criminal behaviour arising out of his homosexual lifestyle and had spent some years in America before settling in France at Chateau de Draveil near Paris.

Noleen and her husband John corresponded with the present Earl's estate which led to a meeting at Powderham Castle with the Earl and Dorothy Presswell, the archivist of the estate. Dorothy spent much time analysing and putting the letters into chronological order.

John Wilkinson employed at least four clerks to copy these letters and 'some letters are written with greater clarity than others, each clerk has his own style of abbreviating words and the work was, at times, penitential to transcribe.'

The folio consists of about 450 letters, spread over 479 foolscap sheets, addressed to Viscount Courtenay in Paris, his agents in Exeter and Ireland, The Viscount's cousin and heir, William Courtenay, the Government tax office and assorted Trustees and gentry.

Dorothy Presswell writes 'It became obvious whilst analysing the letters that the work load of a nineteenth century lawyer was generic in the extreme. In addition to acting upon legal issues, Wilkinson had to sustain total involvement in an unwearied devotion to Courtenay's welfare... Wilkinson undertook many personal commissions for the Viscount; oysters were dispatched; fumigating bellows for the chateau's garden were manufactured and the latest gardening books ordered and sent across; soothing remarks were written in reply to the Viscount's distress on reading adverse remarks published in newspapers and pamphlets about him.'

'A most interesting issue for the reader was the matter of his Lordship's shirts. This became an on-going saga as the lawyer was obliged to make arrangements to smuggle through France handmade shirts manufactured in England. His Lordship had ordered some three dozen shirts from his London tailor. Although there were agents employed at Dover and Calais to undertake the payment of customs taxes (Wilkinson considered them a parcel of sharks and rascals) in the matter of importing silk shirts, there was a complete embargo by the French.'

The correspondence in itself is most interesting in that it sheds a new light on the character of Viscount Courtenay who previous historians had written of as a 'recklessly extravagant, flamboyant homosexual.' Again Dorothy Presswell writes 'Through these letters we can appreciate Courtenay as having been a kind, caring and generous man who must have been charismatic in the extreme. His servants were devoted to him and, in return, the Viscount treated them not as his household but, in the trauma of exile, as members of

his family and made provision for them accordingly. He was far from indolent and played a very active role in the affairs of his estates. Whilst he was one of the absentee landlords so criticised in Irish social history, he was certainly not a rapacious one and he demonstrated that he had the welfare of his tenants at heart with the provision of a dispensary and the maintenance of a school. A man of great courtesy, he was also intelligent and cultured but, his great weakness was a lifelong self-indulgence that affected all aspects of his life.'

The Kerrys point out 'Mr Wilkinson emerges from his letters as an assiduous worker on Lord Courtenay's behalf. They are on excellent terms. Mr W is always very respectful and deferential towards his Lordship.' Miss Presswell adds 'Wilkinson was an honourable man who worked tirelessly in the endeavour to ease the trauma of the Viscount's excile and it is difficult to be dispassionate regarding the fate of the ninth Earl of Devon after reading these remarkable letters.'

In the meantime, John and Noeleen Kerry were pursuing their own enquiries as to how the cache came to be at 55 Elmfield Avenue in the first place. The discovered that the house was built in 1927 and occupied successively by the owner S George Skinner until 1933; during 1934-6 by a tenant, Edgar Bertie Hall and from 1937 by Mrs Amelia Read, wife of Sam Read from whom she was separated. On her death, her son Chris Read took over the tenancy and later bought the house from George Skinner's widow in 1969.

There were other items in the house belonging to Sam Read that had been acquired at auction. It is possible that the letters were acquired in the same way but it does not explain why they were hidden in the coal shed.

The Kerrys also explored the possibility that a previous tenant may have acquired the book, as Sam Read never actually lived there himself.

Between 1934 and 1936 he and his family resided at No 39 Teddington Park, the road that backs onto Elmfield Avenue. In 1934 a 'Jas. Lake Jn.' also moved into 65 Teddington Park where he was listed in Kelly's Directory until 1940 when the directory ceased publication. Is it possible that he was somehow connected to the firm of Smith, Lake and Wilkinson and at some point passed the book to his neighbours Sam and Amelia Read? The connection, although tenuous, is being investigated with the Law Society archives.

John Wilkinson outlived William Courtenay by ten years, dying in 1845 aged of 57. How his correspondence found its way into the coal shed in Teddington built 82 years after his death remains a mystery.

The Teddington Trades Exhibition

MEMORIES OF THE Great Exhibition of 1851 must have clearly lingered in the minds of Teddingtonians long after and in October 1907 the Teddington Tradesmen's Association decided to open their very own exhibition entitled not surprisingly The Teddington Trades Exhibition. This was held in a huge marquee erected for the purpose in the grounds of the Clarence Hotel (now the Park Hotel).

The opening ceremony was performed at 3pm on 1st October 1907 by Mrs Langdon Down who was accompanied by Dr Percival Langdon Down JP, Chairman of the Teddington Urban District Council. As they entered the tent, the Blue Hungarian Band, struck up the National Anthem. The Chairman of the organising committee, Mr J Robertson, said that 'the tradesmen of Teddington had organised this exhibition. They regretted they had no suitable building in the town in which an exhibition of this kind could be held, but they had organised that for the purpose of showing that Teddington as a shopping centre was second to none.'
(Huge applause)

In thanking the committee, Dr Langdon Down said he was pleased to help the trade of the town in any way he could and 'that when the land on the other side of the Thames was built upon and another bridge erected, that would bring a good deal of trade to the town.'
(More applause)

The Thames Valley Times wrote 'The success of the Teddington Trades Exhibition, was assured almost as soon as the proposal to arrange one was first mooted. As soon as the decision to hold an exhibition was arrived at, the demand for stalls came in so rapidly that it became evident that a very large tent would be required. The result was seen yesterday in a large tent well filled with the tradesmen's exhibits, every available space being occupied.'

It was said that considerable artistic taste had been displayed in the general decorations with art muslin in white, apple green and yellow being used to good effect.

The good and the great of Teddington business were in attendance; Messrs Wintour Phelps and Sons, house furnishers of the Broad Street; Mr C E Lemon, refreshment caterer and contractor; Mr C E Poupart's Electric Laundry at Twickenham; Messrs Poupart & Sons, dairymen of the High Street (now the Cigar Shop), Mr W Haine, the photographer of Park Road Studios; the Hampton Court Gas Company, demonstrating their speciality with their gas stoves and incandescent burners; Mr T W Childs, stationer and printer, Messrs Deaytons Limited, grocers, the Clarence Hotel themselves and almost every other trader in Teddington. The exhibition ran for four days and despite unfavourable weather, reported a 'Most gratifying attendance'.

Basking in the success of their exhibition, the Association met the following May whereupon it was agreed that the exhibition should be held again that year and last for a week. It was also decided to hold the event in a field abutting the railway on the Station Road side as this was extremely central and would make 'an ideal spot'. 500 views of Teddington were distributed amongst the trains travelling to and from Teddington to make passengers aware of the considerable historical associations of the town.

The second exhibition opened on September 22nd 1908 and the Thames Valley Times tells us 'A large and lofty marquee, over a hundred yards in length and forty foot wide, had been erected parallel with the railway. Down each side of this ran a row of shops or stalls; whilst one end is filled with a well appointed refreshment display, the other with a large display of furniture. Here also, one finds a small but sufficient bandstand and further on, another railed-in platform. It was here the opening ceremony took place yesterday afternoon, and concerts are being given here every evening.'

The paper went on to say 'It is not possible to describe every department of the exhibition in detail – and indeed our readers would hardly thank us if we did so, but a few of them do claim special attention. First and foremost there is the Teddington Cottage Hospital (in Elfin Grove). Apropos, one may remember that if the advertisement of the Teddington Traders is the main object of the show, the advancement of the cause of the hospital itself plainly runs it a good second.'

Once again the exhibition drew in virtually every business in Teddington. The article goes on to list another thirty traders from grocers to wheelwrights, photographers (including Young & Co whose pictures illustrate this piece), cycle makers, hosiers. Hatters, ironmongers, water engineers, coal merchants, tailors, tobacconists, china and glass merchants, drug stores, electric laundry, toys, sewing machines, shoemakers, bookbinders, sausage makers and auctioneers; just about every type of business imaginable.

A Souvenir Programme was produced by the Association Secretary, Mr E Proctor who reminded everyone that the Teddington and District Tradesmen's Association, to give it its full title, had only been in existence for less than two years but has a membership in excess of one hundred. Since its formation, the Association has interested itself in the improvement of the Broad Street, the Causeway, the Lock Island and in securing better travelling facilities on the railway for residents. It had seen a uniform hour for the closing of various businesses and was engaged in the formation of a town band. The programme gave an outline history of Teddington and was well illustrated.

When a newspaper reporter visited the exhibition at 8pm on the opening night, he noted that it was well attended with some visitors inspecting the stalls whilst others were listening to the popular songs of the day knocked out on a giant gramophone, specially procured for the occasion. Mr Proctor declared 'It has surpassed my expectations. Why up to the present we have had 3,000 visitors. Tomorrow (Wednesday) being early closing, we will have a record attendance. It is the finest advertisement that Teddington has ever had since it merged into a town.'

So successful was the exhibition that the committee decided to keep it open for one more day and were vindicated in their judgement by a further 1,202 visitors passing through the turnstiles on the last day, taking the total number to be in excess of 10,000. The last event was a musical programme on the Monday evening. At the conclusion, the whole of the stallholders and their assistants, together with the committee and their lady friends, sat down to a supper in the marquee, provided by Messrs H & W Humphrey, there being about eighty-five persons present.

I have never seen the 'Souvenir Programme' referred to and if anyone holds a copy, I would very much like a sight of it.

R D Blackmore

"Who wrote Lorna Doone?" asked the keen young teacher.
"R D Blackmore!" replied the class as one.
"What else did he write?" asked the teacher, capitalising on the former question.
Deafening sound of silence from the class.

THIS SUMS UP the average knowledge of Blackmore. Most people know of him as the author of Lorna Doone but few people can name another of his fourteen novels, let alone that he ran a market garden in the centre of Teddington for forty plus years. Most impressions of him are of an anti-social humourless recluse, locked into his own estate and dealing with outsiders in a fairly grumpy manner.

Whilst there is some truth in this, he did not receive a kind deal of the cards when he was born. His elder brother had died two years before his birth and his mother and her twin sister were taken off in an outbreak of typhoid when he was only four months old. He moved around the family until his father remarried and he moved back home in 1831. This only lasted a couple of years before he and his brother went to boarding school in Bruton, Somerset and after that to Blundell's School in Tiverton. Here he fell foul of the fagging system and was badly bullied by Frederick Temple, a future Archbishop of Canterbury. This took the form of striking Blackmore around the head with a brass headed hammer, a treatment that was to bring about epilepsy and upset the balance of his life.

Despite all this, he went on to Exeter College, Oxford, where he gained a Second Class degree in Classics and joined the Honourable Society of the Middle Temple to pursue a career in law. However the deterioration in his health, which had already denied him a First Class degree, struck again in 1854. He wrote to a friend 'ill health drove me from chamber practice; my once excellent health has become impaired. My medical advisor said I would have to give up my profession, seek an outdoor employment or die young. As I was unwilling to depart just then, I took his advice.'

R. D. BLACKMORE.

Blackmore was twenty-nine, recently married to Miss Lucy Maguire and unemployed. He answered the advertisement for a Classics Master at Wellesley House Grammar School in Twickenham and set up home in a 'comfortable villa' at 25 Lower Teddington Road, Hampton Wick. He did not take to teaching particularly well but the walk to and from Twickenham every day gave him the exercise his doctor recommended. He also published his first book of poems Poems by Melanter and made a lifelong friend of the headmaster, T J Scale.

After two years, he received some life changing news that his favourite uncle, Rev Henry Hey Knight, had died and left Blackmore a considerable legacy. This would enable him to fulfil a lifelong ambition to 'become a gardener and horticulturist' specialising in the growing of pears. By coincidence, he became aware of a 16 acre site in the Southfield of nearby Teddington that was for sale. Having satisfied himself that the soil was suitable for his purposes, he acquired the land and set about building a house for Lucy and himself. This was to be Gomer House, named after his favourite dog.

Unfortunately what he did not know was that the London and South Western Railway were planning their rail route from Richmond to Kingston through Teddington. They required a strip of land for this purpose and this would cut through Blackmore's 16 acres, separating a 5 acre plot to the south west from the remaining 11 acres to the north and east. What is not clear is whether LSWR beat Blackmore to the purchase of this strip as they had acquired other lands from the Manor Estate at the same time; or whether there was some sort of compulsory purchase involved taking the strip off Blackmore. Either way, he lost out and decided to dispose of the 5 acres that would be below the railway line.

This was the start of his long running feud with LSWR. He wrote to his father on 5th August 1858 'My building goes on slowly but satisfactorily. The engineer of the Menacing Railway Company was with me on Tuesday. I pointed out to him how easily they could give me the go-by which was all I wished. He paid much attention to my remarks and promised to clear me if possible.' The 'go-by' required was access to his garden from the south of the proposed station yard, as there was a path from this corner to his house. He did not get the 'go-by.'

Then, to his horror, he saw that the railway station was being built almost opposite to Gomer House, although on the far side of the railway track, possibly as a fob to his anticipated protests. Various court cases followed over the years with the verdicts going mainly in Blackmore's favour but even in 1898, he was still grumbling about them. One would have thought that Blackmore would have seen the railway as an asset and easy means of getting his produce to the London markets but such was his dislike of them, he continued to use his horse and cart, often driving it himself.

He does not appear to have been a very good man manager and his biography is littered with stories of sacked employees. In 1889 he had to prosecute his head gardener, Tooley, for stealing £5 worth of pears. Another employee had stated that he had seen a well-known greengrocer, Alfred Woodward, drive to Tooley's cottage and receive two large boxes of pears which he then took to his shop in Teddington, concealed under some hay. Blackmore had then gone to the shop, purchased some of the pears and with his expert knowledge, he was able to identify the variety, which could only have come from his orchard. Tooley was given three months hard labour and Woodward was sent for trial.

It is amazing that the market garden lasted for so long as in the forty odd years he worked it, it only turned in a profit in two. 'All I make with the pen, I cast away with the spade.' When asked why he continued with the garden when his books were doing so well, he replied 'Any ass can write novels; but to make a vine needs intellect.'

He was devoted to his wife and despite his own ailments, nursed her to her last days at the end of January in 1888. On her death, his nieces, Eva and Dolly Pinto-Leite came to Teddington to keep house and look after him.

A Canadian visitor said that 'I felt I was in the house of a friend' when visiting him and that the majority of people in the neighbourhood knew nothing of him. Charles Deayton, the grocer of the Broad Street said 'He has dealt with me for thirty-four years but I have never been inside his garden walls.' The ticket collector at the station knew him as the man who grew pears. The Coward family were close friends although Blackmore declined to become Noel's godfather after the death of his godson, Russell, (Noel's brother) from meningitis. Alexander Smith had good cause to remember him as he received a flogging at Teddington School having been caught scrumping in Blackmore's orchard.

Many other stories exist showing both sides of the man but he seems to have a troubled soul for most of his life. In January 1900 he was struck down with an attack of influenza and passed away on 20th whilst his nieces were reading him a story.

Unfortunately his will dictated that all letters, journals, diaries and personal correspondence were to be destroyed and this has meant that we will never know more about the man who was the author of Lorna Doone and market gardener in Teddington.

St Mary's Church and Churchyard

DESPITE DISCOVERIES FROM earlier periods, it is fair to say that Teddington started life as an Anglo-Saxon settlement and that when converted to Christianity, would have had its own church or chapel. The present church may be traced to the early 16th century with many subsequent alterations. St Mary's Church has some very unusual burials as the parish register will confirm. The Rev Daniel Lysons compiled a survey of these in 1795.

Frederick Christian Rhynhart de Ginkell (1743 - 1808), 5th Earl of Athlone was living in Robert Udney's old house when he died. He was heavily in debt and it was feared that his body might be seized, even from the grave, until all of the debt had been settled, as was the custom of the day. The body was therefore buried within the church, under the communion table at four o'clock in the morning on 19th December 1808. He was succeeded by two sons, the second of which retrieved the family fortune and to his great credit, came forward and paid off his father's outstanding debts. Earl Athlone's remains were dug up on 27th March 1828 and reburied in Ireland.

Another case is that of Paul Whitehead (1710 - 1774), playwright and satirist. He had married Anna Dyer in 1735 and moved to Colne Lodge on Twickenham Heath. His patron was Sir Francis Dashwood of Medmanham Abbey, West Wycombe, founder of the infamous *Hellfire Club*. Whitehead became its steward and secretary. When he died, most of him was buried at St Mary's, apart from his heart which he left to his patron, Dashwood with £50 for a marble urn in which it would be placed within Dashwood's mausoleum. This was done and there it remained as a popular tourist attraction until stolen by an Australian tourist in 1839.

Richard Bentley (1708 - 1782) also found himself in St Mary's. He was the son of Dr Richard Bentley, Master of Trinity College, Cambridge. Bentley is best remembered as an artist and writer. He was a friend of Walpole, although they later fell out, and was responsible for some of the artwork at Strawberry Hill. He also illustrated an edition of Thomas Gray's poems, printed by Walpole at Strawberry Hill in 1753.

Probably the most remarkable burial at St Mary's is that of Sir Orlando Bridgeman (1606 - 1674). A staunch Royalist, he was the Keeper of the Great Seal of Charles II and had been a judge at the trial of the regicides. He fell from favour with Charles and retired to his country seat at Teddington where he died in 1674 and was buried in the church. His ancestors were to become the Earls of Bradford. In 1833 some alterations were being carried out to the church and Sir Orlando's coffin was found to be open. As his body had been embalmed, Sir Orlando was lying in his coffin, with pointed beard and looking as fresh as the day he died. The current Earl Bradford was sent for and had the opportunity of seeing exactly what his illustrious ancestor looked like. Sir Orlando was reburied in the Manor vault.

Margaret "Peg" Woffington (1720 - 1760) the famous Irish actress with the fabulous legs is here. Her career started on the stage in Dublin before crossing the Irish Sea and taking London by storm with her 'breeches' parts. She had a long relationship with David Garrick until 1748 when they parted company. Her last performance was on 17th May 1757 at Covent Garden where she had taken the role of Rosalind in *As You Like It*. As she was speaking the Epilogue, she suffered a seizure and left the stage, speechless. She never acted again. Her memorial is shared with Master Horace Cholmondeley, who had died in infancy.

Teddington's most famous vicar, the Rev Dr Stephen Hales (1677 - 1761) is, not surprisingly, also buried here. 'Plain Parson Hale' as Pope called him was vicar of Teddington for 51 years and is buried in the porch under the tower. In his time he was responsible for much of the rebuilding and maintenance of St Mary's. Apart from his religious duties, Hales was a renowned scientist making remarkable discoveries in plant physiology, blood pressure and ventilation in prisons, to name but a few. He also improved the sewage system in the High Street by introducing a continuous ditch from the village pond to the River Thames which flushed all rubbish into the river.

One of Hales' most devoted admirers was Isabella, Dowager Countess of Denbigh. After his death, she took steps to ensure that she would remain close to him and acquired a plot in the churchyard closest to the church, where she was buried in 1769. Her tomb is enclosed by railings. A lesser known character is Richard Parsons Esq., of Taunton, at one time 'escheator' for the county of Somerset and an attorney of the Court of King's Bench, who died in 1613. The office of escheator was one of considerable power and importance. According to the feudal system all land belonged in the first and last instance to the Sovereign and when any of the king's tenants forfeited their land, either by default or by gross misdemeanour and crime, his land became an 'escheat' to the king who kept a number of lawyers throughout the country, ready to seize such escheats for the king. How Mr Parsons ended up in Teddington is not known.

Also here is William Perseman 'Gentleman borne at Whimple in Devonshire' who was yeoman in ordinary to Queen Elizabeth I and for many years afterwards usher to King James I. These yeomen are better known as Beefeaters (a corruption from Buffetier, a waiter at the Buffet or sideboard). Mr Perseman died in 1618 at the age of 78.

An unusual burial is that of James Parsons on 7th March 1743. Mr Parsons liked his food and the parish register has recorded 'who has often eat a shoulder of lamb or a peck of hasty pudding at a time."' He was 36.

Henry Flitcroft the well known architect was buried here in 1769.

John Walter (1739 - 1812) ended his colourful career at Teddington. He had started out as a coal merchant and from there, he became a Lloyd's Underwriter. Due to the American War he lost a fortune and was made bankrupt. He decided to go into printing and founded The *London Daily Universal Register* in 1785. This later changed its name to **The Times** and is what we know today. Handing the paper over to his son, also John, Walter retired to Teddington and acquired The Grove. However when he went to claim his pew at the church, he found that none had been allocated, the previous occupant of The Grove having been Moses Franks, a Jewish businessman, had no need of a pew at St Mary's. Walter sued the churchwardens and won the day. He became a churchwarden himself in 1801 and introduced a new allocation of pews which caused men and women servants to be separated. Probably not a popular move with the servants.

The parish registers began in the reign of Queen Elizabeth I and have been kept up to date ever since. The first christening is dated 1558, the first burial in the same year and the first marriage in 1561.

The registers together with the Vestry minutes have allowed us to paint a picture of the town as it has evolved into the Teddington we know today.

Teddington, Hotbed of Crime

MOST OF THE ESTATE agents' talk about Teddington relates to the good schools, lovely parks and open spaces, the river Thames etc etc; they do not mention the criminal past although in fairness, most of this was a long time ago.

An account in the Middlesex Sessions of 2nd February 1555 tells the story of Robert Marshall – 'At Teddington, in a certain meadow near the Thames, Robert Marshall, late of Kingston, labourer, assaulted William Lancaster and murdered him by giving him diverse mortal wounds with a hedginbyll, of which wounds he then died mortally. Robert Marshall threw the body in the river. He pleaded guilty and was sentenced to be hanged.'

Murder was not the only crime committed and William Hill of the Manor House writing to a friend on 6th February 1608 had this to say – 'My servant, Thomas Mosse, had to attend the Middlesex Sessions today to prosecute John Cowley, a yeoman of London, who took away a certain cloak and sword from him. "Took away" – that's how this event was described at the Sessions but I call it stealing. Fortunately he was found guilty of petty larceny and is to be whipped."

However murder was to raise its head again a few years later in 1611 Robert Astoll, soon to obtain his badgers, kidders and drovers licence, witnessed the following – 'It was three or four o'clock in the morning, I was looking for the badgers when I heard a noise and saw Thomas Weldon assaulting Thomas Nicholson. He mortally wounded him on the right side of the belly with a sword worth 2/-. Nicholson died at 12 o'clock that same morning. Weldon was found guilty, has no goods and is to be hanged. He was led off to gaol by Robert Johnson.'

In 1612 William Wilshire of Teddington was branded and led to gaol for stealing one and a half baskets of barley worth 3/- from Thomas Hall and at the same court Joab and John Ryde, birdcatchers, were accused of taking pigeons with nets. John came to court and swore that Joab was too ill to attend so the charge was postponed until the next Sessions.

A more unusual crime concerned Margaret, wife of Thomas Ruddy, who was accused of having two husbands. William Robinson gave evidence that Margaret claimed to be his wife as well as being the wife of Thomas Ruddy. The punishment for this offence is not recorded.

A quick look at the Richmond & Twickenham Times today makes one feel that we live in a lawless society. 'Oh for the good old days!' you might say – but you have forgotten the highwaymen. 'Not in Teddington, surely?' but alas yes. We were very much on the borders of Hounslow Heath which began just to the west of Stanley Road, which was little more than a track. There were no houses in Hampton Hill or Fulwell.

Most of the information we have comes from the pen of that well known letter-writer, Horace Walpole. He had moved into Strawberry Hill in 1747 and in between bouts of house building, he embarked on a massive correspondence with his associates and he kept them well up-to-date with all of the local gossip.

One of his correspondents, the actress Kitty Clive wrote to him – 'I have been robbed and murdered coming from Kingston. Jimy (her brother) and I in a postchey at half past nine, just by Teddington Church were stopped by footpads. I only lost a little silver and my senses, for one of them came into the carriage with a great horse pistol to 'sarch' me for my watch, but I had not it with me.'

Very soon after this, Walpole had his first brush with highwaymen and described the encounter in a letter to Lady Ossary on 17th June 1776 –

'As I came home, two footpads just at the entrance to Strawberry Hill, stepped out of the bushes and up to my footman, damned him and bid him stop. Luckily it was not David, the regular one but a young fellow- James Sibley, who rode up to the coachman and bid him drive on – fast! I expected to hear pistol fire after us but Sibley saw nothing more than a large stick which one of them pointed at him.'

Walpole was robbed again in 1781 as he wrote to Lady Ossary: 'Lady Browne and I were as usual going to the Duchess of Montrose at Twickenham Park at seven o'clock. The evening was very dark. In the lane some twenty yards from the gate, a small figure on horseback pushed by between the carriage and the hedge on my side. I suspected it was a highwayman and so, I found, did Lady Browne, for she stopped speaking. To calm her fears I was about to say "Is that the doctor going to the Duchess?" when I heard a voice say "Stop!" and the figure came to the carriage. I had the presence of mind. Before I let down the glass window, to take out my watch and stuff it within my waistcoat under my arm.

He said "Your purses and watches!" I replied "I have no watch." "Then your purse!" I gave it to him. It had nine guineas – it was so dark I could not see his hand but I felt him take it. He then asked for Lady Browne's purse and said "Don't be frightened, I will not hurt you." I said "No, you wouldn't frighten the lady?" He replied "No, I give you my word I will do you no harm." Lady Browne gave him her purse and was about to add her watch, but he said "I am much obliged to you, I wish good night" pulled off his hat and rode away. "Well" said I "Lady Browne, you will not be afraid of being robbed again, for as you see, there is nothing in it." "Oh! But I am" said she "and now I am terrified lest he should return for I have given him a purse with dud money which I carry solely for such a purpose. Bid the coachman drive faster!"'

Writing again the following year, he was commenting on the effect that highway robbery was having on the social scene: 'I am awaiting a visit from Countess Soltikoff but her terror of highwaymen near her kept her within her own walls and my recent attack of gout prevents me from travelling – tis an ill highwayman that blows no good!'

He continued: The Hertfords, Lady Holderness and Lady Mary Coke dined here last Thursday but with a company so well armed as to storm Gibralta.'

Robberies were still taking place in 1785 and he again wrote to Lady Ossary: "John Cosens, parson of Teddington, and his wife were robbed at half an hour after nine last night by three footpads with pistols at my back gate. My housekeeper heard the bustle from her room that is over the Holbein Chamber. I was in the library, but knew nothing of the matter till today. It is agreeable to have banditti on one's doorstep."

It is not known how many of the local highwaymen were caught but at least two went to goal in 1789. John Bunce of Stanley Road Teddington was robbed of his silver watch and seven and a half guineas in gold as he returned home across Sunbury Common. He stated in evidence that the footpads were armed, one with a pistol and one with a stick. They said to him somewhat dramatically "Deliver your money or we will have your life." The two footpads were subsequently arrested and sent to Southwark goal.

With the increase in population and growth of Teddington in the late 1800s, law and order gradually took over and fortunately have held the upper hand ever since.

Frances, Lady Waldegrave (1821-1879)

FRANCES ELIZABETH ANNE BRAHAM was born on 4th January 1821. Her father was the German Jewish tenor, John Braham, who performed at all the main theatres and opera houses of Europe and America. Although of very comfortable means, Braham was tied into building St James's Theatre in London and this was proving to be a drain on his finances.

As a result of her father's theatrical connections, Frances was invited to a dinner party at Strawberry Hill in the summer of 1838, along with her parents. Strawberry Hill House was then in the occupation of the 6th Earl Waldegrave, John James Henry, and his family. By all accounts Frances was a strikingly beautiful young lady and as this was her first visit to Strawberry Hill, she set out to explore the house. Whilst doing so, she was observed by the Earl's two sons, John James and George who both fell in love with her on the spot and set about finding out who she was. John had declared his love for her before the night was over.

Frances and John started to spend a good deal of time together, despite objections from her mother. John is described as 'extremely good looking but uncouth – and illegitimate,' the 6th Earl and his fiancée having jumped the gun. However, Frances was not interested in the family fortune which had passed to John's brother George who became 7th Earl. Frances and John were married on 25th May 1839.

At George's insistence, they both stayed for long periods at Strawberry Hill and were told to treat the House as their own. Both brothers were thoroughly dissolute and Frances applied a very motherly care to them. John was an epileptic and his fits grew progressively worse until he failed to recognise her. He died within a year of being married. Frances retired to friends and family in London.

Meanwhile George drew himself into the Waterford set, a circle of friends of dubious repute whose only interests seemed to be in drinking and gambling. During Derby week 1840, George and three friends went to Kingston Fair 'which outdid Greenwich for riotousness.' On the way back to Twickenham after midnight, one of the party decided 'to knock up a woman who kept a mangle' in Hampton Wick. We are told that door knockers had an irresistible fascination for Lord Waterford and an unholy racket was being created in the early hours of the morning.

When PC Charles Wheatley tried to quieten them, a scuffle took place outside the Swan Inn and the policeman was badly knocked about. The miscreants all succeeded in getting away but a hat was left at the scene. From this George and a Captain Duff were traced and arrested but they refused to divulge the names of the other two. It was noticeable that Lord Waterford left by sea for his castle in Northumberland the following day.

Out on bail, George went to see Frances and express his profound love for her. He declared that he had found a way around the Marriage Act of 1835 which prevented a man from marrying the spouse of his deceased brother and he proposed to her immediately. Taken completely by surprise, Frances accepted and they were married in Edinburgh on 28th September 1840. The infamous Captain Duff was best man at the wedding – and the worse for drink!

GEORGE, 7TH EARL WALDEGRAVE, 1842

George, Lord Waldegrave and Captain Duff appeared at the Queen's Bench on 3rd May 1841 and pleaded guilty to the charges and were sentenced to six months imprisonment in Newgate and fined

£200 and £20 respectively. Showing an amazing degree of loyalty, Frances insisted on joining her husband in jail for the period of his sentence. Despite being imprisoned, 'they led a very social life and hosted many dinner parties.' However all through this period their financial problems were mounting; the estates were not being properly managed. This growing stress caused Frances to miscarry and sadly her condition was such that she would never have children.

When they left Newgate, Waldegrave had been used to drinking excessively and was given to bouts of bad temper. Whilst thinking about satisfying their creditors, he hit on the idea of selling Walpole's lifelong collection of treasures. Thus the Great Sale of 1842 commenced where Walpole's works were disposed of to the far corners of the United Kingdom. Whilst the sale was underway, Frances and George slipped away to the Continent.

On returning to England, they went to their Somerset home, Strawberry Hill having been stripped of its furniture and furnishings, where Frances wanted to live quietly with her husband. George however wanted to show off his Countess to 'the London Season' and began a round of socialising which went neatly with his excessive drinking. He was taken ill in February 1845 and Frances insisted on nursing him herself. Family friend Dr Cutler declared that George had cirrhosis of the liver and that time was short. George died on 28th September 1846.

Frances, now Countess Waldegrave, twice widowed and only twenty five found herself extremely wealthy but entirely alone. At this point in time she re-met an old friend of her father's, George Granville Harcourt, a widower of 61 and son of the Archbishop of York. Harcourt was clearly smitten, despite the 36 year age gap and pressed his troth. Although Frances wanted to endure a year of widowhood to consider her future, she succumbed to his intentions and they were married by special licence on 30th September 1847.

Under Harcourt's careful guidance, Frances was introduced to the British political scene. Operating from Harcourt's family home of Nuneham, Frances gradually set out to make her mark on society, where she blossomed as a hostess and caught the eye of Liberal hopeful, Chichester Fortescue, an old friend of Harcourt's. As Harcourt's influence waned, Frances set about restoring Strawberry Hill which had remained empty since the Great Sale. A huge amount of money was expended on the project and by the time Harcourt died in 1861, Strawberry Hill was the epicentre of Liberal politics in the country.

Lord John Russell, Gladstone and Disraeli were all regular visitors to Strawberry Hill and an invitation there was the most coveted prize of the season. Fortescue wasted no time in proposing to Frances by way of a 13 page letter. Frances wanted to allow a respectable year of mourning to pass and so became secretly engaged to Fortescue. They married on 20th January 1863.

The social and political whirl of the 1863 – 1866 culminated with Fortescue, now a Privy Councillor, being appointed Chief Secretary for Ireland and

moving out to Dublin with Frances. On the occasion of a visit to the theatre, a wag from the audience shouted 'And would your ladyship be after informing us, which of your four husbands do ye like the best?' With an exquisite and inimitable turn of her head, she looked at the questioner and, without a moment's hesitation, her clear, lovely voice flashed back 'The Irishman, of course.' which brought the house down.

At last, with a husband her own age, Frances enjoyed many happy years with Fortescue until she was struck down 'with rheumatic pains in my chest, arms and back' and she died in the arms of Fortescue on 5th July 1879.

Rev Stephen Hales: Vicar & Scientist

ON 4TH JANUARY 1761, the longest running ministry in Teddington was brought to an abrupt end; Stephen Hales had died.

Hales was born into minor gentry on 17th September 1677 at Bekesbourne in Kent. His parents, Thomas and Mary had eleven children, Stephen was the tenth child and sixth son, and a long way removed from the baronetcy of his grandfather, Sir Robert Hales. Stephen's father died at an early age and Sir Robert took on his guardianship and saw him placed at Bene't Collage (the forerunner of Corpus Christi) Cambridge in 1696 at the age of nineteen.

The country was still recovering from the Civil War, the Commonwealth, the Restoration and the Great Plague and the college was predominantly theologian. Little is known of his life at Cambridge other than that he graduated and was elected a Fellow of the college in 1703 and in the same year, he was ordained a Deacon. In this period Hales became interested in every aspect of science and physiology which led to his study of anatomy and the dissection of frogs, dogs and other animals.

On August 10th 1709, he was appointed Perpetual Curate of the parish of Teddington. Although he still continued his experiments on blood pressure and on live horses. Mindful of the distaste with which his parishioners viewed these experiments and not wishing to be considered cruel to animals, he moved his attentions to the life of plants and how they lived and breathed. His work became better known and he was elected to the Royal Society in 1718 and on March 15th, he delivered his first paper to the Society. This appeared some time later in his book *Vegetable Staticks*.

At the time of Hales' appearance in Teddington, it was a small village of about 400 people, a small manor house and a rundown church. There was no parsonage. The 'living' of the church was normally in the hands of the Lord of the Manor but in this case, it had been taken on by a wealthy and influential family, the Bridgemans, to whom Hales was distantly related. This explains his presence in Teddington in the first place. This living was the princely sum of £87, twice the value of his Fellowship.

In 1720 at the age of 43, he married Mary Newce, the daughter of a Hertfordshire clergyman. They were married in St Paul's Cathedral under a special licence by his old college head, Dean William Stanley. Nothing is known of Mary and sadly she died a year later. He conducted the service himself and wrote in the register 'Mary Hales, my dear wife was buried. Oct.10.1721.'

He set about restoring the fabric of the Church of St Mary which had fallen into disrepair and in the years of his ministry, he virtually rebuilt the church himself. His sermons were moral dissertations, based on the gospels and stressing the Christian values of charity and love. To these he added some of the arguments he had noted for himself, drawn from natural science. The effect of this combination was to draw large attendances to the services to the extent that within five years, it had become necessary to enlarge the Church.

He kept very full records of his ministry and his registers contain much more detail than one would normally expect. One of the more unusual aspects of his tenure was the application of

Public Penance for acts of immorality. This involved the poor penitents being clothed only in a white sheet, given a white rod and made to stand barefoot, outside the church until the Litany, at which point they were brought inside to be prayed over. The registers show :

Anne Clarke, Spinster for Adultery, 10 Feb 1722
William Whiting, for Fornication)
Hannah Hill, Widow for Fornication) 18 Apr 1732
Frances Honeywell for Fornication)
Sarah Fuller for Fornication, 13 June 1733
Frances Honeywell for Fornication, 6 Oct 1737
Eliz. Mansell of Hampton got with child
By Joshua Mitchins of London, Feb 8 1740

It was the job of the parish to deal with the poverty of the parish and in addition to support other national tragedies and these, Hales seems to have skilfully dealt with without imposing any huge levies.

One of his particular dislikes was drunkenness not only for the harm that it did to men's bodies but because of what he called the 'bewitching of Naughtiness in these fiery liquors.' He ordered 200 copies of a tract *Against Drunkeness* and 250 of a similar tract *Against Swearing* and distributed these around the village. When he took on the living of Farringdon in Hampshire also, he noted that at Farringdon he found himself placed among a sober and industrious people but the people of Teddington were more remiss. In 1741 he calculated that the expectation of life at Farringdon was one third longer than at Teddington which being unhappily within the Gin Bills of Mortality, grows continually from bad to worse.

He undertook some experiments on food preservation and was particularly concerned with the effects of air supply on both human health and stored foodstuffs. He wrote a paper for the Royal Society in 1741 promoting the use of ventilators 'whereby Great Quantities of Fresh Air may with Ease be conveyed into Mines, Gaols, Hospitals, Work-Houses and Ships, in Exchange for their Noxious Air.' This slowly became a popular feature of everyday life with ventilators in granaries speeding drying and eliminating mould and putrefaction. The first major prison installation was at Savoy Prison where the subsequent drop in prisoner deaths was so marked as to prompt new installation in a number of prisons.

The Admiralty finally took up ventilators following some success in reducing illness and death in the merchant fleet, particularly on slave and transport ships. An order went out in 1756 to fit ventilators to all His Majesty's Ships. Hospitals followed starting with the Navy hospitals at Portsmouth, Gosport and Plymouth to Hyde Park Corner and the Middlesex small-pox hospital.

During the Seven Years War with France, he wrote to the French authorities in charge of English prisoners of war to urge them to install ventilators in their prisons and prison ships. This they did, to the benefit of English prisoners. Hales hoped none would accuse him of treason for corresponding with the enemy.

Back at home in Teddington, he improved life in the village with a method of flushing the drain in the High Street which ran the full length from the village pond to the River Thames with a supply of fresh water fed into the pond.

Hales died on 4th January 1761 after a short illness at the age of eighty four, having been parish priest at Teddington for fifty two years. He is buried under the tower of the church and in 1986, a memorial plaque was placed on the floor of the porch.

Sources: Stephen Hales DD, FRS by A E Clark-Kennedy, Stephen Hales DD, FRS 1677-1761 by David G C Allan

The Chestnut Avenue

ANOTHER CHESTNUT SUNDAY has passed and the weather was fairly kind to us as thousands of people flocked to Bushy Park to admire the 'candles', the blossoms of the lines of magnificent horse chestnut trees on the main avenue. it is worth taking a look at how they got there in the first place.

For this we have to go back to the time of the Glorious Revolution of 1688 when Princess Mary and her Dutch husband Prince William of Orange deposed James II to take the throne of England. This unique pairing, the only couple to ever rule jointly, decided upon Hampton Court Palace as their place of residence and proceeded to upgrade the Palace and its grounds, probably the first major upgrade since the days of Wolsey in the early 1500s.

Their success was a little short lived as Mary died in 1694 leaving William alone at the Palace. However William had some very ambitious ideas for Hampton Court and was not going to let his widower status get in the way of these plans. He had appointed Sir Christopher Wren as the First Commissioner of Works in 1689 and together they came up with a grand design that would have transformed Hampton Court into one of the finest palaces in the world. It involved the demolition of the old Tudor buildings and in their place, a new grand William & Mary range was to appear.

As one can see today, this was not completed, due to a rather tragic accident. In 1702 William had been riding his favourite horse, Sorrel, in Home Park when the horse stumbled on a molehill, throwing William. He broke his collarbone in the fall and then contracted pneumonia from which he died.

THE ROYAL CHESTNUT SUNDAY, BUSHEY PARK, 1909.

Had William lived, the Great Hall as we know it would have come down, along with the Tudor kitchens and other buildings in that block. The main entrance was to have been moved from the West Front to a new entrance at Lion Gate. This was preceded by a new road from the Teddington Gate to the Lion Gate, flanked on either side by a line of horse chestnut trees. Behind these were three rows of lime trees. The length of the Avenue in a straight line from end to end, including the diameter of the great circular pond, but not reckoning its circumference – is exactly one mile. The chestnut trees, which line it, are 274 in number, that is to say, 137 on each side, planted at 42 feet apart.

There had always been some speculation as to how much of the design was down to Wren himself or whether the royal gardeners, George London and Henry Wise had been involved or even William Talman, the Comptroller of H.M. Works. However in 1909, some rough sketches of the design came to light with notes and measurements in Wren's own handwriting, proving beyond doubt that the plans were entirely his, even though they were never completed as Wren had intended.

An old bill was discovered amongst the records in the summer of 1699 that the scheme and estimate was put to King William III by Wren 'for transforming a flat and then uninteresting piece of ground, timbered with little else but indigenous hawthorns, into one of the most agreeable parks in the neighbourhood of London.' The work was carried out at a pace and completed by the end of the year. The bill presented by gardener Henry Wise amounted to £3,300 for making the road and planting more than one thousand trees.

A round pond was dug at the Lion Gate end using water diverted from the Longford River. This work was well advanced at the time of William's death. As William and Mary had no issue, the crown passed to Mary's younger sister, Anne. A short time after her accession, the statue of Arethusa was removed from the Privy Gardens in Somerset House to the new pond in Bushy Park and henceforth was known as Diana.

Poor Anne inherited the throne and a mountain of debt from her brother-in-law. His grandiose ideas were extremely costly and had spiralled out of control. She was forced to put a block on all works in the parks, gardens and palace at Hampton Court. Wren's plan for the new approach had to be abandoned at least for the present time.

Since the creation of Bushy Park as a deer park by Cardinal Wolsey in about 1500, it has always been a private or a royal park. It was not widely open to the public. When Queen Victoria took to the throne, one of the first things she did was to make some of these places accessible to the public. First she opened Hampton Court in 1838 and then Bushy Park in 1840. The new Victorians were the first Britons to have properly organised leisure time and they quickly availed themselves of facilities like Bushy Park.

This was particularly so when the blossom of the horse chestnut trees was at its height, usually reckoned to be the second Sunday in May. Word of this event spread rapidly in The Illustrated London News and very soon vast numbers of people were coming to the park taking picnics with them and making a day of it. The railway came to Hampton Court in 1849 and this provided access for even more people. It was noted on Chestnut Sunday 1894 that over 3,500 tickets

were collected at Hampton Court station alone.

On 1st June 1908 a great storm or whirlwind struck the south east of England and swept across the open ground and in the space of one minute, uprooted eighty of the great trees in the Avenue – seventy limes and twelve chestnuts – all perfectly sound and some of them 12ft in girth and 100ft in height. It was said that the tree trunks lying in an interlocked mass on the ground provided an extraordinary sight. The park was visited by King Edward VII to inspect the damage and by many thousands of people curious to see the devastation. Strong, young replacement trees were planted in the autumn of 1909.

From that time onwards, royalty became regular visitors to the park and the event was then dubbed as Royal Chestnut Sunday. King Edward came several times and after him King George V and his cousin the Kaiser. Up to the outbreak of the Great War the Chestnut Avenue was honoured by the visits of many Kings and Queens, and almost every member of the Royal Family.

After the war the tradition fell away and it was not until 1993, after another World War and a Great Storm in 1987, that Colin Pain and the Hampton Wick Association revived the event and Chestnut Sunday has once again become a prominent date in the Teddington calendar. I think Wren would be pleased with his achievement.

Source: *The Chesnut Avenue, Bushy Park, Hampton Court By Ernest Law (GeorgeBell) 1919*

Sir Orlando Bridgeman

LOOKING AT THE name Bridgeman in Bridgeman Road, it is easy to assume that the name commemorates some famous man of the past. Well yes and no. The connection is Sir Orlando Bridgeman but he has hardly ever been considered famous. In fact for the length of time he was in Teddington, it is perhaps inaccurate to call him a resident.

Orlando Bridgeman was born in 1606, the eldest son of Dr John Bridgeman, rector of Wigan and later Bishop of Chester. It is true to say that he lived through a troublesome time of political strife and religious controversy. He read law at Cambridge from 1619 to 1624. He married Judith Kynaston on 30 January 1627 and they had two children, Mary and John.

Orlando was called to the bar in 1632 as a member of the Inner Temple. He demonstrated a great understanding of the law which brought him considerable success. So much so that Lord Campbell called him 'a profound master of the Common Law.' In 1638 he became Chief Justice of the County Palatine of Chester, later Attorney to the Court of Wards, and then Solicitor General to the Prince of Wales. He was a staunch royalist, a devout 'Churchman', a 'bigoted Protestant' with some sympathy for Non-Conformists.

In April 1640 Orlando was elected MP for Wigan in the Short Parliament and re-elected in November 1640 to the Long Parliament where he maintained the Royalist cause against that clever Parliamentarian, John Pym. This involved voting against the unjust conviction of Thomas Wentworth, Earl of Stratford, and to endeavour to maintain some balance of reason in a body where passions ran high. As said, he was a staunch royalist and in 1642 he assisted Lord Strange at Chester against Parliamentary forces. As a result of this, he was expelled from the Parliament 'as a deserter'.

However he was called to the King's Oxford Parliament where he was knighted by the King in 1643. Certainly not a soldier, the civil war passed by him although his loyalty to the King was never in doubt. On the execution of Charles I, he reluctantly submitted to Cromwell. Cromwell seems to have been a secret admirer of Bridgeman and provided he kept out of London, he was pretty much allowed to do as he pleased.

Orlando's wife Judith had died in 1644 and he moved to Beaconsfield in 1650, continuing in private practice. His speciality was conveyance and with so much land confiscated and so many estates forfeited, there was much work to be had. He wrote the standard legal text book on the subject and this was the accepted standard until the 20th century when reforms simplified land holding. On 30 May 1660 the Stuarts returned to England and to power. Orlando was made Serjeant-at-Law, and two days later he became Lord Chief Baron of the Exchequer, under his friend and mentor, the Earl of Clarendon, the Lord Chancellor. During the next week, he was created a Baronet, of Great Lever, in the County of Lancaster. Soon after he was appointed to sit as Speaker of the House of Lords in the absence of the Lord Chancellor. In October of the same year, he presided at the trial of the regicides, the late King's judges. Whilst demonstrating a strong loyalty to the crown, he exercised a policy of moderation and instead of the expected blood-bath, only twelve of those found guilty were executed.

As soon as these trials were over, he was promoted to be Chief Justice of the Court of Common Pleas. By 1662, he had acquired a house in Teddington, later called Bridgeman House on the South side of Teddington High Street, to the

east of Field Lane (on the site of the present Telephone Exchange). Hearth Tax Lists for 1664 to 1672 indicate that the house had twenty hearths – the biggest house in the village. The house survived until about 1911 when it was demolished.

In 1667 Lord Clarendon fell from grace and was dismissed from office. Charles II needed a trustworthy lieutenant to administer the Great Seal and Orlando fell in line for this. It was not to be a great position for Orlando, who being timid by nature, tried to please everyone. However as a judge his decisions in equity and his management of the business of the Court did not measure up to the great expectations the king had of him. We know that he was seriously ill for a period and left his house in Essex Street and retired to Teddington to recover.

At some stage he met a widower, Dorothy Saunders, and went on to marry her in May 1670. This seems to have caused some malicious gossip around the Court: 'It is said also that his wife was a most violent intriguess in business, and his sons kept no good decorum whilst they practised under him. His family gathered like a snowball while he held the Great Seal.' I have not been able to discover what intrigues Lady Dorothy had been guilty of and his sons would have been too young to make any serious dent in his character.

Two political events were to undo Orlando's favour at Court. The first involved the question of religious tolerance; Charles was seeking an opportunity to declare himself a Papist and was advised to publish a royal declaration granting 'indulgence to tender consciences' and Orlando was asked to apply the Great Seal to this. He refused until a clause was added 'that the benefit of public worship should not be extended to Catholics, who must confine their assemblies to private houses'.

The other was far more serious; Charles' extravagant lifestyle had brought the nation to the edge of bankruptcy and his close advisors proposed that the Exchequer be closed for a year and that no payment should be made to any public creditor for a twelvemonth. Unsurprisingly, Orlando would have nothing to do this and refused to administer the Great Seal. Like his predecessor, he was sacked from office on 17 November 1672 and he retired quietly to Teddington.

Here he turned his attention to the impoverished clergy of the parish. He made several endowments to the 'living' (the term meaning the annual income of the parish priest) amounting to about £80 in the form of fee-farm rents, the stipend from the Lord of the Manor being only £6 per annum. He and Edward Hill, Lord of the Manor, entered the unusual arrangement of jointly agreeing on the appointment of a chaplain for the parish. He died at age 66 on 25 June 1674.

Some years later in 1833 during alterations to the Church, 'his coffin was found accidently open, and his remains, which had been embalmed, so perfect, with pointed beard etc, that the representative of his family, Lord Bradford, was sent for; and he saw him. The coffin was then resealed, and placed in the new Manor vault.' Not many people get to see what their ancestor of some 250 years ago looked like.

Writing in his parish history notes, Rev Daniel Trinder, who seems to have taken a liking to Orlando because of his high sense of morals and his unshakeable honesty, said 'It would have been well for our country, perhaps, if there had been more like him.'

Hollywood on Thames

IN 1880, HENRY CHINNERY, a prominent London stockbroker and Teddington worthy, acquired some property including a mansion known as The Weir along the Lower Road (now Broom Road). He then amalgamated the properties to become Weir House, a large imposing house in its own grounds with lawns sloping down to the Thames.

The story moves to 1912 when Bill Kellino, a music hall artist from Kingston was taking a stroll along the towpath by Teddington Lock and decided to cross the bridge and walk along the other side, down the Lower Road. When he came to Weir House, he was immediately struck by the amount of light there, ideal for the new medium of film-making. Fortunately for Bill, Henry Chinnery also had an interest in the new invention and when approached for permission to film in his grounds, he readily agreed, even going so far as to say that if it started raining, they could use his greenhouse.

Bill Kellino and friends scraped together a sum of £1,000 and Ec-Ko Films was formed. Inevitably the rain followed and they found themselves in the Chinnery greenhouse but far from inconveniencing them, they found it an asset to film under glass where there was no lost time for inclement weather. They leased the house and grounds and built a huge glasshouse so that they could utilise every hour of daylight available for their filming. The long hours and the 'strange' lights gave rise to the locals renaming the building Weird House.

The output was soon quite prolific with about one film per week being made, each film being about 500 ft long, running for about five minutes. The films featured Bill's old music hall ensemble with regular names like The Brothers Egbert and Sam T. Poluski.

In 1914 the house and grounds were acquired by Charles Urban, an American-born film pioneer who specialised in newsreel reportage and scientific and educational films. He traded as

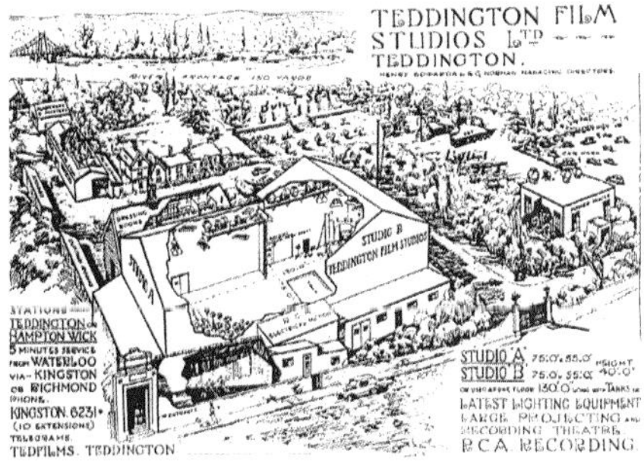

The Kinemacolor Company and had a five year monopoly on the use of Kinemacolor. By 1915 the early success was tailing off and the company moved to Kew Bridge and changed its name to Homeland Films.

At the end of the First World War in 1918, Weir House was leased and later purchased by Master Films Limited who set about redesigning the house - a single greenhouse building with dressing rooms, workshops, scene docks and a small preview theatre – the first enclosed stage measuring 60ft by 40ft and with the most modern cameras and lighting. Master Films was the first company to produce full length feature films at Teddington. Although their output for 1918-1922 was substantial with some memorable films such as *Calvery*, *Corinthian Jack*, *Daniel Deronda*, *Hobson's Choice*, *A Peep Behind The Scenes* and *La Poupee*, the critics attacked the productions as being rather cheap, lacking in skill and care. They complained that 'horizons swayed in unison with boat decks.' By 1925 the company had gone into liquidation.

The Ideal Film Company merged with British Gaumont in 1927 and leased Teddington Studios. This tenancy was cut short by a serious fire in 1929 but not before they had completed *His House In Order* with Tallulah Bankhead and Ian Hunter. The last silent film made at Teddington was *Hours of Loneliness* for Carlton Films. January 1931 saw the development of talking pictures and the studios were purchased by Henry Edwards and E G Norman. They announced their plans to re-equip the studios to produce their own films as Teddington Film Studios Ltd and also to rent space to other filmmakers. Only one film was made under this banner; *Stranglehold* directed by Henry Edwards himself.

The Government had become concerned at the low output of British films in contrast to the huge influx of overseas productions and set in motion legislation to balance matters. In 1928 the Government Quota Legislation came into force ensuring a certain amount of British film footage must be screened at all British cinemas, starting at 5% and rising in annual stages to reach 20% in 1935. The Quota Act ran for ten years and, with the introduction of sound, was to have a profound effect on the British film industry, especially Teddington Studios.

In 1931 Warner Brothers First National Productions Ltd took a lease on and later purchased Teddington Studios to make between 120 – 150 low budget 'Quota Quickies' to satisfy legislation. Although they were not looking for quality as these films were secondary to the main features, it soon became apparent that this was an ideal training ground for producers, directors, technicians and actors alike. Heavy investment was made by Warner Bros with £100,000 spent on a new sound stage, power house, office wing and prop shop. Although no critical acclaim was expected from these films, some new stars were discovered; Errol Flynn made his debut in *Murder At Monte Carlo* in 1934 and was quickly whisked off to Hollywood thereafter. Many other household names served their apprenticeship in films at Teddington Studios including Rex Harrison, Joan Hickson, Cecil Parker, Felix Aylmer, Laura La Plante and Margaret Lockwood. It was said that 10% of all British films made came from Teddington. By 1938 the Quota term had been served which led to fewer films but those that were made were longer and of better quality.

Visit by The Duchess of Kent

The studios closed briefly at the outbreak of war but re-opened shortly afterwards under the control of Studio Manager, Doc Salomon who was drafted in from Burbank. Whilst many other film studios in London were closed during the war and used for other purposes, Teddington was fortunate to be left to carry on the business of making films. These included *The Night Invader, The Hundred Pound Window* and *The Dark Tower.*

On the evening of 5th July 1944 some of the production staff were trying to persuade Doc Salomon to join them for a drink in the King's Head. He declined sadly saying 'All you British think about is beer!' A V1 flying bomb fell into open ground at the studio where it exploded, igniting oil tanks. Doc Salomon was killed instantly, along with two others.

Despite a grand re-opening by Danny Kaye in 1948, the studios never recovered their former momentum and closed down in 1952. Although they once again opened as a Television Studios in 1955, but that is another story.

The Story of Teddington Studios by John Tasker (2002), British Film Studios by Patricia Warren

John MacGregor and the Royal Canoe Club

JOHN MACGREGOR, BORN 1825, was the son of General Sir Duncan MacGregor in a line descended from the famous Highlander, Rob Roy MacGregor. He enjoyed a first class education, graduating from Trinity College, Cambridge. His first ambition was to be a missionary but this was blocked by the family. He then turned to the law and became something of an expert on patent law and wrote several books on the subject.

His great passion was travel and being of independent means, he was able to down tools at work and set off on one of his many journeys. In 1849 he spent nine months exploring Southern Europe, Palestine and Egypt. All of these trips were meticulously recorded in his sketchbooks and as he was also an accomplished artist, they were very well illustrated. Although he must have seen native canoes when he was in Halifax, Nova Scotia, where his father was stationed, no mention was made of this until 1858 when he was on a tour of the United States and Canada.

He retained his strong religious convictions and would not sail on a Sunday. Whilst in America he took an interest in the slavery question and was deeply disturbed by what he saw and heard. Writing to his sister he said 'There will one day be a civil war here about these slaves.' Three years later, he was proved right.

On his return to London in 1859, the Crimea had taken a heavy toll on the British Army and one way of rebuilding this was to form volunteer corps. John MacGregor joined the London Scottish Rifle Volunteers, a battalion of gentlemen-citizen-soldiers. The following April, he had been appointed captain in the East Company, where he proved to be a popular officer. He also proved himself a champion marksman, winning first prize in the regimental shooting contest at Wimbledon in 1861, a feat he was to repeat on at least one more occasion. Unfortunately this particular skill was short lived as 'a smash in a railway carriage' did lasting damage to the 'nerves which one needs for rifle shooting' and turned him towards 'a life on the water.'

In pursuance of this new found love, MacGregor designed his first canoe in 1865. It was 'double-ended', in the Indian style and built in Lambeth of lapstrake oak planking, decked in cedar covered with a rubberized canvas with an open cockpit in the centre; 15 feet long, 28 inches wide, 9 inches deep and weighed 80 pounds (36 kg) and designed to be used with a double paddle. The boat was named *Rob Roy* after his distinguished ancestor. (In fact he named all of the boats he built *Rob Roy*.) The boat proved to be extremely seaworthy.

MacGregor set out on his travels by canoe, writing about them and giving lectures on his return home. He formed a group of interested gentlemen who met in the Star and Garter Hotel on Richmond Hill and on 25th July 1866, he formed the Canoe Club. With many influential businessmen in their ranks, membership grew quickly and a number of Rob Roy craft were to be seen on the Thames.

The first recorded Regatta was held at Thames Ditton less than a year later, on 27th April 1867, when 15 canoes took part in a paddling race. This was followed by a canoe chase in December of the same year when six members took part in the first long distance race over a twelve mile course between Teddington Lock and Putney Bridge.

In 1867, Edward Prince of Wales (later to become King Edward VII) became Commodore of the Club and in 1873, by command of Queen Victoria; the Canoe Club became the Royal Canoe Club. This was a significant honour for the club, which was devoted exclusively to small craft at a time when larger yachts were very much a status symbol.

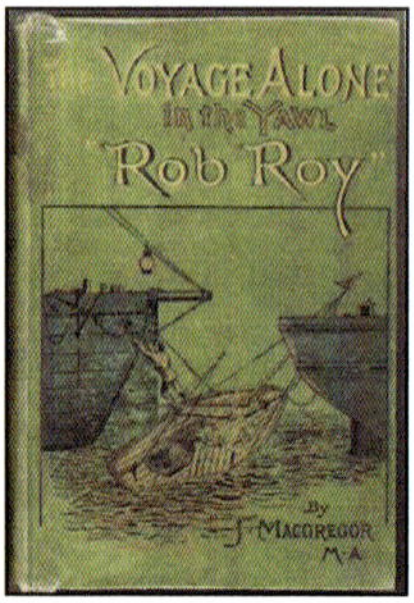

During this period, John MacGregor had turned his hand to the pen. His first offering was *A Thousand Miles in the Rob Roy Canoe on Rivers and Lakes of Europe*. In this he emphasised the concept : in walking you are bounded by every sea and river and in a common sailing-boat you are bounded by every shallow and shore; whereas a canoe can be paddled or sailed, or hauled, or carried over land or water. Quite apart from publicising the sport he dearly loved, the book turned out to become an international best seller. Not that he needed the money, the book earned MacGregor more than £10,000. Further works followed: *The Voyage Alone in the Yawl "Rob Roy"* in 1867, *The "Rob Roy" on the Baltic* in 1867 and *The "Rob Roy" on the Jordan, Nile, Red Sea and Gennesareth* in 1869. It is hard to see where he found the time to do any canoeing.

During the first ten years, the Club regularly held meetings on the Thames at Teddington and established a camping ground there but it was not until 1878 that a clubhouse was obtained. This was in Turk's Boathouse at Kingston. Michael Turk's grandfather had applied for membership to the Royal Canoe Club but was refused as it was considered that he was 'in trade.' To right the wrong done to his grandfather, Michael Turk (the current owner of Turk's and Keeper of Her Majesty's Swans) was made an Honorary Member. In 1897 the Club obtained a lease of land on Trowlock Island, a site which was later purchased. The timber building put up at a cost of £500 is still the main base for canoeing.

The sailing canoe was introduced in the early 1870s and a section still exists within the Royal Canoe Club for canoe sailing, although it is no longer at Teddington; the modern design of the craft and the building which has taken place along the river over the years, have made the water at Teddington unsuitable for such craft.

In 1922, Edward Prince of Wales (later to become the Duke of Windsor), became Commodore, a position he held until he succeeded to the throne.

Royal Canoe Club members have had the honour of representing their country at every Games since the Berlin Olympics when canoeing was first admitted as an Olympic sport.

In 1993 an opportunity arose to acquire premises which had previously been owned by BP as part of their Company's leisure activities. The BP site was ideal, being situated on the mainland whereas the Clubhouse is on the island. The Walbrook Rowing Club was set up by BP as part of the leisure package for its employees. A periodical purge of non-employees from the membership reduced the numbers considerably and kept them fairly small.

With the Royal Canoe Club taking on part of the clubhouse, together with the Skiff Club, who had previously been nomadic, the clubhouse was soon flourishing again. So much so that Walbrook threw off its BP mantle and became an open club and grown from strength to strength.

Anyone with a liking for the river and water sports would do well to pay the club a visit as there are facilities for seniors, juniors, experienced oarsmen and absolute beginners. It is a far cry from the enterprise began by John MacGregor. Having lived an 'Actionman' life, he retired to Bournemouth and died at Boscombe in 1892, aged 67.

Refs : Royal Canoe Club archive.

The FitzClarences of Bushy House

CAN YOU IMAGINE the scene at Bushy Park when the Duke of Clarence and his mistress moved into Bushy House and proceeded to repopulate Teddington. To be fair, they did arrive with three children and just carried on.

To start at the beginning, William Duke of Clarence fell head over heels in love with the prominent Irish actress, Dorothea Bland or Jordan, to give her the stage name about 1790. William was a big spender but, like his brothers, was always penniless. Therefore a liaison with a highly successful and popular actress could only have been a good thing, for him anyway. After having been pursued for many months, Dorothea agreed to move in with William on 13th October 1791, whereupon William wrote to his brother George saying 'you may safely congratulate me on my success'.

George Augustus was born in 1794, followed by Henry in 1795 and Sophia in 1796. King George III seems to have tolerated this relationship and this was demonstrated when he created William the Ranger of Bushy Park in January 1797, both to give him something to do and a source of income. The satirical cartoonist, James Gillray, caught the mood of the nation with his cartoon *La Promenade en famille*. This depicts William and Dorothea en route from Richmond to Bushy Park. William is pulling a carriage containing the three children with young George cracking the whip whilst Dorothea is reading her part as Little Pickle from the new play *The Spoil'd Child*.

Bushy Park air obviously agreed with them as they went on to have seven more children between 1798 - 1807 at Bushy House.

It is hard to see where Dorothea found time to take to the stage but she appears to have been working almost continuously during these years. The separation in 1811 of William and Dorothea was carried out in a very underhand way and her future treatment was nothing short of abominable but that is another story.

William's immediate elder brother, the Duke of Kent died in 1820 and his father, George III a fortnight later. He was succeeded by his son, George IV. Suddenly William was a serious contender for the throne and the Government set about ensuring the succession, resulting in his marriage to Princess Adelaide. George IV was not a well man and on 26 June 1830, he died leaving the throne free for William.

In the meantime, the FitzClarences had been busy. George had joined the army and fought in the Peninsula War. Here it was said that he had the makings of a good officer showing 'great quickness, intelligence and activity'. His brother Henry went into the navy although this was not very successful and he was later commissioned in the Fusiliers. They were soon in trouble as part of a group of officers who accused their commanding officer of cowardice and a neglect of duty. At the subsequent court-martial, the C.O., Colonel Quentin was acquitted and the two FitzClarences were packed off to India for their troubles. George made the best of his circumstances and had good reports about him sent back. Henry was less fortunate; he clearly did not take to the climate. After a protracted illness, the Governor General decided to send Henry home but he contracted a fever on the way and died a few days later.

William was very proud of his children, especially his daughters – 'and I am now come to that time of life that I must make sacrifices I would not formerly have done; but then I am the father of ten children and it is my duty to provide for them.' The girls all made good marriages; Lady Sophia to Philip Sidney, 1st Baron de Lisle, Lady Mary to General Charles Fox, Lady Elizabeth to the 18th Earl of Erroll, Lady Augusta to Lord John Kennedy-Erskine and Lady Amelia to the 10th Viscount Falkland.

Even before taking the throne, the boys had shown signs of the overweening arrogance that was to become their trademark in later years. In society parlance they were called 'Les Batards' and their pretensions were the subject of unfavourable comment. Now that William was to be crowned, the boys jointly demanded honours and allowances vehemently. They wrote to William 'We are well aware of the cruel position in which we are placed as natural children.' William partially gave in and passed on one of his titles, Earl of Munster, to George and ranks that are in line with the sons of a marquis to the others. This did not satisfy George and he demanded the Order of the Garter in recompense for the part he expected to play at the coronation, 'Let me carry your crown at the Coronation – for who is more fit than your own flesh and blood.' The squabbling went on into the next year until George was made Constable of the Round Tower.

George was never happy with his lot and was completely dissatisfied with the provisions made for him despite gaining the rank of Major General and becoming Aide-de Camp to Queen Victoria. He married Mary Wyndham in 1842 and they had seven children. His increasing mental instability took control and in 1842 he shot himself with a pistol that had been presented by George IV.

Brother Frederick fared a little better. He was also in the army and reached the rank of Lieut General. In addition he was the Lieut Governor of Portsmouth until 1851 when he left this position to take command of the army in Bombay where he died in 1854.

The next brother, Adolphus, became Rear-Admiral Lord Adolphus Fitzclarence, GCH, ADC, RN. He had a fairly undistinguished career culminating in command of the Royal Yacht, the *Royal George* and died in 1856.

Augustus, the last son, proved unsuitable for military life on the grounds of poor health, although it is said that he inherited his mother's histrionic talents. He followed the time worn pattern of entering the Church and became Vicar of Mapledurham. He died in 1854.

To return to George and the Munster line, George was succeeded by his son, William, and then by his own son, Geoffrey who died in a mining accident in South Africa. The title passed to his brother, Aubrey, who died unmarried in 1928, to be succeeded by his nephew Geoffrey as the 5th Earl, who died in 1975. Edward the 6th Earl then died in 1983. The 7th Earl, Anthony, ignored his lineage to become a publican, a graphic designer for the Daily Mirror and latterly an expert on medieval stained glass. He was the last of the FitzClarences and died in the year 2000, ending the line of the House of Munster.

John Walter: Man of 'The Times'

WHEN I THINK BACK to my time travelling on the 7.24am to Waterloo each day, I noticed as many broad sheets as redtops being avidly read by my fellow passengers. In particular was *The Times* which seemed to have the edge on The *Daily Telegraph* and in those early days, I did not know then that it originated at the behest of Teddington man – John Walter.

John Walter was born in the City of London in 1739, the son of a Richard Walter, a successful coal merchant. On his father's death, John succeeded to the business and by 1755, he was the head of Walter, Bradley & Sage. The firm prospered and he made a considerable fortune, taking a leading part in the establishment of the Coal Market or Coal Exchange, an institution of which it is recorded that he was 'the principal planner and manager.' He was chairman of the committee of this institution for many years but he resigned the position in 1769, when he abandoned the coal business to become a marine underwriter.

At first he only concentrated on ships involved in the coal trade. As he became more successful, he also became more involved, joining Lloyd's of London (then Lloyd's Coffee House). He was to write in 1799 'I was twelve years an underwriter at the Coffee House, and subscribed my name to six millions of property; but was weighed down, in common with above half those who were engaged in the protection of property, by the host of foes this nation had to combat the American war.' This was the American War of Independence and it was enough to snuff John's ambitions.

In the beginning of 1782, John called his creditors together and announced his bankruptcy. This was handled in an honourable way and the creditors agreed for John to collect all debts due to the estate, such was their confidence in his integrity. This he did ensuring that the creditors suffered very little but he himself was ruined. With a wife and six children to maintain, he rapidly needed to find a new venture.

John Walter

Later in the year, he met Henry Johnson, a printer who had patented new methods of printing. Greatly impressed with these, John purchased the patent rights from Johnson and in 1784, he acquired the King's Printing Office in Printing House Square, Blackfriars. Initially, he intended only to print books using the logographic process which he confidently expected to become of national benefit. Despite printing some forty volumes, including *Robinson Crusoe* Vols 1 & 2, printing was not delivering the anticipated profits.

However at this time John Wilkes had established the press's right to report Parliament and a thriving London press now boasted eight morning papers with a combined circulation of about 25,000. Their content consisted of parliamentary reports, foreign news culled from continental papers and advertisements and they were all very strongly Whig (Liberal) or Tory.

In May 1784 John wrote to his former creditor and current patron, Dr Benjamin Franklin 'I am going to publish a newspaper' and on Saturday the 1st January 1785, the presses rolled for Issue 1 of *The Daily Universal Register* which three years later was to become *The Times*. At four pages and sixteen columns printed by hand and priced 21/2d (11/2d of which was stamp duty), John Walter had arrived as a newspaper publisher. His editorial proclaimed *'The Register*, in its politics, will be of no party... Due attention should be made to the interests of trade, which are so greatly promoted by advertisements.' Unlike his

rivals, he would not hold over advertisements to make room for windy Commons debates.

The Register plodded on in its way. John's high-minded principle of putting advertising revenue before affairs of state was all very well but it did not make money. When, in 1789, he accepted an under-the-counter Government salary of £300 per annum, he was only doing what every other newspaper proprietor in London was doing. In his case, it was a fee for publishing paragraphs favourable to the King's party but it was to backfire badly.

In 1789 George III was declared cured of his madness, much to the relief of his Prime Minister, Pitt the Younger, who knew that a Regency under the Prince of Wales would soon see him out of office. A letter containing two paragraphs of copy arrived at Printing House Square, bearing the agreed secret mark of the Secretary to the Treasury. The screed attacked the conduct of 'Prinny' and the Duke of York whilst at the King's bedside, implying that they had not shown due respect for the monarch and were not especially pleased that he had recovered. John duly published and the King's sons duly sued.

John expected Pitt to bail him out of trouble but Pitt remained silent. The case went to court and John's defence was that he could not be personally held responsible for every word printed in the paper, an excuse as lame then as it would be now. Nevertheless, he established the stout journalistic principal of refusing to divulge his sources. He lost the case, was fined £50 with a further £50 for a libel against the Duke of York, and sentenced to two years in Newgate prison. He bemoaned his lot protesting that he was locked in his cell at eight every night 'without a sixpence for all the expenses I am at.' However he continued to draw the £300 each year and in a moment of remorse, the Prince of Wales gave him £250 for his trouble and won him an early release after sixteen months.

As the years moved on, John began to relinquish power to his son William and by 1795 he retired

The Grove. as extended. in about 1910

to Teddington leaving William with the printing business and his other son, John Jnr, managing *The Times*. John acquired a house named The Grove which had been built by Sir William Chambers for a prominent Jewish merchant, Moses Franks. Being Jewish, Moses Franks did not attend St Mary's Church and so when John arrived at Church to claim his pew, he was informed that there was not one. John was much aggrieved with this and set about suing the churchwardens of the parish, Messrs Gunner and Drury, calling on them to show cause as to why they had not seated the plaintiff and his family in the parish church in accordance to his situation and condition. He won his case, thereby setting a precedent for ecclesiastical law.

Despite crossing swords with the establishment, again, John became a churchwarden himself in 1801. Having regard to his own experiences, the first thing he accomplished was a complete re-allocation of the pews, part of which caused male and female servants to be separated. Apart from this he seems to have enjoyed the quiet life of Teddington until his death on 16th November 1812. He is buried in Teddington Church. It would be interesting to know what he would have made of his present successor at *The Times*.

Refs: VCH Middlesex Vol IV, Momentous Times by Alan Hamilton, Times Past by Rosemary Atkins

Robert Udney (1725-1802)

ANOTHER UNUSUAL STREET name in Teddington is Udney, as in Udney Park Road. The mystery man Robert Fullerton Udney was born in Udny Castle, Aberdeenshire (in Scotland they have dispensed with the 'e') in 1725. He was the second son of James Udney and fourteenth in succession to the property. He became a very successful West Indian merchant and built up a considerable fortune in his dealings. His brother, John, had entered the diplomatic service and had risen to the rank of British Consul at Leghorn and Venice. The Udneys have a complicated family tree with many James, John and Robert entries.

Already living in Mayfair, Robert decided upon a country retreat and acquired a house on the corner of Teddington High Street and Kingston Lane in 1789. The architect, William Niven, who lived in the house for eight years, described it thus: 'In Robert Udney's time the land in connection with the house is said to have extended to the river (Thames) and to have consisted of some 70 acres. ...It was a good specimen of the pleasure-house which it was fashionable to build in the last century within a drive of London.'

Writing in 1984, local historian Paddy Ching challenged this: 'In the Enclosure Award of 1800, Udney owned a house, offices, yard and gardens, both freehold and copyhold, of about 3.5 acres, which was on the corner of Kingston Lane and the High Street; a garden on the opposite corner of Kingston Lane and the High Street, 16 perch; 2 houses and about 0.75 acre of land on the west side of Watt's Lane; a piece of land with a summerhouse in Bleachfield Meadow on the banks of the Thames, copyhold, about 4 acres and 3 allotments of freehold land in Southfield totalling 11 acres. The total amount of land was just over 17 acres, not the 70 acres reported by Mr Niven.'

He was married twice; first to Mary Hougham on 26th October 1749, by whom they had a daughter, also Mary Hougham and second in 1787 to Martha Jordon. We are not sure what happened to his first wife but Martha Udney certainly caught the eye of his neighbour, Horace Walpole. In a letter to Mary Berry on 29th July 1790, Walpole wrote 'I have seen Mrs Udney. O! She is charming, looks so sensible, and unluckily, so modest. Mr U---- looks as old and decrepit as I do.' Given his own persuasion, this was high praise indeed; the letter went on to say "... At my return I found a note from Mrs U---- to invite me to a concert on Sunday.' A further letter of 6th September 1795 states 'I sent the U-----s half a buck. They wanted me to partake of it, which, luckily, I declined; and well it was I did, for they had invited that surfeiting flatterer, Lady D----, and such a hogshead of sweet sauce would have overloaded any stomach that has not a royal digestion.' Walpole was clearly becoming very possessive of his friendship with Mrs Udney and when he heard that the miniaturist artist, Richard Cosway, was staying with the Udneys he wrote that 'Cosway romanced with his usual vivacity.'

At some point in time, Robert started upon his art collection. His brother, John, as British Consul in Italy, was ideally placed to act as Robert's agent in the purchase of many paintings by the Italian old masters. In fact John should have taken a good part of the credit for assembling this collection which became internationally well known. Word certainly reached the ears of George III and on more than one occasion he and

Queen Charlotte visited the house for breakfast, en route to Windsor and to view the paintings. On leaving on one winter's morning, the king is reputed to have said 'I will put on my great-coat Udney, for it is better to sweat than to cough eh – better to sweat than cough.'

Given that the art collection was internationally known, it is very strange that we do not know exactly where the gallery was sited. Clearly it must have been a large expanse of building; was it purpose built or was some part of the house converted? Niven made the following suggestion 'Upon the brickwork of the house itself were the initials I.K. and the date 1768. The house gave one the idea that it had been built more with a view to entertaining than for residence, the bedrooms being rather inadequate compared with the reception rooms which measured about 30ft by 20ft. The drawing room was on the first floor, a handsome room 14 ft high... Beyond the drawing room was an elliptical room with domed ceiling, which probably served as the ante-room to the picture gallery, which seems to have formed a west wing and was taken down apparently about 1825.' A different account by Robert Fuller stated that the picture gallery was a separate building, standing alone, on the opposite side of the High Street (perhaps Udney's other land to the west of Watt's Lane). Whichever was the true location, we will probably never know.

One of the Mary Udneys became under-governess to Princess Charlotte; we do not know for sure which one – Niven feels that it was the daughter

but Ching is equally sure that it must have been the mother. Whichever Mary was involved gave rise to the local legend that the Royal carriage was often seen on the street of Teddington carrying Mary and her charge.

Robert Udney died at his Mayfair house in Hertford Street in January 1802. The Gentleman's Magazine ran an obituary on him which described him as 'a gentleman much distinguished for his taste in the fine arts, and ranked with our best judges of painting ... and possessed a fine collection of pictures.' After his death the art collection was put up for sale and was auctioned at Christie's. Unfortunately it was a bad time marketwise with prices being very depressed and sold for far less than the values their new owner, Sir William Cunynghame – Udney's son-in-law, had put on them, to the extent that the executors went to court on the issue and the case ran the full course of the law.

The estate remained intact under Cunynghame for the next fifty years but after then, parts of it were disposed of. The major part of its dispersal was in 1920 when the local council acted on the government initiative to build 'Homes for Heroes' and the estates between Kingston Lane and Fairfax Road were developed.

Robert Udney remains something of a mystery man, not even worthy of an entry in the Oxford Dictionary of National Biography.

Pioneer of Mountaineering: Edward Whymper (1840-1911)

WHEN ONE THINKS of mountaineers, the usual case that comes to mind is of Hilary and Tenzing who managed to conquer Everest just in time for the Queen's coronation. Or perhaps George Mallory who didn't quite make it despite an heroic effort. Or maybe Chris Bonnington who has climbed every mountain ever heard of. But today we need to think back to the 1850s, to a time when the Himalayas and Everest were unknown to Western climbers; to a time when the world's most famous unconquered mountain was the Matterhorn in the Swiss Alps. Enter Edward Whymper.

Edward Whymper was born in London to Josiah and Elizabeth Whymper. Josiah was a Dutch wood engraver who had anglicised his name from Whimper to improve his business prospects. Although solvent, his business was hardly a great success and the family lived on the breadline. Edward joined the family business and developed as an illustrator embracing general artwork as well as engraving. He established a reputation and caught the eye of publisher William Longman, who, in1860, commissioned him to go to the Alps and make on-the-scene sketches of the Alpine peaks for a forthcoming book on mountaineering.

Whymper had a vague ambition to be an arctic explorer but had never seen a mountain in his life, not even a Scottish or a Welsh one. This commission gave him the opportunity to break away from the drudgery and tedious routine of the family firm. On 23rd July he set off on this new adventure. Naturally he was introduced to mountaineering whilst in Switzerland and he took to it like a duck to water. In his first summer there, he covered 600 miles on foot. He visited the Monte Rosa Hotel in Zermatt, the 'Mecca' of every climber in Europe, and mingled with international names in this new and fast growing sport. By early September he had reached Chamonix, an ancient town on the Mont Blanc range, overflowing with the tourists of the day.
His journey took him to La Bessee where he sketched Mont Pelvoux for Longman. Here he met some of the people who most influenced him over the next few years; Michel Croz – a guide who would take Whymper on his most successful campaigns, Jean Reynaud – a Frenchman and 'a right good fellow' who would be his climbing companion the following year and Prof T G Bonney who was to write Whymper's obituary many years later.

He had enjoyed a most successful first season. Whilst reflecting on his introduction, he soon realised that with his innate self-confidence, he could enter the society of the class of men whom he so admired and hold his own with them.

Whymper returned to the Alps the following year and climbed the previously unbeaten Mont Pelvoux, the first of a series of climbs in the area which added to the mapping of the range. All the time his reputation was growing. He was elected a member of the Alpine Club and enlarged his circle of friends. During this time he experimented with climbing and camping equipment. However Whymper was to be frustrated eight times in his attempts to climb The Matterhorn.

In 1865 he again planned a further attempt on the Matterhorn but was hampered in his efforts by a rival expedition led by the Italian, Felice Giordano who had secretly engaged the best guides and porters in the area and effectively stole a march on Whymper. However they were heavily provisioned and would move slowly. A chance meeting between Whymper and Lord Francis Douglas brought about a plan to climb the east face which was thought unassailable. Douglas had two experienced guides, 'Old' Peter Taugwalder and 'Young' Peter Taugwalder. Before they had completed their arrangements Whymper and Douglas discovered a further English expedition was in progress led by Rev Charles Hudson with Michel Croz as guide. A third member, Douglas Hadow who was only 19 completed the party. Whymper approached Hudson and both parties agreed to join forces to outpace the Italians.

Whymper's group left the Monte Rosa Hotel on July 13th – four climbers and three guides. Some hard climbing over very difficult peaks followed for the ascent and the stark realisation that they had succeeded was overwhelming. Wymper and Croz rushed to the summit and ended at a dead heat. The Italians were some 1,200 feet below them on the other side of the mountain. Croz planted a tent pole in the snow and attached his shirt to it whilst Whymper shouted and sent rocks tumbling down to attract the Italians' attention. The Italians, shocked and completely deflated by the sudden appearance of the English on the summit, turned and headed down the mountain.

Then began the descent. Hudson and Whymper agreed the order; Croz would lead, Hadow, the least experienced next, then Hudson, Douglas and Old Peter. Whymper and Young Peter stayed behind to write their list of names and leave them in a customary bottle on the summit and then caught up the rest of the party. Disaster struck when Hadow, who had shown signs of difficulty on the ascent, lost his footing and fell against Croz, knocking him over. 'I heard a startled exclamation from Croz, then saw him and Mr Hadow flying downwards. In another moment Hudson was dragged from his steps and Lord Douglas immediately after him. ...Old Peter and I planted ourselves as firmly as the rocks would permit. The rope was taut between us and the jerk came on us both as one man. We held but the rope broke.' The descent continued with Whymper at odds with the two Taugwalders over their attitude to the accident.

A search party went out the next day but Whymper knew that survival was impossible. The four

had fallen over 4,000 feet bouncing from one precipice to another on their descent. Three mangled bodies were found in the order of their climb but of Lord Francis Douglas there was no trace. As *The Times* was to put it, the deceased were not 'common men' and despite the strong denials of the survivors, there were strong suggestions that the rope had been cut to save their lives. Queen Victoria even suggested that the sport should be outlawed altogether.

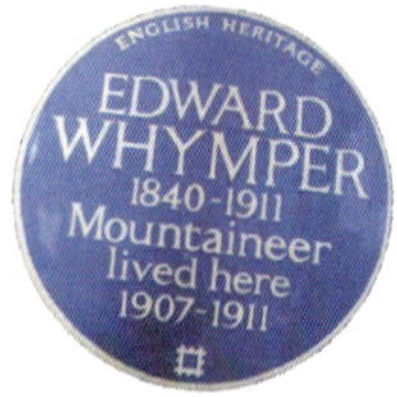

The accident always haunted Whymper and he later wrote 'Every night, do you understand, I see my comrades on The Matterhorn slipping on their backs, their arms outstretched, one after the other, in perfect order at equal distances – Croz the guide first, then Hadow, then Hudson, and lastly Douglas. Yes I shall always see them ...'. The profound effect it had on him led him to drink, something which stayed with him to the end of his life. Whymper rarely climbed the Alps again, although he visited regularly and in 1871, he published his account of The Matterhorn expedition in *Scrambles amongst the Alps*.

To the surprise of his contemporaries, in 1906 he married Edith Levin, the daughter of his landlady in Southend and forty-five years his junior. They moved into 82 Waldegrave Road, Teddington, the only house he ever owned. Unfortunately the union did not last and although they had a daughter, Ethel, who was also to become a mountaineer, they separated in 1910.

In later years, probably due to the Matterhorn experience and his alcoholism, he managed to antagonize all who worked with him. Although he continued to climb in Canada and Europe, he was becoming more physically restricted in what he could achieve.

On 16th September 1911, Edward Whymper died aged 71, shortly after a climb in the Alps. Although obviously ill, he had refused medical attention by locking his hotel room door and here he died. He is buried In Chamonix. A Blue Plaque was mounted in Waldegrave Road in 2011.

See TW11 website for references.

The Black Act and John Guy

AT THE BEGINNING OF the eighteenth century, poaching from deer parks up and down the country was rife. Two particular gangs were notorious for their daring; the Windsor Blacks and the Waltham Blacks. 'Blacks' was attributed to them for the practice of blackening their faces when out at night. The landlords were starting to suffer heavy losses and were not going to take it lightly. As usually happens in such circumstances, the landlords banded together to lobby Parliament to bring in new legislation to combat this threat. This brought about a new law – 9 George I c.22 – which came to be known as 'The Waltham Black Act' 1723, or simply 'The Black Act'.

This law was entitled 'An Act for the more effectual punishing wicked and evil disposed persons going armed in disguise, and doing injuries and violencies to the persons and properties of His Majesty's subjects, and for the more speedy bringing the offenders to justice; it is (among other things) enacted, that if any person or persons, from and after the 1st day of June, in the year of Our Lord 1723, being armed with swords, firearms or other offensive weapons, and having his or their faces blacked, or being otherwise disguised ...'

This hastily passed piece of legislation was to be a deterrent and carried draconian penalties for the hunting, wounding or stealing of red or fallow deer, and the poaching of hares and conies (rabbits) and fish. The first category of offenders cited in the Act is of 'persons armed with swords, fire-arms, or other offensive weapons, and having his or her face blackened'. The penalty for breaching this Act was death by hanging. However it was not only a requirement of the Act that the poacher was caught 'red-handed'; a suspect could be accused on sworn testimony and if he failed to so surrender and was then apprehended, be deemed guilty and sentences to death without further trial.

Not surprisingly, this was one of the most unpopular acts of legislation ever passed in this country.

Little is known of John Guy, a young man of about 25 from Teddington. Taking supper one evening with his sweetheart at an inn, 'a discourse arose concerning the expeditions of deer-stealers, which Guy's mistress took occasion to express great admiration of, and to regard them as so many heroes, who had behaved with courage enough to win the most obdurate heart, adding that she was very fond of venison, and she wished she had known some of them.' In an attempt to impress the girl, Guy seems to have sought out the company of poachers and joined them on their exploits. They would go into a park on foot, sometimes with a crossbow, and sometimes with a couple of dogs, being armed always with pistols for their own defence. When they had killed a buck, they trussed it up and put it upon their backs and walked off.

John Guy joined forces with a London wheelwright named John Berrisford, or Biddisford, known as Jack the Wheeler, who was a well known deer stealer who had been proclaimed under the Act in March 1724 after an affray on Enfield Chase the previous October. A game keeper was wounded in this attack. On one occasion the game keepers were tipped off by a local innkeeper that Berrisford and Guy were to poach in their park. They summoned help from the local gentry and two grooms arrived at about 11pm. They tied their horses in a little copse and went to the place the keepers had appointed to keep guard. The poachers were confronted but broke loose and entered the copse where the horses had been tied. Cutting the bridles, they mounted the grooms' horses and rode off as fast as they could, turning the horses loose as soon as they were in safety.

This escape and similar incidents of the same nature enhanced their reputation and made them bolder than perhaps was good for them. In a very short space of time John Guy seems to have risen from a lowly apprentice to a master criminal with a price on his head. Not content with their raids on chases and such places, they broke into the paddock of Sir Anthony Duncombe (later Lord Faversham and nephew of Charles Duncombe, the Lord Mayor of London) on 5th September 1724 and killed some fallow deer.

One Charles George, the Head Keeper, heard the noise that they made, and with his assistants, followed the sounds and came upon the poachers. A fight ensued and in the exchange of fire, Jack Berrisford was hit in the stomach. As the Northampton Mercury put it the following day 'On Tuesday morning died, in Kingston Jail, John Berrisford alias Jack the Wheeler, a notorious deer-stealer, who received his death's wounds in an encounter with the keepers of Richmond Park early that morning.'

Guy was captured by the keepers and taken to Kingston Jail. He eventually came to trial at the Old Bailey, was found guilty and sentenced to death. According to the journal of Newgate Jail, to which he sent to await execution, 'his conviction was very much contrary to his expectation; and after sentence was passed upon him, though he was far from denying his guilt, he was also far convinced in his own mind that he should escape the Law.' When he finally saw his name

on the Death Warrant, he began to appreciate the enormity of the sentence. 'He applied himself heartily to prayer and other religious duties, seeming to be thoroughly penitent for the crimes he had committed.' He also sent letters to his companions, guilty of the same crimes, to prevail upon them to give up their ways to avoid 'the same fate which he suffered, for so inconsiderable a thing perhaps as a haunch of venison.' He was hanged at Tyburn on 29th April 1725, the first Londoner to be executed under the Black Act.

John Guy's place of burial is unknown.

The Black Act was repealed but not until 1827.

There is some confusion as to the whereabouts of Sir Anthony Duncombe's paddock. Some accounts hold that the poachers were caught in Richmond Park, whilst others hold that there was a separate attack in Richmond Park on the same night, placing Berrisford and Guy elsewhere. There is no record of a private deer park amongst Duncombe's lands in Teddington although it is not inconceivable that he held a lease on the hunting rights of Bushy Park.

Ref.
London Gazette 7-10 March 1724
Lives of the Most Remarkable Criminals
by A L Hayward

Education in Teddington

EVEN WITH MY GREAT love of Teddington, I cannot claim the town as a great seat of learning. Yet it has existed since before Saxon times and has been in constant occupation since those times, so there must have been some form of education in place.

The earliest legend is that Dame Dorothy Bridgeman left an amount of £40 in her will in 1697 to the parish for the purchase of a plot of land, the rent from which was to pay for the education of 12 girls. The old Parish Magazine of 1875 confirmed that this was so and that the land was now in the occupation of the Vicar and produced an income of £5.00 a year. An amusing aside in the parish register notes that a Mr Abraham Clark is mentioned in later years as having been paid 25/- (£1.25) a quarter for giving such education. Unfortunately he spelt 'write' as 'wrighte' and 'teaching' as 'techin,' so one may be excused for doubting his professional qualification. In 1720, his pay was suddenly stopped for, it is said, his being in debt for rent.

In 1711 20 other parishioners gave an amount of £22.4s.0d. towards the teaching of the children of Teddington. However perhaps they should have started with the teaching staff as we are told that one mistress could not write her own name legibly and another signed with a mark. In 1718, Mr Wm Alexander received £3.1s.4d. for teaching 28 children to sing during three months. No charge appears for pens, light or fuel, but mending broken glass occurs. In 1741 the list of subscribers had dwindled to only five although by 1761 the number of children was 44 from 21 families. The situation was so bad that the Vestry passed a resolution that every family could send only one child each to school.

Things obviously drifted along and there were a number of dame schools in existence at that time. A dame school was an early form of a private elementary school, usually taught by women and usually located in the home of the teacher. The curriculum was very basic; reading, spelling,

Teddington Public School 1906

writing and some mathematics if you were lucky (or not). One such dame school was run by Miss Elizabeth Acton at Faversham House in Teddington High Street and continued into the 1870s. By 1824 part of the Bridgeman legacy was being used for other purposes as only 12 children were being educated in two dame schools.

The inadequacy of the Vestry efforts in the direction of education came to a head in 1831 and in August of that year, the residents formed a committee to finance a new school and oversee its building. Its patron was Queen Adelaide, living nearby in Bushy House, and she personally donated £100. The target was met fairly quickly, building commenced and Teddington Public School opened for business on 30th January 1832. The principles of the school were as laid out in Chris French's *A History of St Mary and St Peter's Primary School* – 'To provide a good plain education suitable to their wants and condition, for all boys of the village, including those of the immediate neighbourhood whose parents or guardians desire to give their children the benefits of the institution; and secondly in its system of discipline, to inculcate religious principles, correct moral conduct, duty to parents, diligence, fidelity and contentment in their future stations in life, and gratitude to God and obedience to His Commandments. Instruction on these heads being drawn from the pure source of the Holy Scriptures.'

Teddington Public School

The first master was Mr Salisbury on a salary of £60 per annum and he had a charge of 51 boys. The school was for boys only at this stage and they were required to attend Mondays to Fridays 9.00am to 12.00 noon and 2.00pm to 5.00pm. There was a charge of 2d per week payable on Monday mornings. The committee insisted on a high level of discipline and the school master was judged on how he maintained such discipline. Unfortunately Mr Salisbury did not come up to the committee's standards and he was dismissed after only six months.

Chris French describes an extreme case of harsh discipline that took place in September 1832 – 'two boys – Joseph Walters and Thomas Hammerton – were punished for stealing ten shillings kept in the Donation Box in the schoolroom. Not only did they have to stand in front of the whole school holding a sheet of paper with the word "THIEF" on it whilst the rest of the boys chanted "thief", but Joseph Walters – the main instigator of the crime – was to be publicly flogged and receive two dozen lashes.'

Despite this, the school flourished with a girls' section added in 1843 and an infants' section in 1848. However there was a high turnover in the number of masters and the problem was exasperated by the master's wife usually taking the role of mistress of the girls and infants. This was largely a matter of salary; a skilled worker could earn a much higher wage than a school master. The problem was resolved by the school being awarded a government grant in 1853 which made up the master's pay to a commercial level.

1863 saw the coming of the railway to Teddington. This brought about a huge increase in population which was to continue to the end of the century, and the subsequent demand on more school places. Various Education Acts of 1870, 1880, 1891 and 1902 closely monitored the progress made in Teddington schools as they opened:
1865 Station Road Undenominational School
1875 St Mark's School opened
1883 Sacred Heart RC School opened
1884 St Paul's RC Convent School opened

Stanley Road School 1907

1899 Victoria School opened
1903 Summerleigh School opened
1905 Teddington Council School opened.

All the time the Public School was being expanded and it continued to receive good reports. When the new parish of SS Peter and Paul was created, the school changed its name to St Mary and St Peter and when the buildings were resited, the new name moved with it.

The Council School became Stanley Road School in 1907. It lost its senior wing in 1962 and now is an infants and junior school.

The legendary Sarah Collis was headmistress at the Station Road School. She served here from the school's beginning in 1865 to her retirement in 1906. Her place was taken by her niece, Miss Mary Collis and in 1936; the school became Christchurch County Primary School. In view of the esteem in which the Collises were held, the school finally changed its name to Collis Primary School in 1960 and moved to its present location in Fairfax Road in 1972.

A major development took place in 1962 with the opening of Teddington Secondary School. This establishment opened as a boys only school and added girls a couple of years later.

In recent years, the standards of Teddington schools have been highly praised and places are much sought after. Altogether a bit different from the £40 donated to educate 12 girls.

Teddington and the Black Death

IN OCTOBER 1347 twelve Genoese galleys put in to the port of Messina in Sicily. Normally such vessels would have carried valuable cargoes of silks and spices from the Far East but on this occasion they were empty, having fled in a hurry from an attack by the Tartars to their fort in Tana on the Crimean coast. The Tartars were blaming the Genoese for the spread of an unknown disease that was devastating Asia Minor.

When the port officials went to check the ships, they found to their horror that hardly anyone on board was left alive and those that were, suffered from a strange sickness 'that seemed to cling to their very bones.' They displayed black boils, some the size of apples, in the groin or armpit and everything that came out of their bodies – breath, blood, pus – smelled awful. The officials immediately turned the galleys away to find another port but already it was too late; the Black Death had arrived in Europe.

The Black Death or bubonic plague was probably the biggest pandemic the world has ever seen. It seems to have originated in China in the 1330s and wiped out more than five million people. Carried by the fleas of black rats, the main symptoms were black boils or buboes in the groin, armpits and neck. It is estimated that eight out of every ten people infected, died from the pestilence.

By the summer of 1348 the Black Death entered England, probably at the southern port of Melcome Regis, a popular trading port for the wool trade. It spread rapidly through England and into Wales, Scotland and Ireland. In those days England was mostly rural with London as the capital and Norwich as the second city.

Medieval Teddington was an unusual manor; it did not appear in the Domesday Book of 1086, nor in the Poll Tax of 1381. It had been awarded to Westminster Abbey allegedly by Edward the Confessor, by way of atonement for breach of a promise to pilgrimage to Rome if he gained the throne. Without the Domesday Book and Poll Tax Roll, it is impossible to state the population of Teddington in 1349. However in an early document called the Commission of Array, a list was compiled on the orders of the king to establish the number of men in each village eligible for military service. The document for the Hundred of Spelthorne, of which Teddington is part, exists for 1338 and shows each village produced about 20 men. 'The Teddington men all had daggers but only 5 had swords, 1 a spear, 14 had axes and 2 hand bills; not a very war like bunch – more like the Dad's Army of 600 years later. Most vills produced the same sort of turnout, bows and arrows being in short supply in this area. Teddington, Halliford, Ashford and Littleton had none, Shepperton and Feltham 1 each, 2 in Harlington, 3 each in Hampton Wick and Sunbury, 4 each in East Bedfont and Hanworth and a staggering 20 in Harmondsworth but they did not carry the almost universal dagger.'

'The men from Teddington were John Goose – sun constable with sword and dagger; William Heryng, vicenar (commander) with spear, sword and dagger; Richard West, Ralph Mabon and Thomas le Notyer with sword and dagger. William, son of Andrew East, and William Notyer had a bill and dagger and the following all had an axe and dagger : Richard le Notyer; John Stalworth, John, Thomas and Richard Elham; Thomas Peek; John Beaumond; John Mordon and John Mordon junior; Simon Mordon; Richard Freeman; Thomas Pestel; John Balle senior and John Balle junior. Richard de Bec, knight (who appears nowhere else)."

In Teddington the Lord of the Manor would have been the Abbot of Westminster and one of the brothers would have been the bailiff who was not resident in Teddington. There was a reeve, a man elected by his fellow tenants to run the day to day business of the manor; 5 free tenants; 15 villein tenants (an "unfree" tenant); 12 cottars (a cottager with a small holding); various manor servants and their wives and children. 100 people would carry out the lord's boonworks (labour given by a tenant to his lord; a day's work at specific times such as ploughing or harvesting) each year.

In 1338/9 the reeve, Walter Notiere, reported a loss of 4d on the rent of John Trewelove as John had died and no heirs had come forward to claim the land and pay the rent. By 1349 the reeve was William Lorchon who had taken over from Walter for reasons unknown; perhaps he had fallen victim to the plague. 'The new reeve reported a default in the rent and tallage of Richard West, William Alleyn, Matilda ate Doune and William East and a default in tallage of Margery Squires. Rent was also due from Roger Basset, Richard Constantyne and of course, John Trewelove. All their land was "in hand" there being no one to pay the heriot or to tend or claim their holdings." Were these people all victims of the pestilence ?

Margery Squires had held her lands by works and therefore paid no rent but paid tallage of 6d at Michaelmas on her virgate (about 30 acres) of land. In 1349 her dues of one-fifteenth amounting to 3d, payable to the king, were paid by the manor. She no longer supplied one peck of rye at Churchscot and one bushel and one peck of rye at Cornbote, nor half a hen and five eggs as part of her rent. Her share of 57 manual works between September and June, 12 summer works, 18 works in autumn and two autumn boonworks was not forthcoming. These deficits were recorded until 1376.

The shortage of men led to increases in prices. The villeins were quick to see that they had an opportunity to better their lots and the following increase in wages was noted. However these higher prices were not to be maintained and by

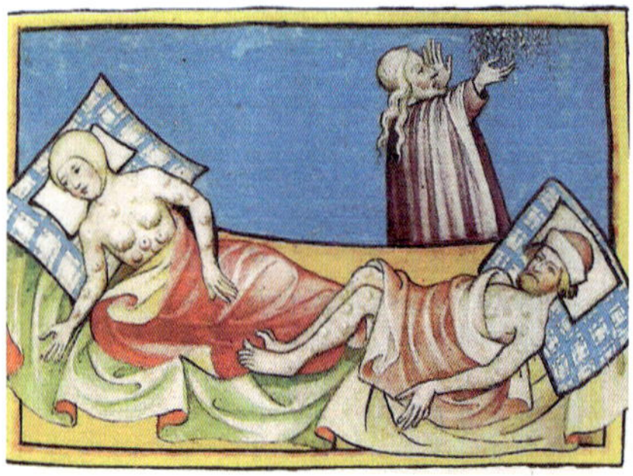

1358/9 had fallen but were still higher than 1349 :

	1335/6	**1349/50**	**1358/9**
Carpenters	31/2d	6d	4d
Ploughman	5/-	11/-	7/-
Maintaining Ploughs	6/-	11/-	7/-
Cowherd	4/-	11/-	7/-
Dairyman	2/-	4/-	

When one does not know the original population figure, it is simply impossible to say how many victims the Black Death claimed in Teddington, but on an estimate of between 100 - 200 people, it seems likely, (based on national figures) to be between one third and one half.

Several other outbreaks of the plague occurred in 1361, 1368, 1371, 1375, 1390 and 1405 but they did not compare with the horrors of that first awful Black Death. The Great Plague of 1665 did not trouble Teddington.

Sources :
Victoria County History of Middlesex Vol II
Medieval Teddington by Mary Clark (BOTLHS 78) 1999
The Black Death by Philip Ziegler (Sutton) 1997
The Black Death by Derek Turner (Longman) 1988
The Black Death by Sean Martin (Pocket Essentials) 2001

Prophetess or Trickster? Joanna Southcott (1750-1815)

I CAN REMEMBER A friend of mine telling me that a surefire way of making money quickly would be to form a new religion. I don't think he could have said that to Joanna Southcott although she may have been of like mind.

Joanna Southcott was born at Taleford and brought up in the village of Gittisham, East Devon, the only daughter of William and Hannah Southcott. Her father was a small farmer and Joanna received very little formal education apart from being required to read a chapter of the Bible every day and discuss it with her father. Her mother died when Joanna was quite young and at the age of 21, her father became very ill and she was obliged to take on the running of the farm. She accomplished this very well for the next two years until her father recovered.

On his recovery, Joanna left the farm and went into domestic service at the house of an upholsterer in Exeter, where she became skilled in that trade. The first 42 years of her life seem to have been very ordinary with nothing to mark her out as a revolutionary. At some time in the 1790s, she heard the preachings of a revivalist Methodist minister who seems to have turned her head. Despite being a regular member of the congregation at Exeter Cathedral, she now left the Church and joined the Wesleyans, 'as she affirmed – by Divine command.' She was now seeing visions and had several apocalyptic dreams.

A 'voice' told her 'The Lord is awakened out of sleep. He will terribly shake the earth.' She suddenly found herself writing messages without any conscious guidance: 'The writing comes extremely fast, much faster than I could keep up by voluntary effort. I have to turn over the pages and guard the lines of writing from running into each other, but, except for this, I need not look at the paper. I can talk on other subjects whilst writing.' Many of her prophecies were made known and more to the point, were fulfilled.

She approached a Church minister, Joseph Pomeroy and passed many of her revelations on to him. She predicted that the Bishop of Exeter, then in good health, would not see Christmas; he died on December 12th. Lord Malmesbury went on a peace mission to Paris in 1796; Joanna predicted that it would fail and it did. She predicted the successes of the young Napoleon Bonaparte in conquering Italy.

News of her predictions was spreading and Joanna was gathering many followers, keen to know if they were in God's eye and what lay in store for them. Joanna appears to have found a die or seal with the letters JC on it between two stars and from this, she would stamp copies of the seal onto blank squares of paper and sell them to her followers as *Certificates for the Millennium*, *Sealings of the Faithful* and *Passports to Heaven* at a charge varying from twelve shillings to a guinea a time. Of these, between six and seven thousand were sold. The stamp was also used to validate her written revelations.

In 1798 she moved to Bristol and she began to publish books of her prophecies and warnings which were eagerly snapped up by her followers. Her output was quite prolific and in all, she published 65 books, many of which are still in print today. Her writing style is unusual, being partly in prose and partly in rhyme.

Her works came to the attention of William Sharp, the engraver, who in 1801, invited her to come to London to continue her ministry. She also had several influential friends in London and was generally well received. She clearly moved around the city and established several centres of faith and chapels in the Home Counties.

One of these was the Millennium Chapel in Teddington. This appears to have been established by Edmund Baker sometime between 1801 and 1811. He left Teddington in 1811 to minister another Southcottian chapel in Dawlish. Some records of the Teddington ministry survive in London Metropolitan Archives which show that the congregation was formed of 125 adults – persons over the age of 14 – who are listed by name and 88 children under the age of 14. Of the adults, 72 were women and 53 were men.

It was interesting to note that some of the members came from as far afield as Windsor, Kingston, Barnes (include Edmund Baker himself), Mortlake, Walton, Sunbury, Richmond, East Molesey, Turnham Green and even Andover. However approximately half were from Teddington, Twickenham and the Hamptons. The Teddington people are listed as living either at The Clarence Arms or Clarence Arms Lane or Clarence Arms Street. No address is given for the chapel and this remains a mystery to this day. Could it have been in the vicinity of The Clarence Arms?

Cobbett in his *Memorials of Twickenham* claims that '...in a small cottage which adjoined Coles' Nursery on the Staines Road, which was pulled down about five years ago (i.e. 1867) lived and preached Joanna Southcote ....' Unfortunately nothing further has been found to verify Cobbett's statement.

The well known Hampton historian, Bernard Garside 'believed that one old Southcottian chapel was in the building still standing next to the Jolly Gardener (now redeveloped as housing) in the Uxbridge Road and was until recently used as a builder's store.' More work needs to be done to expand this theory.

In 1812 a legacy from a rich disciple left Joanna financially secure but in the following year, her 'voices' told her that she would become pregnant at age 64 and give birth to Shiloh, the new Messiah. The due date of 19th October 1814 came and passed and nothing happened. It was reported that she was in a trance and rarely left her bed after that. She became weaker and died on 27th December 1814. At a postmortem four days later, doctors 'examined the body and found no organic disease beyond a condition of dropsy, which had enhanced the false pregnancy.'

Part of Joanna's legacy to the world was a wooden box of sealed prophecies which was only to be opened at a time of national crisis and in the presence of all 24 bishops of the Church of England. Attempts were made to persuade the episcopate to open the box during both the Crimean War and the First World War but to no avail. In 1927, a psychic researcher named Harry Price received a box purporting to be Joanna's from one of the descendants of her trusted friend, Rebecca Morgan (nee Pengarth). After consulting the Archbishop of Canterbury and other bishops, Price opened the box. It contained 56 articles which included a number of books and pamphlets, a lottery ticket for 1796, a paper souvenir 'printed on the River Thames, Feb 3rd 1814,' a fob purse containing a variety of coins, a rusty horse pistol and a woman's embroidered night-cap.

In 1966 the box was passed to the British Museum for safe keeping. They allegedly opened the box, removed some documents to their library and stored the box and remainder of the contents in part of the basement but they have now lost track of it. A rather sad end to an extraordinary life. And we still do not know the location of the Teddington Millennium Chapel.

The Udney Park Playing Fields

WHEN ROBERT FULLERTON Udney died in 1802, he was the owner of 70 acres of Teddington, quite an accumulation in 12 years. These were in different plots in Teddington and mostly unconnected with each other. For the purposes of this discourse, we are only concerned with the 11 acres that stemmed from his house in the High Street and was contained by Udney Park Road to the east, Kingston Lane to the west and the Southfield, later to become Cromwell Road, to the south. This land had been awarded to him under the Teddington Enclosure Act of 1801 and had not been developed.

His house and estate were inherited by his daughter, Mary and her husband, Sir William Cunygham and on his death in 1834, everything passed to their son, Capt George Augustus Frederick Cunygham. Further sales took place with the lands passing to Henry Gouger, Charles Mackenzie, John Chamberlain and W H Hubbard. William Niven, the architect of St Albans and uncle of screen actor David Niven, acquired Udney House in 1880 although he only remained there until 1890. The house had been demolished by 1900.

The 11 acres still pretty much intact and undeveloped was acquired by the Belgravia Land Co Ltd in 1906. Strangely no attempt seems to have been made to develop the land for the next two decades.

In the early 1920s the Old Merchant Taylors' Sports Club (the old boys association of the Merchant Taylors' School founded 1561) raised a Memorial Fund, partly to provide for the education of sons of the fallen OMTs in the First World War and partly to establish a war memorial. They had been looking for playing fields as they had outgrown the facilities shared with Rosslyn Park RFC in Old Deer Park. As their Dr Cove-Smith reported '.... eventually owing to the zeal of H M Wyatt the site of Udney Park Road, Teddington was selected – a tumbled heap of allotments some fifteen acres in extant, necessitating much levelling and turfing but on a good gravel bed.' The Old Merchant

Taylors' War Memorial Sports Ground opened for business in October 1922 and the following year, The Old Merchant Taylors' Sports Club was formed.

The School moved from the City of London to Hertfordshire in 1937 and the Sports Club followed shortly afterwards to a new location at Croxley Green leaving the Teddington site vacant.

Local legend has it that Lord Beaverbrook underwent some serious surgery at St Mary's Hospital, Paddington and after his successful treatment, he asked the hospital if he could do anything for them. Dr Charles Moran, personal physician to Winston Churchill, told Beaverbrook that the Hospital could do with a Medical School. Lord Beaverbrook duly obliged with a donation of £63,000. The Medical School was built but out of this bequest, the playing fields at Teddington were also purchased. Dr Moran considered it necessary to have good rugby facilities to attract the best students from Oxbridge. This created something of an atmosphere in the Rugby Union circles as scholarships were being offered to talented rugby playing would-be medical students and this smacked of professionalism to some of them.

The 1938 local directory shows that the site was renamed St Mary's Hospital Medical School Athletic Ground. For some unknown reason, there were already a series of restrictive covenants applying to the sale of this land from 26 March 1908, which of themselves do not appear to be too onerous for any potential buyer. The conveyance of this land in the agreement of 30 April 1937 is between (1) the Vendors (2) the Rugby Union Trustees and (3) St Mary's Hospital Sports Ground Ltd.

Further covenants were added to the new conveyance : -
'THE Purchasers hereby COVENANT with the Rugby Union Trustees AND IT IS HEREBY AGREED AND DECLARED as follows : -
THAT the Purchasers shall not without the consent of the Rugby Union Trustees use the property hereby assured or any part thereof for any other purpose during the appropriate season than as a sports ground for the playing of games by Amateurs the chief game to be played thereon being Amateur Rugby Football and will not during any part of the year other than the appropriate season use the property or any part thereof for any other purpose than the playing of games by Amateurs.'

The next covenant is a confusing jumble of words which states what would happen in the event of a breach of covenant 1. In some circumstances, the Rugby Union Trustees would have the right to repurchase the ground from the Purchasers i.e. St Mary's for a fee simple of £24,900. This all seems to be relevant to any such breach occurring '....at any time before the expiration of Twe4nty years from the death of the last survivor of all the children now living of His late Majesty King George the Fifty (sic).' I have no doubt whatsoever that a good (or even a bad) lawyer could make something legible out of that - for a fee but I can only feel that the intention is not to alter the basic purpose of the original conveyance.

Covenant 3 provides for a situation if the Rugby Union Trustees do not arrange a sale within nine months of the breach and Covenant 4 defines that 'an appropriate season' shall be between the First Day of September in any year to the Thirtieth Day of April the following year.

Notwithstanding these covenants the conveyance was completed and this commenced a long and fruitful association between St Mary's and Teddington. Their prowess as a rugby football club was enormous and they certainly became the most successful club in the hospital circuit and with such superior facilities, St Mary's hosted many other cup finals and other representative games including a fund raiser for Teddington Memorial Hospital on January 19th 1986 where Peter Yarrington's Golden Oldies (a scratch team of internationals) captained by Roger Uttley took on a select Teddington XV picked from five or six Teddington area clubs. The score has been lost in the mists of time but over £5,000 was raised for Teddington Hospital on the day.

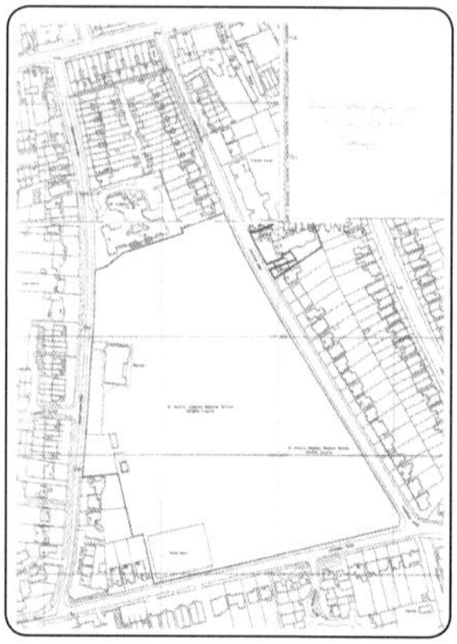

In the years following, St Mary's became a constituent school of Imperial College London in 1988. ICL acquired a new sports ground in Heston in 2014 and the Teddington ground has been put up for sale. The Teddington Society have asked ICL to honour the intentions behind the original Beaverbrook gift and leave the playing fields as they found them. The ICL Trustees for their part do say that they 'have a legal responsibility to ensure that all its assets are managed as effectively as possible.'

I understand that the bids are under consideration and it is a shame that the views of the students do not seem to have been considered. One Imperial Medic has said 'Teddington is steeped in history and has been part of our club for decades and from when we were St Mary's Medical School. Many traditions were born there and it would be a shame to lose its history and worth to our medical school for purely profitable means.'

Watch this space.

I am indebted to Paddy Ching and Dr Christopher French for use of their unpublished manuscripts.

The Building of St Albans

ANY STRANGER VISITING Teddington on the Twickenham or Kingston Roads must wonder how a small riverside town like Teddington ended up with a 'Gothic Cathedral'.

For centuries the parish church of Teddington was St Mary's and we like to claim its Saxon origins but blanch when asked to point them out. The earliest chapel had been founded by Benedictine monks from Staines and certainly by the time of the Norman Conquest, there existed an established church building. Over the years, it was extended and much altered, particularly in the time of the Rev Dr Stephen Hales (1709-1761), who funded much of the work out of his own pocket.

The nineteenth century saw an expanding town, particularly with the coming of the railway in 1863. This brought about a substantial increase in population from 699 at the turn of the century to 1,183 in 1861 to 6,599 in 1881. SS Peter and Paul was created as a chapel of ease to St Mary's in 1865 and became a separate parish in its own right later. During this period Rev Daniel Trinder (1857-1878) was parish priest and he caused a huge rift in the congregation because of his 'popish' ways. This led to a number of parishioners leaving the church and setting up the Free Church of Christ (Station Road) in 1864.

In 1884 the 28 years old Rev Francis Leith Boyd, accepted the 'living' at Teddington from the Earl of Bradford. Boyd was a very ambitious young man and immediately realised that, even with the help of SSPeter and Paul, the structure of the church was too small for what was still a growing congregation. To make any further extensions was not a practical proposition; he decided that a new church was required.

Fortunately he was supported by a staunch and wealthy group of parishioners and with their backing, Boyd set about the challenging task of raising funds for the new church. One of the most important considerations was to appoint an architect worthy of such a project. Boyd sought the advice of local parishioner, William Niven, who had come to Teddington a couple of years earlier. Niven suggested two well established architects to Boyd, who secretly had Niven in mind for the job and continued to press him, until he reluctantly agreed to accept in October 1884. The commission was to be modelled on an existing medieval building and Niven agreed to defer his fees by up to two years if necessary.

Fundraising now began in earnest. It is said that Henry Chinnery donated £10,000 as the first gift. Niven produced his drawings in the Gothic style, based on a French Cathedral, which also reflected Teddington's early monastic connections. Work began in 1885 but Nevin's role was never easy as early donations exceeded expectations and Boyd then wanted Niven to expand and enlarge the original design. In May 1886 Boyd wrote to all parishioners saying that building would be 'from East to West, proceeding as far as funds allow.' Even at this stage it was suggested that the West end would be left unfinished.

A fighting fund of £19,000 had been raised and work went ahead. On 29th April 1887 the foundation stone was laid by the Bishop of London, the Right Revd William Temple (coincidently a contemporary of Blackmore's from Blundell's School).

That autumn Boyd and Chinnery visited the Holy Land to look for a suitable souvenir from Jerusalem for inclusion in the new church. Whilst there Boyd visited the Church of the Holy Sepulchre where he was much taken by the 10,000 silver lamps which lit the church and hit upon the idea of obtaining seven of these for Teddington. These could not be sold, being consecrated property but if Boyd could find something of similar intrinsic value in Damascus to replace them he could have the lamps. Suitable replacements were found with the help of the British Consul.

The building works, as far as funds would permit, was finished in the summer of 1889. There was an outstanding debt of some £6,000, so the consecration could not take place. Instead a service of dedication was held by the Bishop of London on 8th July 1889. A procession then moved out of St Mary's and into the new church of St Alban the Martyr. St Mary's was then closed.

Although this was a massive structure compared to St Mary's, it was substantially smaller than originally planned. To the East there should have been another bay leading to the High Altar and two further bays to the West end where a 'temporary' corrugated iron structure closed off the West front.

With the main body of the Church built, the next task was to furnish it and once again the parishioners came to the rescue. The pulpit, designed by A H Skipworth and made by L A Turner, was given by John Pullman; the reredos, Fontana candelabra, the lectern and the altar frontals were also presented by members of the parish. Mrs Cavendish Bentinek of Ham Common (the late Queen Mother's maternal grandmother), donated candlesticks. Alas many of these items have disappeared completely but attempts are still being made to trace them.

St Alban's was up and running. The rail network had made travel much easier and more affordable. The population was still rising, from 6,599 in 1881 to 14,038 in 1901. Unfortunately such change was not what the gentry wanted and with tram lines being laid before their front gardens, they felt their world becoming enclosed and their privacy evaporating. They therefore moved out to less populated parts of Surrey. The newcomers from the middle and working classes did not have the means of their forebears and the Church's income suffered.

The First World War robbed the British church of many of its old congregations. So much so that the smaller St Mary's was adequate for the reduced size and reopened in 1936 for services. Meanwhile services also continued in St Alban's but with a much reduced congregation. Another World War and a further fall in congregations saw St Alban's struggle on until the last service in 1975 and on 1st January 1977 the church was declared redundant. A Grade II listing had been sought and obtained in 1952. A debate then took place as to what should be done with the old Church and fortunately, Landmark Arts Centre won the day. The 'temporary' corrugated iron structure remained until 1993 when a grant of £500,000 from English Heritage was made for repairs to the exterior and re-roofing to make the building secure and weatherproof. A further £250,000 came from sale of land to complete the West end and to secure a stained glass window from the redundant church of St Peter in Islington. The Church was completed one hundred years after work had first started.

Landmark Arts Centre is now in their 20th year of running the old church and has made a valuable contribution to the local social scene.

The Collis Family

IN THE EARLY PART OF 1838 John David Collis, his wife Mary and their children Jane, Mary S and Thomas moved out of the family home in Newington, where John had a grocery business in Dorset Street, and came to make a new home in Teddington. They moved into a bakery shop with living accommodation, in American Buildings, 5 Broad Street, next to the Britannia beer house. Just why they came here, we do not know but it may have had something to do with John's health and was possibly a reason for them to seek a healthier climate to that of the inner city. Mary was pregnant and gave birth to their fourth child, Robert, on 5th February. A fifth child – Sarah Emma – followed on 29th April 1840. Life seemed to be moving along smoothly until the following April when John died at the relatively young age of 32. He was buried in St Mary's churchyard on 18th April 1841 (the cemetery did not open until 1879).

Mary seems to have adjusted to this early tragedy although she was only 30 herself, and continued to run the grocer's shop and bring up her five children. Her eldest daughter, Jane, went into the business alongside her and in the 1851 census, both Jane and Mary are shown as 'grocers.' The second daughter, Mary S, seems to have gone to live with Mary's brother and wife in Lambeth but by 1851 she had returned to Teddington where she was a domestic servant, living at the home of the curate, Alfred Wilkinson, in the High Street. By 1846, the business had become a grocers and Mary had added the term of 'cheesemonger' to her profession. The business of grocer often incorporated the work of the post office and we see Mary Collis described as Postmistress and Jane Collis described as Sub-postmistress of Broad Street, Teddington.

1861 saw some significant family changes. Mary senior and Jane were still running the grocers and post office in the Broad Street; Mary S and Sarah were both teaching at the Carlton Girls School in Lindrick, Nottingham; Thomas had emigrated to try his luck in New York and Robert had moved back to Kennington where he was teaching.

Having gained some educational experience, Sarah returned to Teddington and opened the Park Road Girls School at 31/33 Park Road in 1865. This had modest beginnings and starting with only 16 girls but rising to 71 by the end of that year. Miss Jane Collis lent a hand by becoming a Sunday School teacher there. This venture was successful and in 1867, larger premises were required and the school moved to Station Road. There is a reference to boys being admitted to the school in 1871 but there is no other reference to boys; indeed all advertising for the school until long into the future declares that it is a 'School for Girls and Infants.'

There is some conflict as to the size of the school; one directory claims they had 318 pupils in 1875 whereas another in 1882 states a capacity of 250 with an average attendance of 179. Whatever the number, the school continued to prosper and in 1885, Sarah's niece – Mary Jane – joined the school as an assistant mistress. By 1890 the school had been enlarged and the capacity had increased to 400 with an average attendance of 300. 1899 reveals that Sarah was assisted by Mary Jane and seven others. 1902 saw the school renamed the Station Road Day School for Girls and Infants with a capacity of 440 and an average of 400.

Meanwhile, at the grocer's store, Mary and Jane continued to run their business efficiently and successfully. The addition of Post Office was clearly a prestige appointment and something to be cherished. Mary showed no signs of slowing down and in 1890, at age 80, she is still shown as Postmistress. She died in 1893, presumably without having retired, and is buried in Teddington Cemetery. Jane then took over the running of the business and herself became Postmistress for Upper Teddington. She did retire from her post in 1899, having probably worked there since the death of her father, giving her a 58 year career. She stayed in Teddington and died in 1913, joining her mother in the family plot in the cemetery.

At some point between 1891 and 1901, probably in 1899 and certainly after Mary Jane had joined the family in 1885, the two sisters, Jane and Sarah moved dwellings to 'Coleraine' 15 Victoria Road, a road leading to the railway station. For a time they employed a servant; presumably this was whilst they were all working.

In 1906, Sarah Emma Collis retired from the school she had founded forty one years earlier but the family connection remained as Mary Jane took over the headship. Sarah continued to live at 'Coleraine' until her death in 1917. She is also buried in the family plot in the cemetery. In the true family tradition, Mary Jane continued to run the school until her own retirement in September 1928. She died in 1930 and was buried in the cemetery. Within the same plot is her sister, Annie Sarah, who died in 1933. It is believed that Annie came to join Mary on the death of Sarah and stayed in Teddington.

As any good Teddingtonian will tell you, the school went from strength to strength. In 1937 the school was renamed Christchurch County Primary School and then, having due regard to the founders and the esteem with which they are still held, the name changed again to Collis Primary School.

1965 saw the school's centenary and in 1972 it moved to its present location in Fairfax Road. The old building was in use as a teachers' centre for some time and is now an Asquith children's day nursery. Now in 2015 the school is celebrating its 150th anniversary and in the light of what has gone before, it will celebrate many more to come.

Sadly, with no living relative nearby, the graves in the cemetery look a little neglected. A poor testament to a remarkable family of ladies who in nearly 100 years gave so much public service to the town of Teddington.

Sir John Fitz and 'The Bloudie Booke' - Part 1

THIS MONTH I AM stepping a little out of the town boundaries but the story is one of great interest as I hope you will see.

It all began when I was staying with friends in Tavistock and one morning I decided to take a look at the monument to Sir Francis Drake as a distant ancestor had something to do with the unveiling of it in 1883. Standing behind the statue is a rather austere block building with crenellated walls but nothing else of any substance around it. I asked my host for the story behind it and he replied that I should know all about it as there was as much of the tale in Twickenham as in Tavistock.

The building, much resembling a prison or barracks was in fact the old gatehouse to Fitzford House, a sumptuous Elizabethan mansion no longer standing and the home of the Fitz family of Devon.

Four generations of the Fitz family had lived on this site and had all been very successful in the law and had all married well, increasing their property and estates with each generation, so that apart from the Devon estates, they owned property in Cornwall, Kent and Southwark. John Fitz, the father of the subject of this story, was a counsellor-at-law and married Mary, daughter of Sir John Sydenham of Brimpton, Somerset. He had managed to add to the wealth of the family and retired from public life.

Devon folklore has it that one day he and his wife were returning to Tavistock across Dartmoor from Moreton Hampstead and they lost their way; the account states that they were "pixy-led" and went around in circles until they came across a clear running stream. Both exhausted and parched with thirst, they dismounted and quenched their thirsts in the clear waters. Immediately John's head cleared; he knew where he was and was able to pick up the trail to Tavistock. In recognition of this, he built a granite structure to enclose the well and bearing his initials and the date 1568,

this still stands today. Such was his superstition; he had water from this well piped to his mansion at Fitzford.

John Fitz then become increasingly interested astrology and the casting of horoscopes. So much so, according to the Rev John Prince that when his wife was about to give birth in 1575, he studied the stars and 'finding at the time a very unlucky position of the heavens, he desired the midwife, if possible, to hinder the birth but for one hour; which, not being to be done, he declared that the child would come to an unhappy end and undo the family.' Thus young John Fitz came into the world.

Young John's early days are not documented but he seems to have had a normal upbringing in Devon. Unfortunately John senior died on 8th January 1589, aged sixty-one. His will made his wife executrix and guardian of their son, who was a little over fourteen years old.

Despite John senior's will, Mary was not granted guardianship of her son. He was a ward to the Queen and was placed in the care of Sir Arthur Gorges, an associate of Sir Walter Raleigh. Young John seems to have been well looked after and there were no early signs of any of the antisocial behaviour to come.

John then married into the nobility before attaining

his majority. His bride was Bridget, sixth daughter of the 3rd Earl of Devon, Sir William Courtenay of Powderham. They had one daughter, Mary born on 1st August 1596 when John had reached his twenty-first birthday. Now that he was of age, he considered himself free of all restraint. He was the owner of large estates, and 'was without stability of character or any principle, and was inclined to a wild life.'

Over the next two to three years, his reputation grew as a boisterous reveller with a fearsome temper who would draw his sword in anger with little provocation.

On 4th June 1599, he was breakfasting with friends at Tavistock and according to 'The Bloudie Book', wine was flowing freely and 'with great varietie of merriments and discourse they outstript the noontide.' As the day wore on, John Fitz had drunk a great deal of wine and started to boast about his possessions, stating that every foot of land in all his estates was owned in freehold, save that owned by the Queen herself. At this point his friend, Nicholas Slanning of Bickleigh, interrupted Fitz to politely remind him that he occupied a small parcel of land that rightfully belonged to Slanning who could claim rent for it should he so wish.

On hearing this, Fitz seems to have gone berserk, leaping up to call Slanning a liar and in a blind fury drawing his dagger and moving as if to stab Slanning. Slanning swiftly drew a large knife he was carrying and parried the thrust. Before any further action could take place, other members of the party interceded to separate the two and calm was restored, at least on the surface. Shortly afterwards, Slanning probably thought that it would be an opportune time to leave and quietly departed for Bickleigh with his servant on horseback.

A short distance into their journey, they came to a steep and rough descent. They dismounted so that the servant might lead the horses whilst Slanning walked through the adjoining field. Suddenly he noticed John Fitz and four others

bearing down upon him. Slanning awaited the arrival of the party and asked Fitz why they had followed him with such urgency. Fitz answered that he was determined to avenge the insult he had suffered earlier and ordered his men to draw their swords, whereupon all five fell upon Slanning who was forced to draw his own sword in defence. There was a brief skirmish and then Fitz's men withdrew, sheathing their swords.

There the matter might have rested but for the cajoling of one of Fitz's men called Cross who shouted 'What play is this? Why child's play; come to fight and now put up your sword!' With this Fitz, who had sheathed his sword, now drew it again and rushed towards Slanning. Slanning was wearing long riding spurs and as he stepped back, they caught in a tuft of long grass and unbalanced him. As he staggered backwards, Fitz ran him through the body and another of Fitz's men struck him down from behind where he fell 'foully killed.'

'Great was the lamentation that the countryside made for the death of so beloved a gentleman as Maister Slanning was.' His children had not yet reached their majority and had to bide their time to take action.

This is by no means the least of the ignominious incidents to involve John Fitz's, I will tell you more of his infamous tale in next month's issue.

Refs: 1. The Bloudie Booke, Or the Tragical and Desperate End of Sir John Fites by J Roberts 1605
2. Worthies of Devon by Rev John Prince 1701
3. Devonshire Characters and Strange Events by Rev Sabine Baring-Gould 1908
4. The Twickenham Museum

Sir John Fitz and 'The Bloudie Booke' - Part 2

WE CONTINUE OUR STORY from last month's edition and rejoin the tale after the dramatic events surrounding the death of Nicholas Slanning.

John Fitz, now 24, feared prosecution for the murder of Slanning so fled across the Channel to France to avoid arrest. Here he stayed until the good offices of the Courteney family managed to procure a pardon from the Queen. He returned home, unsubdued, insolent, riotous and haughty. Queen Elizabeth died in 1603 and James I was crowned the same year. At James' coronation, John Fitz was knighted, not for any service to the Crown but because he was of good family, well connected and a man of property, and 400 members of the gentry were honoured in a similar way.

Sir John Fitz returned to Fitzford and started to continue with his dissolute life. He found that his wife and child were something of a hindrance and curb upon his activities in his wild and dissipated career, and so in a fit of pique he turned them out of his house. Bridget and Mary were forced to seek shelter from Sir William at Powderham Castle. The path was now clear for Fitz and his evil associates, 'Men of dissolute and desperate fortunes, chief amongst them was "Lusty Jacke", one whose deeds were indeed meane, whose qualities altogether none. The Towne of Tavistocke, though otherwise orderly governed with sobriety, and likewise of grave magistrates, was thereby infected with the beastly corruption of drunkenness.' A long string of crimes were committed in the town and after having abused the townsmen and disturbed their neighbours, the gang would return to Sir John's house as a place of sanctuary. There is some dispute as to whether or not Fitz killed one of the town constables.

Matters changed in the summer of 1605 when Sir John Fitz was summoned to London to appear before the courts, to answer a claim for compensation for the murder of Nicholas Slanning, brought by his children. The Queen's pardon did not absolve him from this. There can be no doubt that the intervening years had weighed heavily on Fitz and he set off to London on horseback with one servant, his mind greatly disturbed. Not only was he concerned that a heavy fine would be imposed on him for killing Slanning, he was also under pressure from the Earl of Devon for the treatment of his daughter. He convinced himself that his life was in danger, with the Slanning and Courtney families preparing to ambush and murder him on the route.

At length he reached Kingston-on-Thames and decided to put up there for the night. However he could not sleep; noises disturbed him and he finally arose and insisted that his servant make ready his horse. His phobia had now convinced him that his servant was in the pay of the Slannings or the Courtenays and would lead him into a trap. He therefore ordered the servant to remain at Kingston whilst he proceeded over Kingston Bridge alone. He rode through Hampton Wick and Teddington and became lost on Hounslow Heath. He called at a large unnamed house and was turned away, moving on into Twickenham. He arrived at the Anchor Inn, a modest tavern kept by Daniel Alley and his wife Agnes, who resided there with their three children, a maid servant and a lodger named Robert Goddard.

Daniel and Agnes had been married at Kingston in 1597 and had run the tavern ever since.

By now it was 2am and the town was asleep. Fitz's servant had followed Fitz and caught up with him. He now hammered on the door, shouting for attention. Daniel put his head out of the window and enquired what the gentleman wanted at such an hour. When told that a bed and shelter was required, Daniel Alley begged to be excused, saying that he had no spare room and the inn was small and not suitable for the reception of persons of quality. Fitz was insistent and no doubt offered higher than the going rate for Alley then vacated his own bed, changed the sheets and sent his wife to the children's room.

Fitz then sent his servant on to Brentford where he found lodging, and fell into a restless sleep. He tossed and turned; the host and hostess heard him cry out about his enemies pursuing him and eventually he called for Daniel Alley to sit with him, which he did. The household did not get much sleep that night and at 5am Daniel arose to start a day's work cutting hay in a nearby field with Robert Goddard. They planned their course of the day but their voices reached Fitz who persuaded himself that his enemies had arrived and were surrounding the inn. He rushed downstairs in his night gown with sword in hand and fell upon Daniel Alley and ran him through. Goddard made his escape but Agnes Alley was wounded in the arm. He now discovered what he had done and in a rare fit of remorse or perhaps despair, he set the hilt of his sword into the wall and ran onto the blade, twice.

By now the neighbours had been awakened by the commotion and attended the scene. Daniel Alley was dead. Fitz had stabbed himself and was taken back to bed and his wounds bound. A surgeon was sent for but Fitz angrily refused his services. Word of this tragedy reached the ears of the Earl of Northumberland at nearby Syon Park and he sent his private chaplain 'to put him in mind what he had done, how grievously hee had offended his maker in committing so detestable murders .... and persuading him to repent.' Fitz agreed to make a payment of £100 to Agnes Alley and he died two days later.

Daniel Alley was buried in St Mary's Churchyard on 6th August 1605. Despite being a suicide and being of gentle birth, Sir John Fitz was buried beneath the chancel of St Mary's Church, Twickenham. Possibly the Earl of Northampton may have persuaded the vicar, the Rev Thomas Goose, to allow this, although there is no record of any service being held. Nor is there any memorial. Whether any of his family from Devon attended the ceremony, we do not know.

Agnes Alley recovered from her stabbing and on 8th September 1606, she married George Clarke. Her £100 compensation would have allowed them to live in reasonable comfort.

Young Mary Fitz inherited what was left of the Fitz fortunes and led a remarkable life of her own. She was clearly a great believer in matrimony and married :
- 1608 Sir Alan Percy, son of the Earl of Northumberland
- Thomas Darcy, heir to, the Viscount of Colchester
- Sir Charles Howard, son of the Earl of Suffolk
 1629 Sir Richard Grenville

The epitaph of Nicholas Slanning in Bickleigh Church is in Latin but was translated by Rev John Prince :

'He author of my murder was, and the revenger too,
A bloody murderer of me, and then himself he slew,
The very sword which in mine first, he bathed in his own blood,
O ! of the highest Judge 'twixt us, the arbitration good !'

Refs: - see December '15 Issue

Teddington Hospitals

EVERYONE CAN EXPECT a visit to the hospital at some time in their life and it has become so matter of fact that we hardly take any notice of it. This was not the case for life in Teddington in the 1860s. This was a time when the manor had been sold (1861), the London & South Western Railway had arrived (1863) and the population had increased from 699 in 1801 to 4,063 in 1871. For the purposes of Poor Relief, Teddington was part of the Kingston Union – the Kingston Board of Guardians of the Poor. There were a number of doctors in the town and also some barber surgeons and in the main, one would be administered to in one's own home. For any serious illness or injury requiring surgery, the patient might have been taken to Kingston or even West Middlesex Infirmary.

The old village might have put up with this state of affairs in 1801 with less than 700 people to support but in 1871 and onwards, it was a different story. This brought about some of the leading residents of Teddington calling for a review of matters and so it lead to Thomas Chappell, the head of the world famous family firm of piano makers and music publishers, to take action.

On Friday 10th July 1874 he called a meeting at his home, the magnificent 40 roomed mansion 'Weir Bank' in Broom Road (now absorbed in the Lensbury Club), of the good and the great of Teddington including the vicar, the Rev Daniel Trinder, the newly appointed minister of Christ Church and four physicians to discuss the motion of 'the desirability or otherwise of establishing a hospital for the reception and treatment of the sick poor of Teddington.' The doctors and clergy soon convinced the assembled company of the virtue of the proposal and a steering committee was formed to undertake a feasibility study of the local population as a whole. A public meeting at the Clarence Arms was held on 7th August passed the resolution 'That it is desirable that a Cottage Hospital be established for the benefit of the sick poor of Teddington and Hampton Wick....' and to this end Thomas Chappell

pledged a pair of villas in Elfin Grove for use as the hospital.

A building specification was drawn up to convert these buildings to a hospital at a cost of £149.7s 0d, probably funded by Mr Chappell. The work was completed as quickly as possible and on 6th February 1875, the first matron, Mrs Caroline Casper, took up her duties at a salary of £30 per annum all found, and the first four patients were admitted. The official opening took place on 20th March, the ceremony performed by Lord George Hamilton M.P. for Middlesex. Operations were set to charge the patients 1s (5p) per day and night with the power to reduce the charge according to the patient's means.

Finance was always at the route of the hospital's existence and the meagre fees recovered from the patients did not cover the costs of food, heat and power let alone staff wages and members of the committee were regularly asked to dip into their own pockets to balance the books.

The population continued to grow and more was required of the hospital and out-patient services were set up for the poorer members of the two towns. The hospital was expanded; a dispensary, provided by Mr Chappell opened in 1883 (although it closed in 1903), the number of beds increased to six and then to ten, the staff increased to a matron, two trained nurses, three probationers, a cook and a porter. When Thomas Chappell died in 1902, his family gave a donation of £500 for a new ward to commemorate his name and when this opened in 1904, the number of beds increased to 22.

The constant battle of expenses continued into the twentieth century and regular public appeals for more funds being surprisingly met. Valentine

Knapp, editor of the Surrey Comet must take some of the credit with his launch of 'The Shilling Fund' and other appeals. Hospital Sunday was another very welcome donor to the fighting fund with the Amalgamated Societies parading around the town, collecting boxes at the ready. The activities of the 1914 Demonstration Sunday broke all previous records but before anyone could decide how to spend the proceeds, we were at war with Germany.

The Management Committee placed the hospital at the disposal of the War Department but they politely declined the offer. Some troops however did receive treatment here. A bigger problem was the reduction in funds with no more Hospital Sundays and competing war charities such as the Belgian Refugee Fund and Serbian Relief.

At the end of hostilities, normal life resumed and the Hospital Management Committee renewed their discussion on the desirability of a new hospital. 'Wallace Elmslie, who had been present at the May 1914 meeting and whose only son, Lieutenant Kenward Elmslie, had been killed in action that same year, suggested that the town's most fitting memorial to its 337 dead would be a new hospital, and this was endorsed by the Committee without dissent.' At about the same time, David Anderson, nurseryman of Hampton Road, announced that his family firm was winding up and offered 21/2 acres of land for the new hospital at a price of £2,000.

However the enthusiasm with which the announcement of a new hospital was made did not last and after the dedication of the memorial monolith in January 1921, donations shrank to a trickle. Only £76 was donated in 1921. It was clear that at the present rate, the new building was a far off prospect. It needed someone of outstanding zeal and ability to marshal the forces of the town and drive the project forward. The Honorary Secretary, F Hugh Munby, was elected Chairman and from this position, he proceeded to attack the apathy shown towards the fund-raising.

Starting with a public meeting at Elleray Hall which attracted nearly 300 people, he and his panel made some impassioned speeches. An amount of £16,000 would be required for the first phase, of which only £2,800 was in the bank. The response was immediate and effective; a Hospital Fete gave a profit of £87, The Grand Hospital Carnival Procession and Fete produced £523, the Brick Scheme brought in £40 in its first month. Hugh Munby seemed to be busy, whipping up support and cajoling more money into the building funds. Finally on 29th June 1927 the contract for the building works was signed for a sum of £17,777, a generous donation of £1,000 from David Anderson having clinched the target. A list of 1,863 'persons, firms and organisations who had actively promoted Teddington Memorial Hospital and Health Centre and made its creation possible' was placed beneath the foundation stone for posterity.

This of course, was only the start of the story of the hospital and the ups and downs that followed but it should never be forgotten that the Hospital was built on the public subscriptions of the people of Teddington and Hampton Wick.

Teddington in WWII - Part 1

IT IS HARD TO imagine that a small town like Teddington would have had much to contribute during the 2nd World War but that was not the case as we shall see.

When Neville Chamberlain's grim words announced that we were at war with Germany on 3rd September 1939, the nation was taken by surprise. After the affirmation of the Munich agreement, it seemed that 'Peace In Our Time' had been achieved. Teddington, along with other towns in Britain, tested its air raid sirens, formed its Home Guard units and generally tried to act as if we were ready for war. The initial fears died down as we entered the 'phoney war' period. Life returned almost to normal and complacency seemed the biggest danger.

The year turned to 1940 and the long awaited troubles struck. The French line collapsed and the British professional army, the British Expeditionary Force was in a trap by German Panzer divisions and forced back to the coastal town of Dunkirk. The BEF dug in around the sand dunes awaiting the next onslaught. Dunkirk did not have much of a harbour left after heavy German bombing and the many sunken wrecks and the shallow waters off the coast meant that the heavy naval ships could not get close to the shore to evacuate the stranded troops.

In London, Admiral Ramsey was put in charge of an emergency evacuation which the Admiralty hoped would liberate 30,000-40,000 soldiers. He quickly realised that smaller craft were needed to get into the shallow waters and ferry troops to the big ships. A decree went out to all boat yards along the Medway, Solent and the Thames for suitable craft to be commandeered. At Teddington Lock, Douglas Tough of Tough Brothers received a cable from the Admiralty, ordering him to collect all suitable boats on the Thames and in view of the shortage of experienced seamen with a knowledge of the Channel, some of their owners also. He assembled more than 100 craft and towed them to Ramsgate where they were fitted out for the

Dunkirk crossing. A couple of the boats had to be returned as these were the permanent homes of persons who had been away at work at the time Douglas Tough called. One pet cat almost went on the mission.

Between 26th May and 5th June, under constant enemy fire, the small ships sailed in and out of the shallow waters, taking load after load of soldiers off the beaches and to the comparative safety of the heavy ships anchored offshore. By the time the operation was finished by extensive enemy fire, 332,226 British soldiers and about 58,000 French had been rescued to fight another day.

There were losses and about 100 of the 'little ships' failed to return. However at the 50th anniversary of the evacuation, Bob Tough sailed the cruiser 'Minnehaha', a vessel that his father had found at Ramsgate with her wheelhouse virtually burnt out but with her chart drawer intact. I am pleased to say that son John Tough skippered the boat in the 2015 crossing.

The first enemy bombs to fall in this area were on Tudor Avenue, Hampton on 24th August 1940. They caused much damage to housing but there were no casualties. As the blitz gathered pace, the concentration in the area increased, particularly as enemy aircraft returning home followed the route of the Thames and unloaded any spare bombs on whatever looked a likely target.

Teddington's worst night was 29th November 1940 and is still remembered by some elderly residents. The raid started at 7.20 pm that night and altogether 257 separate incidents were recorded in the Borough's Incident Book. It was the night when high explosive bombs rained on Teddington and Bushy Park; over 100 delayed action bombs

were amongst the fall. The Willoughby Hotel in Church Road took a direct hit. It was a busy night with the payout of the Christmas Loan Club. The landlord, Frank Tomlin, and his family and several customers – in all seventeen people – perished at the pub which was never rebuilt. Half of Argyle Road was demolished. The Baltic Timber Yard in Stanley Road was hit and the blaze lit up the sky. The Baptist Church in Church Road was also bombed and set alight. More deaths occurred in Railway and Tranmere Roads and in Shacklegate Lane, fourteen people died. Families from Walpole Crescent were evacuated to the supposed safety of the air-raid shelters at the National Physical Laboratories but unfortunately one of the slit trenches sustained a direct hit with six fatalities. In total forty-three people lost their lives that night with a further ten hospitalised with serious injuries.

From the very start of the war, extensive activities were taking place at the Admiralty Research Laboratories. There a young scientist from Hampton Wick called Peter Wright perfected a 'degaussing' system which was to protect our shipping from magnetic mines. In fact this proved to be so successful that not a single naval ship at Dunkirk fell victim to a magnetic mine. He further developed this system to make midget submarines to foil German magnetic detectors on the seabed and in this way, our X-Craft submarines were able to penetrate the enemy defences in Norwegian fiords. In 1944 they attacked the German pocket battleship 'Tirpitz', crippling her and effectively putting her out of the rest of the war.

Sometime after the war, Wright was called up by MI5 and became the scourge of enemy agents during the cold war. Dissatisfied with his pension arrangements, he later went to Australia to write his memoirs and is now universally known as 'Spycatcher'.

Meanwhile at the neighbouring National Physical Laboratories, another scientist was working on a completely different project. Barnes Wallace was developing a special type of bomb to breach the dams of the Ruhr valley, thus depriving the Germans of a good part of their hydro-electric power, so valuable to their steel production. Wallace was already an established aircraft designer for Vickers-Armstrong at Weybridge; he had already been heavily involved with the R100 airship and the Wellesley and Wellington bombers. He reckoned that by disrupting Germany's steel production, the war would be shortened by several months.

The 'spherical bomb – surface torpedo' was to be dropped into the water at low level, where it would then skim along the surface like a seaside pebble to its target, the dam. It would then sink to the base of the dam and explode. The technology for the 'bouncing bomb' as it became to be known was developed at the Alfred Yarrow tank of the William Froude Laboratory of the N.P.L. This was put to devastating effect on 17th May 1943 when 617 Squadron – The Dambusters – attacked and breached the Mohne and Eder dams and severely damaged the Sorpe dam. Sadly the raid did not cause as much disruption as Wallace had hoped for but it gave Britain a tremendous morale boost at the time. Unfortunately recent works at the N.P.L. have removed the Froude Laboratory and the William Yarrow tank is now a car park.

Teddington in WWII - Part 2

THE POUNDING THAT London took during the blitz caused many employers to see if they could continue their operations somewhere more safely out of London. One such firm was Shell Petroleum who had set up their sports and social club – Lensbury – by Teddington Lock. Shell moved all of their key personnel to the Lensbury Club and this continued to be their headquarters for the remainder of the war. During this period, their sportsfields were ploughed up as part of the 'Dig for Victory' campaign and the cricket pavilion became the Air Raid Wardens' post.

Bushy Park, which had played host to many allotments in the First War, was again utilised for food production. There were also several temporary buildings set up along Chestnut Avenue in between the trees to provide office space for workers whose London offices had been bombed out.

After the Japanese attack on Pearl Harbour in 1941, America entered the war. A new but raw army was transported across the Atlantic to be trained to carry the fight to Germany. The 8th US Army Air Force arrived in Bushy Park on 9th July 1942 and established their HQ. Local legend had it that the massive convoy of vehicles arrived at Bushy due to a navigational error, for which the Americans had a reputation, when in fact they should have joined the existing American base at Bushey Hall near Watford. If it was an error, then it was an easy one to make as the nearby railway station had been called 'Teddington and Bushey Park'.

The camp was named 'Camp Griffiss' after Lt. Colonel Townsend Griffiss, the first American casualty of the war in Europe. Ironically he was shot down in 'friendly fire' by a Polish RAF pilot. The camp's codename was 'Widewing' reflecting the wingspan of the giant bombers. One of the provisos of setting up the camp was that when hostilities were ended, the camp would be restored to parkland. The base was not actually vacated until 1963. The establishment of the camp began a sometimes fragile alliance with the local population. It was therefore surprising that the camp commander called a public meeting. Many thought he would explain the protocol of his soldiers mixing with the young girls of the town and the precautions taken to maintain a happy relationship. In fact the reason he had called the meeting was to report that a number of young girls had been caught trying to break INTO the camp and he was seeking the assistance of the town to prevent this.

Morale was given a very high priority in wartime. An interesting development took place in Richmond in 1941. The Mayoress, Mrs Phoebe Leon, was anxious to be able to provide a facility for ordinary people to be able to enjoy a nourishing meal at a reasonable price, within the framework of rationing. She set up several premises as eating establishments and also commissioned a series of recipes for this purpose and the concept of British Restaurants was born. News of the venture reached the Ministry of Food who were much taken with the idea and arranged for Mrs Leon to extend the scope of activity to the whole nation. Soon every town in Britain had its very own British Restaurant. In Teddington, the premises now housing Headmasters Hairdressers in the Broad Street was selected and continued in use until 1946.

From June 1941 bombing raids on England continued but on a much reduced scale. The devastation caused in the blitz of 1940 still needed to be cleared up and building materials were in short supply. Very often an unexploded bomb would be found amongst the debris and this would delay clearance until the offending bomb had been dealt with. Between 1942 and 1943 there were only about thirty raids on London and only one of these reached Twickenham.

Early in 1944 General Eisenhower decided to move SHAEF Headquarters (Supreme Headquarters of the Allied Expeditionary Force) to Camp Griffiss. This was to be his base for planning the DD invasion on the beaches of France. Eisenhower did not want to be based in London as he was worried about heavy bombing and also the potential distractions of London nightlife on his soldiers. Certain ladies of the night moved into the boarding houses in Teddington to be close to the GIs and it was a problem for the local constabulary to keep the situation under control. Whilst the General was looking for suitable accommodation for himself, he stayed at Bushy Park Cottage in Park Road and it was necessary to vacate this house before he moved in. He eventually went to Telegraph Cottage on Kingston Hill.

It must have been impossible to keep such an operation secret and it was necessary to deploy huge camouflage nets over the lakes, the Diana fountain and the main Chestnut Avenue to cover up any landmarks visible to the German aircraft. As there was now about 8,000 troops stationed in and around the park, the chances of keeping the base out of enemy eyes were slim.

On 6th June 1944 the D-Day landings took place on Normandy beaches. Despite some minor setbacks, the operation was largely successful. The assault took place on a section of coastline that had no natural harbours and the German High Command did not think that the Allies would be able to mount an attack there as there would have been no way to support frontline soldiers without heavy armour. However the NPL had devised what were known as 'Mulberry' harbours, a series of interlocking artificial harbours which were towed across the Channel, pieced together and then sunk in situ to prepare for tanks and other heavy armoured vehicles to be put ashore.

The logistics of supporting an invading army depend very much on maintaining a fuel supply and the NPL came up with the solution by providing 'PLUTO' – the PipeLine Under The Ocean. In August two complete pipelines were laid from the Isle of Wight to France and these continued to operate at full capacity until the end of the war.

Back in England, Teddington and elsewhere was seeing the attacks of the Reprisal weapons - the V1 and V2. The first V1 hit Holmesdale Road. Further bombs landed on Normansfield Farm and Bushy Park. Another demolished the Pope's Grotto Pub in Twickenham. On 5th July a V1 struck the Warner Bros Film Studios in Broom Road. The bomb hit a 2000 gallon fuel tank which dispersed and ignited. The production head, 'Doc' Max Salomon, along with Henry Brayfield and Elizabeth Roe were killed instantly. Employees from Toughs boatyard maintained a steady hosing on the bunkers containing the Warner Bros Film Library and succeeded in saving the film store.

On 24th July a further bomb fell on Argyle Road, already severely bombed in November 1940, causing damage over 1000 houses. There were eighty three casualties including nine fatalities that night. Argyle Road was never rebuilt. The final bomb that fell on Teddington was a V2 that hit the railway embankment behind 59-61 Fairfax Road, leaving a 40' wide crater.

Then it was all over and the massive task of getting back to normal started. The Borough of Twickenham statistics show 161 people killed and 275 seriously injured, 654 properties destroyed, 762 properties seriously damaged and a further 29,000 in need of repair.

Over the years I have acquired many snippets of information but a very useful book is :
When The Bombs Fell by Paul Barnfield (BOTLHS No 80) 2001. Available at Waterston's, priced £4.50.

The National Physical Laboratory

TUCKED INTO A small corner of Bushy Park, we have one of the finest and most productive establishments in the world. Until quite recently when the buildings at the front were rebuilt and now look a likely candidate for the backdrop to a Bond movie, this mini estate was hardly noticed amongst its leafy surroundings. I refer, of course, to the National Physical Laboratory.

Its story goes back to the end of the 19th Century. In 1897 the Royal Society decided to establish a National Standards Laboratory and was looking for a suitable site for this. They considered Kew Observatory and also Old Deer Park but dismissed them as unsuitable. Shortly before this, Bushy House had been returned to the Crown, following the death of the exiled Duc de Nemours, who had occupied it since 1865. Queen Victoria was quite happy for the Royal Society to take over the house and the First Commissioner of Her Majesty's Works wrote to the President of the Royal Society to say that 'Her Majesty, the Queen, has granted to the Commissioner of Works, be Her Grace and Favour, Bushy House and Grounds for the use of the National Physical Laboratory under the direction of the Royal Society.'

Thus with a permanent home, the Royal Society set about the organising of a new laboratory. Their first appointment was on 1st January 1900 (not a bank holiday in those days) of Richard Tetley Glazebrook as the laboratory's first Director. In 1901, work commenced on converting the ground floor and basement of Bushy House into a physics laboratory. Other parts of the building were arranged as temporary laboratories for electrical, magnetic and thermometric work, in addition to metallurgical and chemical research. The second floor and parts of the first were set aside as the private residence of the Director and his family.

A grand opening took place in the large bay of the Engineering Building on 19th March 1902 by HRH The Prince of Wales who said 'I believe that in the National Physical Laboratory we have the first instance of the State taking part in scientific research. The object of the scheme is, I understand, to bring scientific knowledge to bear practically upon our everyday industrial and commercial life, to break down the barrier between theory and practise, to effect a union between science and commerce.'

The staff of the National Physical Laboratory (NPL) fell basically into two categories; those engaged in the formulation of standards, the carrying out of tests and the issue of certificates and the others deployed in research. At that time, opportunities for physicists were scare and despite being an unknown quantity, the NPL had no problems in recruiting staff with excellent qualifications, partly due to the reputations of Richard Glazebrook and his Engineering Superintend, Thomas Stanton.

The various test work got under way with the Engineering Department making 40 tests and the Physics Department 229 which included 31 electrical instruments, 38 thermometers, 12 metrological instruments, 22 glass vessels and 94 sets of weights. A good deal of expansion took place in the years 1903 to 1910. A lathe house was built to house a Whitworth standard screw cutting lathe. This building required very close temperature control. By 1905 so much work had been moved to the NPL that it was struggling to survive within its financial framework. A group of MPs met to consider an additional grant : 'The National Physical Laboratory is only partially a State institution. We give it a very small annual grant – just about the tenth of what the Germans give to their corresponding institution and very much less than what the United States and France give. It has a splendid staff, and it is doing valuable work in aid of our industries. But it is starved, and little interest is taken in it. In Germany this kind of institution is regarded as a necessary part of the executive brain. Here we ignore it.' The plea was for a buildings and equipment grant of £30,000 and an increased annual contribution of £10,000. Unfortunately it is not known if they ever got it.

1910 saw the construction of the Ship Testing Tank through a grant from Alfred Yarrow. A second tank was built later as the role of ship research proved to be a large part of NPL's work. This was to become even more so in wartime.

A rough chart of the progress of the NPL is as follows :
1900 – NPL begins
1902 – Opening of NPL at Bushy House
1906 – Department of Metallurgy and Metallurgical Chemistry
1907 – NPL begins testing taximeters
1908 - Begins testing aeroplanes and airships
1911 – No 1 Ship Tank opens
1911 – Begins vehicle testing
1914-1918 – Wartime work
1919 – Duplex wind tunnel built
1920 – Introduction of materials testing
1923 – Improved the ventilation of the House of Commons
1927 – Testing the Schneider Trophy winner
1932 – High precision balance installed
1935 – Radar invented by Robert Watson-Watt

The last two issues have covered the years of WWII and shown the NPL contribution to the war effort so I will not repeat them here.

Peacetime saw a resumption of normal services and the role of testing again came to the fore of NPL activities. Noise was becoming a national problem and to assist in dealing with this, NPL designed and built a mobile acoustical laboratory. This was brought to areas where jet engine noise was being reported, some factories in heavy industry were showing increased levels of noise and any other situation where excess noise was being reported.

In 1953 the NPL received the gift of a graft of Sir Isaac Newton's apple tree, the fall of an apple from which led Newton to recognise the force of gravity. That year also saw the production of

the Royal Command Performance Film of 'The Dambusters'. As many of the original tests were carried out here, it was only fitting that the filming should take place here also.
Two years later, Louis Essen developed the first accurate caesium atomic clock which led to the internationally agreed definition of the second being based on atomic time. This standard is still in use at the present day.

In the 1980s the NPL received another boost when it was joined by the Laboratory of the Government Chemist. This is an Executive Agency of the Department of Trade and Industry set up to provide consumer protection on food and hygiene issues, public health protection and also forensic science. The decision to move to Teddington was taken in 1982 and over the next six years the most advanced purpose built chemistry laboratory in the UK was constructed so that the LGC moved in 1988 with the minimum of fuss.

In 1998 work started on the rebuilding of the laboratories in readiness for the new millennium and that is what you now see on the Hampton Road.

Many other tasks, too many to mention here, have been passed to the NPL for testing and nearly all have been completed successfully.

Watch out for their annual open day where the site is thrown open to the general public who may then see some of these gems for themselves.

Ref. : NPL's History Highlights by the NPL

Hampton Wick Train Crash

FOR THIS MONTH'S EDITION, I am straying over the border and into Hampton Wick, to tell what I hope you will agree, is an interesting story.

Bank Holidays were introduced in 1871 by Sir John Lubbock to compensate for the loss of some traditional religious holidays which were dispensed with in 1834. Sir John was a cricket enthusiast and picked days when he knew cricket was being played; Easter Monday, Whit Monday and the first Monday in August, as well as Boxing Day.

The country was going through a period of change with employee protection being high on the list of social reform. This meant that for the very first time, working people had some leisure time on their hands.

What do we do today at Bank Holiday time? Why, we head away from our homes to the seaside or the country or visit a distant relative. The roads become clogged with traffic and radio and television bulletins are taken over with reports on the progress of the processions of cars leaving and returning to the capital.

Victorian Hampton Wick was no different from any other local population – they did not have the luxury of cars; their mode of travel was the steam train and they went out in droves to take advantage of an additional day's holiday, on the London and South Western Railway.

Bank Holiday Monday 6th August 1888 was no exception. It had been a day of typical bank holiday weather and at the end of it, the fleet of trains that had taken the people away for their day out, were now in action again, returning them to their final destinations.

However, at that point, a terrible event occurred. In the words of the Surrey Comet, 'A collision occurred between the 10.50pm passenger train from Waterloo via Richmond, due at Hampton Wick at 11.42 and a light engine which was returning from Kingston to Twickenham and which by a terrible blunder had been allowed to proceed along the wrong line.' A misunderstood remark between Daniel Pickles, the driver of the light engine and Thomas Parsons, the signalman at Kingston Junction, meant that the points had not been changed for the light engine's return journey to Twickenham. The passenger train consisted of the engine and thirteen carriages which included two guards' vans and a horsebox.

By this time it was very dark and a light drizzle was falling. So much so that the crew of the engine failed to realise that they were on the wrong track. The light tanker, running chimney first, violently struck the passenger train, which was travelling bunker first, at Hampton Wick Station. Next to the passenger engine were a guard's van, a third class, a composite and a first class carriage and these took the brunt of the collision and were piled on top of each other on the bridge.

Walter Pacey of Twickenham, the driver of the passenger train, was taken to the Rose and Crown where he was tended by the landlady and Nurse Chappell; he remained conscious and in great pain for almost an hour before he expired. His dying words, several times repeated were 'It wasn't my fault, mother.' The body of the fireman, James Janvey also of Twickenham, was jammed in the cab and was badly mutilated, so much so that it was taken directly to the local mortuary.

The Mindenhall family had been visiting relatives at Colnbrooke for the day and were returning to Hampton Wick, Mr & Mrs Mildenhall, their two daughters Gertrude and May, and two nieces. Mr Mildenhall gave this account to the inquest : 'We all sat on one seat with our backs to the engine. My wife had been nursing one of the little girls, but just before we got to the station the child got down, asking to be allowed to stand on the seat. Had she not done so she would most certainly have met with the same fate as my wife.'

'All was going well when, just as our part of the train was entering the station, I heard a sharp shrill whistle blowing and I knew something was wrong. My little girl at the same time remarked, "The train is coming, papa". The next thing was the collision. The front of the carriage was forced down upon us, the lights were extinguished, and I could not move hand or foot. We screamed, and the sensation was something awful. Presently I heard the rescue party running over the top of the carriage. We must have remained helpless for nearly half an hour, It was dying by inches. '

'At last they got to us. They first took out the children, and then my wife, who was dead. I was quite helpless, and felt sure I had lost my left arm. I put my right hand over to my left

side to feel if my arm was there. It was hanging down quite useless. My legs were amongst the splintered timber, and my back was very painful. I was lifted out and taken to one of the rooms, where I was laid on the floor and attended to.'

The other fatality was Mrs Lydia Figg of Norbiton who was returning home with her husband and daughters, Lydia and Ellen, all whom received minor injuries. Mrs Figg was taken to the residence of Mrs Usher – No 1 Palmerston Villas, suffering from internal injuries, from which she died, about an hour after the accident. Her body was then taken to the Rose and Crown.

The driver of the light engine, Daniel Pickles, gave this account : 'It was a very dark night. Just as I was entering the station, I saw the train. "Good God!" I said to my mate, "we are on the wrong road." We did all we could to stop the engine. I reversed her, and my mate – well he acted without a moment's hesitation, and tugged at the brake. We knew then it was life or death. We hadn't time to say another word, but looked at each other. I don't know what he did then but I held my breath. Crash!'

There were many injuries, dealt with by the station staff, survivors of the crash and the local police and doctors who were quickly in attendance.

Dr Diplock, the Coroner for West Middlesex, opened the inquiry into the deaths of the four people at Rose and Crown on Thursday 9th August. A Board of Trade Inquiry opened on the following day. It was the biggest tragedy to ever be reported on the London and South Western Railway.

Margaret 'Peg' Woffington

VISITORS TO TEDDINGTON WILL VERY often walk the length of the High Street from the railway bridge and come across Peg Woffington's Cottages. A short while ago these included the Tea Rooms which in itself were worth the walk. At this point the visitor usually asks 'Who was Peg Woffington?'

A good question. Peg, or Margaret, as she was known then, was born into a poor Dublin family on the 18th October sometime between 1714 and 1720. Her father, John Woffington, a journeyman bricklayer, died very soon after she was born. He was given a pauper's burial and left behind a widow, two young girls and a mountain of debt. Young Margaret joined her mother in selling watercress door to door in the city. Whilst doing this, she was spotted by a lady impresario named Madame Violante who operated a variety show. One of her acts was to walk across the stage on a tightrope suspended above the stage, with a basket containing an infant suspended to each foot. Margaret was one of the infants. Fortunately or unfortunately the venture did not extend beyond one season and Margaret rejoined her mother on the watercress run.

However some years later when Margaret was aged about ten, Madame Violante returned with the Lilliputian Theatre Company and she recruited Margaret to the ensemble. Margaret's starring role was Polly Peacham in *The Beggar's Opera*. Her performance attracted the attention of theatre manager Thomas Elrington who signed her to the Aungier Street Theatre. Here she played in *Devil to Pay, Twin Rivals, Old Man taught Wisdom, or the Virgin Unmasked* and *Conscious Lovers*. 1737 saw her at the Smock Theatre where she tackled Ophelia. All of these parts were in addition to Polly in *The Beggar's Opera*. In April she gave what was considered her most bewitching impersonation, that of Sir Harry Wilder, a popular comic breeches part, in the *Constant Couple*.

By this time her fame had spread to London and she was soon booked for Covent Garden and on 6th November 1740 she appeared as Sylvia in *The Recruiting Officer*. The posters had her billed as Miss Woffington. She repeated the part on 8th November but this time the posters had her as Mrs Woffington, a name that she maintained. In playing Sylvia, the part required her to masquerade as a boy dressed in men's hose. If it was not known that she possessed shapely legs before this performance, it certainly was afterwards. She took London by storm! The next few years were a whirlwind of popularity where she was on stage almost nightly taking on new plays and some Shakespearian classics in her stride. She moved to Drury Lane and there met David Garrick. She had returned to Dublin in the summer of 1742 where she was the uncrowned queen of the Dublin stage. She was Cordelia to Garrick's Lear and on returning to Drury Lane she played Lady Anne to his Richard III.

They were known lovers and lived together at No 6 Bow Street WC2 as man and wife. Dr Johnson is known to have reported that Garrick became very cross when Peg, as she was now known, was too generous with sugar. However Fanny Burney praised her qualities when entertaining – 'She was a hostess so attractive that her receptions were crowded with people of distinction, and the table was never presided over so charmingly as when she was at the head of it.' It is understood that she and Garrick had planned to marry in 1744 but this never came to fruition. Some say that Garrick wanted to control her career in every aspect and Peg was far too independent to allow that. They parted company in that year.

Whilst looking for a country residence, she heard that Teddington Place, the former home built by Sir Charles Duncombe, Lord Mayor of London, was up for sale. Peg viewed the property and decided to purchase it. After having settled herself there, she reckoned that it would be the perfect place from which to launch her sister Mary, more commonly known as Polly, into society. With the aid of her friend and manager, the playwright Brinsley Sheridan, she sought to assemble an all star cast of *The Distressed Mother* placing Polly in the lead. They hired a large barn in the neighbourhood (thought to have been in Broom Road) and fitted this out as a temporary theatre. The story goes that the curtain went up to a packed house but that young Polly was a bit wooden in her role and the plaudits went to an up and coming actress – Mrs George Anne Bellamy. This started a feud between Peg and Mrs Bellamy that was not resolved until Peg was on her deathbed.

Peg then concentrated on making a good marriage for Polly and a short time later, introduced her to Captain the Honourable George Cholmondeley, the second son of the Earl of Cholmondeley. After Peg had overcome the family's objections, Polly and George were married in 1746 and moved into a house in Westminster that Peg had acquired for them.

On the stage, Peg was as busy as ever, giving seemingly continuous performances throughout the year with the same blend of comic breeches parts to the classic roles from Shakespeare. She played Lady Jane Grey, a new play with a performance that added greatly to her already high reputation. She went back to Dublin for three seasons and continued to sell out theatres.

In the course of her career, Peg managed to cross swords with the other main actresses of the day, Hannah Pritchard, Kitty Clive and George Bellamy. In 1756 whilst performing Roxana to her rival's Statria, Peg drove Mrs Bellamy off the stage and stabbed her within sight of the audience. The reviewer of the day described as the 'Green-room Squabble or a Battle Royal between the Queen of Babylon and the Daughter of Darius.' Even more bitter than this feud was that between Peg and Mrs Clive – 'no two women in high life ever hated each other more unreservedly that these two great dames of the stage.'

On 3rd May 1757 Peg was playing Rosalind in *As you like it*. It was to be her last performance. She had been in declining health all season and in the fifth act she turned to fellow actor, Tate Wilkinson, and complained of an indisposition. He gave her his arm and took her away. She changed her dress and returned to the stage saying that she was ill. She was into her epilogue when her voice broke, rendering her speechless. 'She strove vainly to recall her words, screamed with terror, and tottered to the door where she was caught.' She had suffered a stroke from which she never recovered. Peg dropped out of public life and resided quietly in Teddington until her death on March 1760. Peg Woffington was buried in St Mary's Church Teddington.

There can be no doubt that in today's celebrity climate, she would have filled the gossip columns apart from being a regular awards nominee. Sadly the view that she donated the Peg Woffington Cottages appears to be a popular myth as no concrete evidence has been found to support this.

Teddington's Public Houses
- Part 1

The King's Head

SEEING THE PRAM RACE IN ACTION around the streets of Teddington recently reminded me of the original Pram Races in the early 1980s where the crew of each pram were supposed to call at every pub in Teddington, have a drink, get their card marked to record the fact and move on to the next one. On crossing the finish line, each team would have called at nineteen pubs. When I was a good bit younger and fitter, I took part one year and I will probably never forget the experience, so good luck to all of the modern contestants!

Does nineteen pubs sound a lot for a small town like Teddington? Actually it was more than that; in fact we can trace evidence of there having been twenty eight pubs in the town over the years.

I will try and tell something about each one but if I make a mistake or if you have a story, funny or otherwise about any of them, I will be very pleased to hear from you.

Firstly we need to establish what constitutes a PUB. All pubs are licensed premises but all licensed premises are not necessarily pubs. For example there are clubs, sporting and otherwise or work related. The ones we will be looking at fall into roughly three categories :
An Inn – such establishments go back to Roman times, a place where a traveller might seek food, drink and lodging for the night for himself and his horse. We usually think of the Tabard Inn in *Canterbury Tales* or the George Inn in Southwark. In the main the Inn has been replaced by the Hotel.
A Tavern – a place of business where people gather together to drink alcoholic beverages and be served food.
A Beerhouse or Alehouse – a place which brews and sells only beers, ales and ciders very often from the front room of a private house.
All of these are now considered as Public Houses or Pubs.

The eighteenth and nineteenth centuries saw the rapid growths of pubs. At this time, the country was in the grips of gin consumption. It was possible to buy a pint of gin for a few pence and this had become the drink of the working classes. Needless to say, the government of the day was greatly concerned for the welfare of its people and set about weaning them off strong spirits and onto something a good deal milder. This brought about the Beerhouse Act of 1830 which enabled anyone to brew and sell beer, ale or cider, either from a public house or from their own homes, on obtaining a moderately priced licence. In must be the only time in the world where a national government has actively encouraged the drinking of beer!

Back to Teddington. Picture the village in 1800 and you will see a small establishment of about 120 houses and a population of approximately 700 people. The earliest Directories by Pigot & Co evidence only three pubs but we know of at least one other.

The first public house that we have traced was Le Queene, which was acquired in 1688 by James Cole, a member of the family of Cole's Brewery of Twickenham. We know that it stood in the south side of the High Street but where exactly is a mystery. By the time of James' death in 1725, the pub was known as The Queen's Head and had passed to James' son Edward. He continued trading and at some point, the name changed again, this time to The Three Bells. Edward died in 1775 leaving the pub to his younger brother, Thomas. It seems that Thomas had little to do with the licensed trade and ownership changed hands a few times until 1797 when the premises were leased out but only as a cottage. The Three Bells then ceased to exist and vanished without trace.

The next pub is The King's Head which was well established when we find our first reference. This was 1689 when the Court Leet, a forerunner of the parish vestry or local council, but acting solely for the Lord of the Manor, was held here. It would meet twice a year and decided several public appointments such as constable, ale taster and pound keeper. It continued to be the base for the seat of local government until 1865 when the vestry was replaced by the Local Government Board of Teddington. The pub is probably the same property described in 1657, 'as a house, malthouse, brewhouse, stables, barns and backside' on the north side of the High Street. It was sold to a Thomas Cole of the Coles Brewery family in 1816. When Cambridge Road was cut through after the sale of the manor lands, the pub was rebuilt to its present style today. It closed in 2010 for refurbishment and was reopened as part of French celebrity chef, Raymond Blanc's White Brasserie Company. Although the head referred to was of Charles I, the current management are showing that of Henry VIII.

The Royal Oak

Almost opposite The King's Head stood The Royal Oak, another of the early pubs which is listed under the Licensed Victuallers Records for 1726. It takes its name from the national surge of loyalty to Charles II, who hid in the foliage of an oak tree after the battle of Worcester. It was sold to the Cole family in 1770 and remained with them for many years. Originally the pub fronted onto the main road but in the 1930s there was talk of building a bridge across the Thames at Teddington Lock, which would necessitate having to widen the road along the High street. Anticipating this, the pub was demolished and rebuilt further back from the road. However the bridge was never built and the pub was left with a huge forecourt which was never fully utilised. A decision was taken to demolish the 1936 building and rebuild fronting the High Street, leaving land at the rear for housing. The building work went ahead but a disastrous flood in the basement prevented the pub from opening on time. After a long delay, it reopened as The Oak and later changed its name to Sammy's but it did not retrieve its earlier popularity. A change of ownership brought back the original name – The Royal Oak – but the stigma of an unfortunate murder outside the pub effectively killed off the trade. The premises were sold on again and are now part of the Cotes Brasserie chain.

To be continued

I am indebted to Paddy Ching for the use of her notes on Teddington Licensed Victualler's Records.

Teddington's Public Houses - Part 2

BEFORE I EMBARK ON THE second part of the story of our pubs, I must point out a correction to the Peg Woffington story. One eagle-eyed reader has pulled me up on Peg's ownership of Teddington Place. She has said that there is nothing in the Manor Court Rolls to indicate that Peg Woffington ever purchased Teddington Place, the former home of Sir Charles Duncombe. This remained in the ownership of the Duncombe family via his nephew, Anthony Lord Faversham, for many years. It is more likely that Peg owned and occupied the eastern most two cottages of the row that now bear her name. So there we have it and I stand (or rather sit) corrected.

Back to pubs, the next earliest on my list is The Greyhound. Our oldest dated record of this pub is 1726. The name has royal connections and the folklore tells us that around the time of the Battle of Worcester, the future Charles II was dining with his most trusted followers and in the event of them having to break up and go their separate ways, they needed something to prove that they were supporters of Charles. With this in mind, he picked up a silver tray which was handsomely decorated with the figures of eight greyhounds racing around the rim of the tray. He broke off each of the figures and passed them to his followers. To this day the greyhound is the symbol of the Queen's messengers.

Normally I abhor the change of pub names but in this case, I can do very little about it as the changes took place a long time ago. Firstly in 1780, the Greyhound pub became The North Arms and this was so named as Lord North, the Prime Minister who lost the American colonies, retired to live at Bushy House since his wife, Anne Lady North, had been created Ranger of Bushy Park. This situation prevailed until 1795 when North succeeded to his father's title and became Duke of Guilford, and the pub duly became The Guilford Arms. North died and the Rangership of the Park passed to William, Duke of Clarence, the future William IV in 1800. The pub was renamed The Duke of Clarence Arms accordingly. This was obviously a successful coaching inn and when hearing that the railway was coming to Teddington, the owners were determined to cash in on the new mode

of transport. The old buildings were demolished and rebuilt as The Clarence Hotel (which it remained until 2000). The opening of the new hotel was designed to take place with the opening of the railway station – 1st July 1863. Close links were established here and railway porters would carry the luggage of some passengers from the station to the hotel.

In the 1950s the Clarence Hotel's reputation began to wane. The gardens were sold for housing and a reduced service was provided. It became the first 'Disco' pub in the area and was refurbished in a rural style with an artificial stream running through it. Unfortunately there were not many disco pubs around at the time and The Clarence came to the attention of the youth of Feltham and Kingston who would meet there on a Saturday night to settle old scores and a mass brawl would frequently ensue. It was rumoured that a panic button was installed under the road to the Police Station opposite. A review of the licensing ended this particular venture and the pub reverted to a two bar establishment again but with the added attraction of strippers on a Thursday night. Although not as disruptive as the disco, this activity did not endear the pub to the great and the good of Teddington and it was quietly removed.

By the year 2000 it had become very run down and it was taken over by Galleon Taverns and given a major refit with an additional annexe built at the side. It reopened as The Park and has become Teddington's premier hotel.

Next on my list is The Duke of Wellington, on the very extremity of the town on the corner of Burton's Road and Wellington Road. This pub opened in 1815 to honour Wellington's victory at Waterloo. Wellington Road had not yet been made

up and took its name from the pub. The first licensee was Joseph Burton and it is quite likely that Burton's Road takes its name from him.

During the tenancy of a Mr Austin, the pub was frequented by a gang of Irish navvies who were building the railway. On one occasion they refused to pay for their drinks and threw Mr Austin into a ditch. A huge fight broke out, the police were called and the Riot Act read. At the next sitting of the Kingston Assizes, over 200 people appeared in court. In spite of that it continued to serve its local community for many years without further incident. In the 1960s it became the local of the Yardbirds pop group who were all Hampton Grammar School old boys. A serious fire destroyed it in 1980 and it never reopened as a pub. Today it is three private houses.

As I mentioned last time the Beer House Act of 1830 brought about many changes in the drinking habits of the community. By 1831 the population of Teddington had increased to 895 living in 200 houses. 1839 saw the opening of The Jolly Sawyer, one of the first beer houses in Teddington. By the time of the 1851 census, it had changed its name to The Queen Dowager after William IV's widow, Queen Adelaide, who had retired to Bushy House after his death and became a very popular figure in Teddington, supporting many local causes. Set in a back street of Teddington, it was not really geared to the demands of 21st century business and closed its doors in 2011, after which it rapidly became a small block of houses.

Also in 1839 the next pub to open was The Britannia in what was then the High Street but which later became the Broad Street after the coming of the railway cut the town in two. It was built in a block known as 'The American Buildings', although today no-one knows why. John Sibley was the beer house keeper and sold beers and ciders. The pub continued trading through a building redevelopment of the area in the early part of the 20th century. In an attempt to attract more up-market customers, the pub changed its name to the Hogarth in the 1960s which also noted its transfer from Charringtons to Fullers. It subsequently expanded internally and opened its garden and today continues to trade successfully.

If your favourite pub has not been mentioned yet, do not despair – there are many more to come. And if you have a story that you wish to share, please get in touch with me.

Once again, I am indebted to Paddy Ching for the use of her notes on the Licensed Victuallers of Teddington.

Teddington's Public Houses - Part 3

I SEEM TO BE MAKING SLOW progress in the perambulation of Teddington's pubs but each one has a story or two to tell. Remember that if you have a memory or know something interesting, please let me know.

We are now in the 1850s; the Beerhouse Act of 1830 had set a new scene for the social drinking of Teddington and gave rise to a number of new public houses. The first of these was The Anglers which started life in 1853 under the guise of The Anglers Tavern and Fishing House. Fisherman Samuel Kemp was the owner of the premises and had only been granted a beer licence. His application for a full licence had been blocked by the landlord of The Royal Oak, William Bliss, who claimed that he would be deprived of trade if such a licence was granted.

Nevertheless by 1861 Samuel Kemp had gained his full licence and was trading actively with his three daughters helping in the business. It was here that plain Mr Henry Morton Stanley met boat builder James Messenger to discuss plans for The Lady Alice, the portable multi-sectioned boat that Stanley would use on his African explorations. By 1885 the premises had become The Anglers Hotel and was featured heavily in the fishing and boating journals of the day. With the close proximity of Teddington Film Studios, The Anglers became a very popular haunt of film and television personalities and production crews, at least until the Studios obtained its own drinks licence. Even then many of the popular stars preferred the freedom of the pub to their own 'factory' bar. With an attractive river frontage and a huge family garden, the pub is still a very popular spot today.

At the other end of town, The Queen was built on the corner of Queen's Road and Broad Street in the early 1860s. It must have been around the time that the railway arrived in 1863 when the whole of the Broad Street was developed. It was probably called after Queen Adelaide but we don't know that for sure. It served its local population for nearly 100 years but closed in the 1960s and is now a betting shop, laundrette and dry cleaners.

Back in the High Street, there was the King's Arms, a beer house which consisted of three cottages. The occupant in 1851 was one Samuel Cole who was a saddler but by 1853 he is described as a 'beer house keeper and harness maker'. The licence then moved to John & William Farnell who had links with the Isleworth Brewery. They installed a tenant, Daniel Edwards in 1862 and he was here at least until 1874. The next landlord was John Marshall Wade, who gave his name to the adjoining road – Wade's Lane. At about this time, the Isleworth Brewery acquired the premises and in 1889 they granted the tenancy to John Barnes and his wife Joanna. John passed the pub onto his son John Harry and his wife Eliza who continued to run it until at least 1939 but it still had not obtained a full licence. This occurred sometime in the 1970s when the couple running it were Rowland and Francis Thanisch. When speaking of the disadvantages of living in a pub of over 100 years old, Francis noted that 'The floors slope quite a bit. If I don't keep the brake on the baby's pram, it runs to the other side of the room.'

There was some controversy concerning the old inn sign. A letter was sent to the College of Arms to offer an explanation of them. Unfortunately the Portcullis Pusuivant of Arms (the Chief Herald) was unable to offer a full account, noting that half of the sign showed three lions representing the Arms of England as with either Henry II in 1154 or Edward III in 1327. The other side showed the quartering as per Queen Victoria in 1837 and a further symbol from the reign of George VI. In 2008 there was a change of ownership and this brought about a change of name to The Clockhouse and also saw the loss of the engraved glass door and window panels of the old Isleworth Brewery.

Moving to Park Lane we had The Prince of Wales at No 22. In 1862 the tenant was one Thomas Ellum, a candle maker, as was his father before him. The property which is one of the oldest buildings in Teddington is now known as 'The Old Cottage.' This property can be traced back to the eighteenth century. There is a record of it being a beer retailer in 1908 but it had ceased to be a pub prior to WW1 in 1914.

A little way around the corner we come to The Adelaide Inn in Park Road and on the west corner of Albert Road. It was built in 1863, hot on the heels of the railway arriving at Teddington. Named after Queen Adelaide, the widow of William IV who had returned to live at Bushy House after William's death. She was extremely popular with the local villagers, being patron of the first school and several other charitable causes. The census of 1871 shows that Walter and Isabella were the innkeepers and also had a barman and two live-in servants. 1881 saw Walter listed as a licensed victualler but by 1891, his widow Isabella is shown as the hotel keeper. She moved on in 1893 and the inn passed into the Bending family. William Bending had been a butler at Worton Hall in Isleworth, (later to become Isleworth Film Studios where the classic *The African Queen was filmed*) before trying his luck in the licensed trade.

A photograph at about the turn of the century shows that the inn sold Isleworth Ales & Stouts. The publicity describes it as 'a good call for cricketers and cyclists' and the other advertising boards show that it sold theatre programmes, railway tickets and trips as well as acting for the house agents Milestone and Collis. William Bending left The Adelaide in 1910, moving to The St Margaret's Hotel where he stayed until 1922 and then retired to Dorking. The Adelaide Inn has seen several licensees come and go since then, usually not staying longer than ten years. Today the inn continues to thrive, having recently undergone a sympathetic restoration and is probably as prosperous as when it first opened.

In the next article I will mention a number of pubs from that era that opened after the Beerhouse Act of 1830 but did not survive 100 years of trading. Many people have asked the reasons for this and it is difficult to give a standard answer. One factor is that most dwellings were rented tenements where two rooms up and two down was a luxury. Therefore family gatherings could not easily be accommodated in a single dwelling. Such occasions therefore took place at the pub on the corner and nearly every corner had one.

Again I am indebted to my friend Paddy Ching for the use of her notes on the Teddington licensed trade.

Teddington's Public Houses - Part 4

As I HAVE SAID PREVIOUSLY, THE Beerhouse Act of 1830 was the springboard for many new beerhouses in the town. We are now in the 1860s and the first pub to consider is The Duke of York in North Lane. There is some dispute as to the date when this pub first opened. I have read that it was built in 1862 but the first landlord I can trace is Thomas Houlding from Clacton, Essex in 1871. His family ran it for about ten years. They were succeeded by Richard Holter and his wife. Two further families, the Rollings and the Butlers took over from 1898-1910 and 1911-1937 respectively. Annoyingly the Butlers were later to be my next door neighbours but I was too small at that time to be thinking about pubs and ask them the leading questions! I have a vague recollection of the pub but cannot recall ever having seen a picture. It closed in 1953.

Another North Lane pub was The Prince Alfred, later to become The Prince of Wales. This opened in 1869 and I think the Haley family were the first occupants. They were certainly there in 1871 for the census. The Haleys were replaced by the Clarkes by 1891 and by 1901 the landlord was William Silver. I am not absolutely sure that William stayed with the pub until it closed in 1914 but the start of WW1 saw its demise. William went on to operate a horse drawn cab from Teddington Station and was a popular local figure. Later still he became the night watchman at the Savoy cinema where he was unfortunately murdered when the cinema was robbed. On hearing that William Silver was dead, the killer – Norris Megaw – was overcome with contrition and gave himself up to the police. He was tried for murder, found guilty and sentenced to be hanged which was later commuted to life imprisonment.

We now come to The Horse & Groom in Waldegrave Road. This pub was also first opened in 1869. In the attached picture (taken during the tenancy of William Strugnell), the description refers to stabling, presumably at the rear of the premises, and so it must have been a substantial establishment in its heyday. It had a succession of landlords and kept going into the 1990s. It suffered from not having a car park and being on a bus route with double yellow lines outside its door. It earned the nickname of 'The House of Gloom' from the other publicans and closed its doors in 1996. It later re-opened as part of the Pizza Express chain.

Moving over to the Hampton Wick end of town, we can see The Eagle in Schoolhouse Lane which allegedly opened in 1869. I know absolutely nothing about this pub other than that it was in the hands of William George Gent and his family for a long period. It closed in 1914 and the building reverted to domestic use. It is looks very much like a pub today.

The Northampton Arms opened in 1871 at No 9 Park Terrace in Broad Street. Again I know nothing about this pub other than that it had a fairly undistinguished history until it closed in 1914, another victim of WW1. The first landlord was Alfred Callaway, succeeded by Walter Padbury, Henry Jones and Henry Minter.

Now we find a confusing situation. In 1866 a building in Park Lane became a pub and opened its doors as The Prince of Wales, not to be confused with The Prince of Wales around the corner in North Lane. This pub was run by Thomas Ellum who worked in Barclay's Wax Candle Factory in Waldegrave Road, and his family successfully ran the pub for over 20 years. The building had previously been a laundry and after it closed in

1914, (yet another closure from WW1), it became a private dwelling. The building is still standing and is amongst the oldest in Teddington.

Jumping back to Schoolhouse Lane, there existed another pub there named The Prince Alfred. This one opened in 1880 and the first landlords were John and Sarah Reaves. Once again the pub prospered without seeming to hit the headlines. When I was researching the opening of the Railway Station, a gentleman by the name of Rob Robb sent me a picture of his grand-mother Sarah Boyer and great grand-mother, also Sarah Boyer, standing at the door of the pub. Sarah the younger's husband James was listed as the 'Beer Retailer' but he was also an engine driver. One day in January 1891, James found himself on a disciplinary charge for running his engine into the buffers at Kingston Station. Whatever the official verdict was, unofficially this was put down to a later than usual night at The Prince Alfred. The pub closed in 1939.

Another of the boom pubs was The Abercorn Arms in Church Road. Built in 1863 by The Kingston Brewery, it was acquired by Young & Co in 1887. The first landlord was Edward Hopwood, although he and his family were there for less than ten years. The Griffiths family were entrenched by 1881 and were still there in 1891. Next came the Mildenhalls who were still in place at the start of WW1. It was clearly successful as in 1940 it expanded into the shop next door but it remained a beer house. It was not granted a full licence until 1950. It takes its name from the Earls of Hamilton and Abercorn, whose coat of arms it used to display but I have not been able to trace the connection.

Almost diagonally opposite The Abercorn stood The Willoughby Arms, built in 1869. This pub was opened by Alfred and Sarah Robinson but they did not stay there long. They were succeeded by the Drummond family and by 1898, by George Byard. It was probably during his tenancy that the status of the premises was upgraded to 'Hotel' and George Byard is described as a licensed victualler. This change was very clearly successful and the pub carried on trading into WW11 until disaster struck on the night of November 29th/30th 1940. It was to be a night that Teddington remembered vividly

as being the heaviest air raid of the war. 130 high-explosive bombs were dropped, as well as three to five thousand incendiaries, completely destroying 150 dwellings and damaging 6,000 more. The loss of life was about 68 persons. That night The Willoughby was having the pay out of its Christmas Loan Club and was very busy. The pub took a direct hit and was destroyed, killing the landlord, Frank Tomlin and seven others. It took at least four days to dig all of the bodies out of the wreckage. The pub was never rebuilt.

That's it for this edition but there is still more to come. Don't forget if you have any interesting stories or other folklore about any of the pubs, I would be very pleased to hear them.

Once again I am indebted to my friend Paddy Ching for her notes and to the Dead Pubs website.

Teddington's Public Houses - Part 5

THANK YOU FOR STAYING WITH ME SO far. I did not fully appreciate how much there was to write about in Teddington pubs and it has become an eye opener to see them all. We are now coming to an end of our virtual pub crawl which I hope you have enjoyed!

I must thank Andy Pirson for correcting me on the closing year of The Duke of York. It actually closed in 1963 and not 1953 as previously stated. Several people have pointed out that many of the pubs are now closed. All I can say to that is I have tried my best but I can't be everywhere at the same time!

My next port of call is The Builder's Arms built in 1865 in Field Lane. This was not opened until 1871 by William Harris and his family. He was married to Isabella with three sons and a daughter all living in. William was a bricklayer by trade and the pub has often been called incorrectly The Bricklayer's Arms although this was truer than the correct name. In addition to a live in servant and pot-boy, three other bricklayers/labourers were lodging there. Curiously the first licence was not granted until 1876. They did not stay there long and by 1881 Dinah Davis a widow, was the landlady. Again her tenancy was not to last and in 1891 the landlord is shown as George Dunkley who ran the pub until about 1910. The next landlord was Edward Hards who was with his wife, Olive. A picture of 1913 shows Olive at the front of the pub on her 21st birthday. The gentleman on the right of the picture was a Methodist minister who always entered the door backwards so that 'no one would see him coming in.' Olive was succeeded by her son, also Edward, and between them, they ran the pub for 45 years. Olive in fact celebrated her 100th birthday in the pub. One old local I spoke to described it more as a club: 'There were three bars; the Saloon Bar was used mainly by business people, the Public Bar by the least well off and the Private Bar by those that thought themselves inbetweens. The Bottle & Jug (off-sales) was between the last two and there was a Club Room at the back.'

Another old pub in the town is The Railway Hotel. This pub is adjacent to the railway station and someone clearly missed an opportunity to cash in on the coming of the railway in 1863 as this establishment did not open until 1867 as The Railway Refreshment Rooms. Whether it had a licence or not at this stage is rather vague and it is probably not until John Pain took over the management in about 1890 and renamed it The Railway Hotel that it held a full licence. John was quite a colourful character - born in Teddington, he witnessed the visit of Garibaldi to Alexander Hertzen at Elmfield House in 1863. He worked at the Wax Candle factory in Fry's Lane (now Waldegrave Road) until moving into the licensed trade. He became a JP and a local councillor, being chairman of the burials board.

He was succeeded in the pub by his son Edward who ran The Railway until his death in the 1950s. The pub continued to flourish until the millennium when to some extent the national social attitude to pubs changed. It closed its doors in 2006 and after a major refurbishment, it reopened at The Bloated Mallard. Apparently the 'Mallard' was a class of the fastest running steam locomotive on that line. This venture lasted until 2013 when the pub changed hands again, had another refurbishment and became simply The Railway.

The Mason's Arms is another of Teddington's back street Victorian pubs that came about as a result of the population explosion. Being an

unpretentious little pub, it very nearly went under about ten years ago when it was closed and up for sale. Rumour had it listed to become a private dwelling. Fortunately Terry Himpfen and Rae Williams of The Roebuck stepped in to prevent the conversion sale and enabled the pub to continue trading as a public house. This simple action has brought about a huge benefit for the local community. There are no fancy frills attached, merely a well stocked bar dispensing a fine range of real ales without the distractions of games machines and live television. In recent years Rae has revived the Teddington Pubs Pram Race which has raised several pounds for charity. And as a bonus The Mason's Arms has just won the Richmond & Hounslow CAMRA Best Pub of the Year award for the second year running.

Speaking of The Roebuck, we should take a look at this pub. It opened its doors on 31st December 1867 and when first built, stood out alone on the Hampton Road. It was the property of William Farnell Watson who later sold the pub to the Isleworth Brewery in 1889. They went bankrupt in 1924 and the pub passed into the hands of Watney Combe Reid & Co. The surrounding area became built up and the pub was a cornerstone of social life. In WW11 a German landmine exploded in Alpha Road and demolished every house in the road except The Roebuck. The pub has since become a freehouse and under the stewardship of Terry Himpfen is very much alive and worth a visit if only to see Terry's amazing collection of memorabilia.

Next is The Red Lion in Stanley Road. This was a trading pub in 1869 to cope with the population expansion. There were few houses around the pub when it was built and those that were there, were not for local people but for the newcomers to the area and clearly a visit to the local pub would have helped them to settle into the local community. In the 1980s the son of the landlord, Finbar Burke, won his first rugby cap for Ireland in Dublin. The well known rugby commentator, Bill McLaren announced on television that 'Paul Burke's father has a pub in Teddington and as a result, there will be a lot of Burkes from Teddington in the crowd today.' Bill Beaumont who was standing beside him quietly said 'Are you sure that's what you intended to say, Bill ?' Despite that and a few other changes, the pub has survived and continues to serve that part of Teddington today.

The Waldegrave Arms is another pub built to deal with an increased population. Sitting at the junction of Waldegrave Road and Shacklegate Lane, it was named after the famous Strawberry Hill socialite, Lady Francis Waldegrave. There used to be a plaque on the wall from the previous brewery claiming all sorts of facts of history which were largely untrue. It closed in 2008 but happily has reopened and is trading happily.

There are still The Lion in Wick Road, about which I know nothing and The Tide End Cottage in Ferry Road of which I know a little. Also known as The Monkey House or The Cottage Inn, this was started by the Kemp family in 1865.

Finally there is a newcomer to the list. On the site of The Tooting Tyre Co and The Italian Place, The Teddington Arms opened in 2002, upgrading the former Green Parrot Wine Bar and continues to flourish.

Once again my thanks to my friend Paddy Ching and to the Dead Pubs website.

A Trip to the Chemist

BEFORE EVERY READER BELIEVES me to be a confirmed alcoholic, I have decided on a slight change of subject this month. What do people usually do when they have overindulged in alcoholic beverages ? – they go to the chemist for some sort of remedy.

It is commonly understood as to what is the oldest profession but do we know the oldest trade? Bakers and butchers have been plying their trades since time immemorial but running them a close third must be the apothecary. This role has existed under various guises in every early settlement since man stopped hunting/gathering and settled down to a life of farming, living in permanent settlements. All such settlements had their own "medicine man" or "wise woman" to whom the group would turn in times of illness or strife.

These people operated under a variety of different names; I have already mentioned the apothecary which was the lowest in status of all of the medical profession, following physicians (at the top), and doctors and surgeons. The Apothecary Society was founded in 1617. There also existed the alchemist who is now largely remembered as one who sought to turn base metals into gold. Then there was the chemist; someone who mixed chemicals in a laboratory unlike the pharmacist who mixed chemicals outside of the laboratory (i.e. in his own pharmacy). There is also the druggist, which is not as sinister a role as it sounds but someone who mixes chemicals. Finally there is the "wiseman or woman" (usually a woman) who was a much respected herbalist acting in rural areas as doctor, nurse and midwife.

So, if you were taken ill in Teddington, who did you turn to? There had been a long tradition of the monasteries of Britain providing a basic medicinal and health care service to their communities and indeed many hospitals can trace their roots back to such institutions. Since 969 B.C. Teddington had been governed by the monks of Westminster Abbey and it is fair to assume that a few of them resided in Teddington to oversee the farming activities. The Black Death wiped out half of the population in 1348 and further outbreaks of the plague occurred in 1361, 1364, 1368, 1371, 1375, 1390 and 1405. Although we do not know for sure, it may be fair to presume that the monks tended to the sick during these desperate times.

In 1536, Henry VIII acquired the village of Teddington and the monks' influence ceased. Alternative arrangements would have to have been made to replace the medical practitioning provided. Further minor outbreaks of the pestilence occurred until the Great Plague in 1665 which was finished by the Great Fire of London the following year.

Sadly. there is very little in the way of written documentation telling us about how the medical profession merged into the villages of Britain. In 1801 the population was about 700 and by 1840 it had crept up to 1,200. The census of 1841 gives us the first detailed survey of the population of every town and village in Britain. Of about 480 adults listed, there are only two surgeons noted and these were very probably 'barber-surgeons' whose medical skills probably went little further than tooth pulling or performing an occasional amputation. There is no mention of either doctors or physicians. So the question arises again, if you were ill, where and to whom did you go for help? Twickenham? Kingston? We simply do not know.

The Poor Laws had been in force since 1349 during the reign of Edward III but these make little or no reference to medical care. It was not until the creation of the Poor House or Work House that any consideration was given this aspect. The only reference being in respect of the inmates who were the sick, infirm and unemployed. The Poor Laws also controlled the movement of beggars and vagrants to stop outside paupers becoming a drain on the parish. Teddington did have some almshouses in Park Lane for the poor but the vestry declined to build a workhouse and farmed out the rest of its poor to Hampton.

The earliest record of a chemist that I have managed to trace is one John While in 1846, who is described as a "Chemist & Druggist." No address is given but it was probably the High Street although the exact whereabouts is unknown. The next entry is George Southam in 1865, who again is listed as "Chemist & Druggist." There is no mention of John While, so can we assume his business was purchased by George Southam? Once more we have no address but I believe the High Street to have been the shop location. Kelly's Directory of 1873 shows John Batt Collins at The Teddington Pharmacy in Broad Street and Charles Swan, Chemist in the High Street. The following year the Collins shop was renamed Chemist & Druggist but the Swan shop was unaltered.

In 1882 John Collins is still trading and Peter Stacey seems to have acquired the business of Charles Swan. In 1890, the Collins business seems to have been acquired by Hornby & Gould who reverted to the title of Chemist & Druggist and show an address of 1 Park Terrace, Broad Street. Peter Stacey is now a Pharmaceutical Chemist and James S Loxton appears at 1 Wolsey Road (later The Causeway). The latter shop was of particular interest to me as this was owned by my father as a Newsagent and Confectioner & Tobacconist from 1929 until it was bombed in WWII. 1899 saw William E Gould at 1 Park Terrace, Peter Stacey in the High Street, and two new entries - Alfred John Last at Wolsey Road and Clarke & Company, Dispensing Chemist at 19 High Street.

This position largely prevailed during the early 1900s, although Clarke & Co had disappeared by 1910, and F Dalton, Chemist had arrived at 4 Alexander Terrace, Stanley Road with W J Bray & Co, Cash Chemist in 30 Broad Street. The businesses stay very much the same during the First World War although Peter Stacey opened a further shop at 9 The Pavement, Kingston Road.

This latter shop completed the development of the business of chemist shops in the key areas of Teddington i.e. High Street, Broad Street, Kingston Road and Stanley Road. All businesses were individual traders until Boots came to town in the 1940s.

The importance of the community pharmacist cannot be overstated. Whilst most people turn to the family mother figure for 'everyday' medical issues, this is followed closely by the local pharmacist who can offer immediate advice and helpful solutions to most problems. Indeed, with their particular expertise they save patients unnecessary trips to their GPs and can offer advice on medication to both doctors and patients. Pharmacies have developed their roles to the point where they are not only hugely beneficial but absolutely essential.

To take Kirby's the Chemist as an example. The premises at 53/55 High Street were built in 1831 but the first chemist, Christopher Roberts, did not arrive until 1927 at No. 53. The business flourished under the names of Gail Potter Pharmacy, Fred Harrison, Walter Fuge and E R Kirby and was eventually acquired by Salim Rajabali in 1975. From being a single fronted shop, the business has expanded into a double fronted one. A physiotherapy service was added in 2012 and an optician joined the team in 2015. Last year saw dentistry added to the business to give an all round medical service.

This is by no means a full listing of the chemists in Teddington but is an attempt to show their development in Broad Street (excluding Boots), High Street, Stanley Road and Kingston Road.

John Charles Buckmaster (1801-1908) - Part 1

ANYONE USING TEDDINGTON LIBRARY can hardly fail to have noticed the refurbished foundation stones listing all of the Teddington worthies who were involved in the building and opening of it. One of these names is J C Buckmaster Esq, it is a name that many people recall but cannot remember the reason why. So who was he?

In fact his history is as much a mystery as anything else. John Charles Buckmaster (JCB) was born in the tiny village of Slapton, Buckinghamshire, about 2 miles south of Leighton Buzzard. Some recorders give his birth date as 23 February 1823 but he used the year of 1819 and so I shall stay with that. Slapton was a very small agricultural community and the Buckmasters had farmed there for over 300 years. Reforms in the social system brought about the enclosure movement and JCB's grandfather, Christopher, was unable to cope with these changes and so gradually sold off portions of the Buckmaster land. This had the effect of reducing their status from yeoman farmers to little more than agricultural labourers.

JCB had a sibling, Richard Price, born 2 years after him. The next part of the story is very complicated. His father, Thomas Buckmaster, is supposed to have married Phoebe Price on 17th October 1824 but JCB was adamant that his mother died of smallpox in November 1822. Writing in June 1933, JCB's second born son, Prof George Buckmaster said to his youngest brother 'I have come to the conclusion that father was illegitimate..... It is an amazing story to learn at 75.' Whatever the case, Thomas was broken-hearted on the death of his wife and took heavily to drink, squandered all of his holdings and thus becoming an object of local scorn. A Mrs Andrews, who was later the maid of JCB's eldest son, recalled how as a girl, she would run to the window to watch the old man making his way home, 'drunk as usual', 'but you always knew he was a real gentleman by the silver buckles on his shoes.' Thomas was incapable of looking after the boys and passed this over to their grandmother Susannah Price, nee Fontaine. Unfortunately the old lady suffered badly from arthritis and could no longer bring up the boys so when he was 7, JCB was sent to live with an uncle in Uxbridge. The behaviour of this uncle was both sadistic and barbaric and it is to be marvelled that JCB survived intact to lead a normal life. He was there for 3 years and during this time his only respite from a cruel and inhumane upbringing was at the local British and Foreign Society Elementary School and Sunday School where it is reputed he stayed from 11am to 8pm every time. At age 10 he was returned to Slapton and deemed fit enough to start work as a farm labourer. He befriended the curate who was very unpopular in the village and was privately educated by him. He was witnessing the great agricultural depression and noticed the rise of Methodism. He reckoned that 75% of the village went over to Methodist teaching and the remaining 25% were non-believers. At this time the 'Swing' riots were breaking out all over the country and at a neighbouring town, JCB saw the local yeomanry called out to disperse a lively meeting.

These events left a deep impression on JCB and at age 13, his father sent him back to Uxbridge to be apprenticed to a carpenter/joiner and to stay at his uncle's house. An uneasy relationship ensued which lasted for 3 years until he broke the apprenticeship and ran away to London. He was caught, returned to Uxbridge and spent a night in the town gaol where he encountered two highwaymen – his first brush with criminals. His grandmother died and left him a bequest of £10 with which he bought himself a second hand chest of tools. He was still determined to break his apprenticeship and planned the second attempt with much more precision. In the spring of 1837 he left Uxbridge, having sent all of his tools ahead, walked 50 miles to Andover eventually arriving in Salisbury. Here he was introduced to the Chartist movement although he did not join it. He did however contract smallpox, which in those days was a killer, but luckily he was nursed back to health by a gypsy woman, a kindness he never forgot.

The following year he moved on to Tiverton in Devon where he became heavily involved with the local Anti-Corn Law Movement. This was a bad time for the national economy and JCB grew to be a formidable public speaker and political activist. He attended the London Conference of the Anti-Corn Law Association in February 1839 and later met Lord Morpeth, who was to have a considerable influence in his life. As opposition to the Corn Laws grew, it became obvious that they would be repealed and JCB then sought the advice of Lord Morpeth as to what his next career move should be. Morpeth said that the Government would next have to tackle the 'Education Question' and suggested that JCB should prepare himself for a career in education.

With Morpeth's help, JCB joined St John's College, Battersea, as a trainee teacher in January 1844. The College was founded by its principal, John Kay-Shuttleworth in 1840 and offered a very difficult course, being only 18 months rather than the usual 3 years. The working hours were 5.30am to 9.30pm daily. Whilst still a student there, he assisted Kay-Shuttleworth in teaching at the Norwood School for Pauper Children. An outbreak of cholera struck the school and out of 1400 children, 342 died in the first week of the attack. The School was closed and the surviving children dispersed amongst other schools. This experience instilled in him a strong sense of public duty.

SANATORY MEASURES.
Lord Morpeth Throwing Pearls before —— Aldermen.

On qualifying as a teacher, JCB took up a post at Parkhurst Prison on the Isle of Wight between 1845-47. Here he was highly critical of the management of the Prison and by chance had the opportunity to show it. On a day when popular reformers Charles Dickens and Hepworth Dixon came to visit the prison, JCB was the only one of the staff present to escort them around the buildings. He was able to give vent to his opinions as to where the regime was going wrong and his listeners were only too pleased to jot it down. This was later in national print and JCB was sacked for his trouble. Although this was clearly an event waiting to happen, the timing was not of his making and he found himself out of work.

There are some blanks in his life which are difficult to fill and this is one of them. I suspect that Lord Morpeth supported him temporarily until Kay-Shuttleworth took him on as one of the permanent staff at St John's College.

Life seems to have settled down for him and the next most memorable thing in his life was his marriage to Emily Anne Goodliffe in August 1853.

What happened next? We will continue to look at the history of J C Buckmaster next month.

John Charles Buckmaster (1801-1908) - Part 2

IN 1851 BRITAIN HAD SEEN THE GREAT Exhibition, which had been an unparalleled success, raising the nation's awareness of the new era of science. The technical schools were anxious to take a hold of this and impart the practical teaching of science subjects to all other schools. Suddenly, JCB found himself advising Sir Robert Peel on how science should be taught. In 1854 he took up a post at the School of Mines and Science (from November 1854 to February 1856). During this period he was also working at Wandsworth Trade School and Poplar Trade and Navigation School, both under the control of the Department of Science and Art.

His work came to the attention of HRH Prince Albert, on whose recommendation JCB was appointed Keeper of the Animal and Food Collection at South Kensington. To assist his teaching, he started to produce text books on various aspects of science, the first of which – *The Elements of Inorganic Chemistry* – was published in 1858. The following year he was given the all-embracing title of 'Organising Master of Science and Art Schools and Classes' at the Department of Science and Art. Curiously the Government only considered this to be a temporary appointment – something which was to rankle with him for many years. (NB temporary posts did not carry a pension whereas permanent ones did).

Family commitments were also growing. Charles Alexander had been born in 1854, followed by George Alfred in 1859, Stanley Owen in 1861 and Martin Alfred in 1862. Finally Phoebe Emily came into the world in 1868. They were all living in St John's Hill in New Street, Wandsworth with JCB's cousin Emily and a maid servant; it must have been quite a busy household! With the expansion of Clapham Junction Station, many houses in New Street were pulled down and Martin Alfred used to joke that 'he was born on Platform 7!'

When it came to promoting the new sciences, most of his colleagues fought shy of presenting themselves away from home and it was left to JCB to travel the country. By 1869 he had established himself as an exceptionally able public speaker; he had an easy way of addressing his audiences, a store of racy anecdotes to enliven the factual content of his lectures and most importantly, a natural inspirational power.

These qualities rose to the fore when JCB heard of plans to develop Wandsworth Common, something he vehemently opposed. He took on the developers and after some protracted legal dealings, won the day. It is thanks to John Charles Buckmaster that Wandsworth Common exists today.

1871 saw an interesting new development in the Department, JCB was persuaded to undertake the delivery of a series of food and cookery lectures. According to family legend, he rushed home to see his wife and tell her that she had to teach him all the arts of the kitchen in the next few weeks. The family claimed that whilst the voice in these lectures was that of John, the words and acts were those of his wife Emily.

These lectures were a great success and caught the attention of the society of the day. It was even said that to attend one such lecture was far more entertaining than attending many of the West End plays. One of the particular attractions was that JCB managed to persuade many famous chefs from the top clubs and hotels to come and demonstrate their signature dishes. Out of these lectures grew The National Training School of Cookery, and the whole concept of 'Domestic Science.' A batch of new cookery schools opened in the capital and later across the country.

Income was always a source of worry to JCB and he was forever coming up with new ideas to increase it. The success of his early text book prompted his publishers, Moffatt and Paige to look to JCB to create others. These were printed on cheap paper and sold for 2d a copy. And so *The Elements of Acoustics, Light and Heat, The Elements of Magnetism and Electricity* and *Buckmaster's Domestic Economy and Cookery* all became familiar additions to the various students schoolbags and continued to be in use until WW1. Such was the take up for these books that JCB later confessed that their sales were the means of putting his sons through higher education.

In 1890 something prompted him to move house and he came to live in 'Ashleigh' a three storey detached house (now part of 252 Kingston Road) in South Teddington. He had barely settled in the house when his beloved wife Emily died and was buried in Teddington Cemetery. His sons had all left home and in 1894 his daughter Phoebe married and moved out to Earls Court.

1894 was a memorable year for JCB. All the years he had worked for the Department of Science, he was not on the permanent staff payroll and was officially regarded as a temporary despite having joined in 1859. He was finally granted permanent status and a pension in 1894. His position was then discontinued and he was made redundant at the age of 75.

It would be quite normal for any man to sit back and enjoy his retirement after such a full life, but not JCB. He became a Justice of the Peace on the Spelthorne Branch in 1893 and in December 1894, he was elected as a Councillor to Teddington Urban District Council. His was the sixth highest election (out of fifteen) to the UDC at his first attempt. His first notable act was to persuade the UDC to acquire Craig Hall in Clarence Road. This was a redundant Baptist Chapel and once purchased, was converted into a Court House and was in regular use for hearings. Apart from Craig Hall, JCB was known to attend all local Police Stations to hear minor cases and administer justice.
He was against the Jubilee Drinking Fountain, calling it ugly and saying that if it was the best design (out of a competition to design the most memorable drinking fountain to celebrate Queen Victoria's Jubilee) then he would dread to see the worst!

JCB urged the Charity Commissioners to check the status of Peg Woffington's Almshouses - to be used for homeless widows - and was pleased to find that all was well.

He refused to pay the Library Rate, stating that the £70 collected was being misused on the cost of newspapers and the Chairman's rent, challenging the Council to prosecute him. At the same time he had been in correspondence with Andrew Carnegie for a grant to open a Free Library. This was finally done in 1904 at a cost of nearly £5,000.

Whilst attending a fete at 'Chesfield' in aid of the Kingston Guild of Cripples, he felt a chill, left early and went home, straight to bed. He did not leave his bed for over two weeks and passed away peacefully from heart failure. The end of a most remarkable life.

I have drawn very heavily on the works of his grand-daughters :
J C Buckmaster : A Study of His Life and Work
by Dr M E Tasker
John Charles Buckmaster
by Hilda Buckmaster

Miss Clara Millard

WHENEVER I WALK TO THE SWIMMING Pool in Vicarage Road, I am always struck by the small house on the right hand side, immediately before the Pool complex. This is named 'The Old Coach-House' and has been there almost since Vicarage Road was cut through in 1881. In a poor state of repair during the 1970s, it was used as a store for building materials but has since been restored as a private dwelling. Who could have been wealthy enough to have owned a coach and a building in which to house it?

After making some enquiries, I discovered that it belonged to a person in the High Street, namely Miss Clara Millard. Miss Millard was one of the earliest antique curios collector and dealer in Victorian England and later came to be recognised as such.

When being interviewed by society columnist Norman Hurst in 1896, Miss Millard was asked what had induced her to start as a dealer in curios. 'At the age of sixteen it became necessary that I should look about for some means whereby I could earn a livelihood. My mother was always a collector of china and curiosities, and from her I learnt as well as inherited a great knowledge of these articles; it therefore struck me that I could not do better than start in that way of business. With this object in view, I prepared a catalogue of that portion of her collection which she wished to sell, and sent it round to collectors and wealthy people. As it turned out, that catalogue, by the attention it attracted, was the starting point in my success, and coupled with the kindly help and valuable advice given me by such celebrated collectors as Lady Schreiber, Lady Currie and Baron Rothschild, which saved me from making many of the mistakes that are so inevitable by a beginner.'

She started business in the High Street and subsequently transferred to Mulberry House in Vicarage Road. By the age of 25 Miss Millard had established a reputation far beyond the confines of the Home Counties – no mean achievement at a time when a woman running any sort of business was something of a phenomenon. As her obituary said: 'To the older generation of collectors, and, indeed, all those interested in antiques, it is no exaggeration to say that Miss Millard's name was a household word.'

In 1893 she married Mr Nathaniel Charles Dance at St Alban's Church. Virtually nothing is known of Mr Dance other than that he assisted her in the conduct of her business all through her commercial life until her retirement. There was a son and a daughter from the marriage but nothing is known of them.

There is no doubt that Miss Millard's remarkable flair brought her to the attention of many royal and distinguished clients, and combined with a pleasing personality, the business grew rapidly until she could boast that almost every collector of note had visited her at some time or another.

When asked about her client list she said 'I have clients for everything conceivable and inconceivable – old playing cards, boots and shoes worn by famous people, walking sticks, match-boxes, snuff-boxes, sun-dials, watches, door knockers, cow-bells, teaspoons, old dolls, and instruments of torture. The Dowager Duchess of Norfolk was my first customer. Then I had the honour of supplying Her Majesty the Queen with some rare books and sometime later I sold her Lord Nelson's written instructions to the Fleet as to how the Battle of Trafalgar was to be fought. Then Mr Gladstone buys books from me. I supplied the present Emperor of Germany with a set of Apostle spoons, Lord Wolseley with miniatures, Prince Christian with royal portraits, The Duchess of Newcastle, Lady Dorothy Nevill, and many more celebrities too numerous to mention.'

She conceded that she had a vast and entertaining post bag: 'To open my letters on many mornings I am sure would amuse you. I speculate over them and wonder; it is quite a lottery – I never know what is coming next. A country gentleman wants a pair of carriage gates or perhaps statuary for his grounds. A fond mother asks for eighteenth century embroidered night-caps. Next comes an application for me to purchase a collection of six hundred old fashioned lamps or an Egyptian mummy, the latter I find I must draw the line at.'

'A collection like mine, that is changing every hour of the day, is impossible to value or keep classified.'

The interviewer asked to see some of her favourite curios that would be of interest to his readers. The face of this energetic young lady brightened in a minute and she became genuinely excited as she flitted from one curio to another giving its history: 'This is the log book kept on board the *Princess Royal* from 1793 to 1796. It contains many interesting notices of the movements of the *Agamemnon* and the good old *Victory*. This bust of Nelson is made from timber taken from the *Victory*. I believe it was carved during the Admiral's lifetime but it has only just seen the light, after having been treasured in a Devonshire mansion for nearly a century. Here is a locket containing a piece of hair cut from the head of the Great Duke of Wellington; this is a loop of hair from the tail of his horse *Copenhagen* which carried him in the battle of Waterloo.'

'I suppose you are frequently asked for impossible articles?' remarked the interviewer. 'Well' said Miss Millard it is my boast that I have never yet been defeated in my search for anything, however rare it may be. Here is a wonderful instance; I wanted for a collector a particularly rare pack of old playing cards. I had agents in every corner

ONE OF MISS MILLARD'S ROOMS.

of Europe looking for them, and still they defied me. One morning a gentleman came in to sell me some trifling object of jewellery, and just as he was leaving he pulled out of his pocket a small pack of cards. "I suppose these are of no value are they?" he asked. It was the very pack I was in search of, and this is the strangest part of it – the gentleman was almost my next-door neighbour.'

A search for rare books held no qualms for Miss Millard and time and again she produced the required book for her client when the established book world had given up hope of ever finding such an item.

She also demonstrated her flexibility in dealing with her customers by one day accepting payment of an exquisite sapphire ring, by a sow and a litter of nine piglets. She sent her butcher to meet the train carrying them and on arrival at the station, he purchased the lot outright. It was said that there were descendents of those pigs running around Teddington for many years.

At some point Miss Millard and her family retired from the business and moved to Milford-on-Sea where she died 6 years later.

Unfortunately there are so many unanswered questions about her life and very little chance of building a full picture of her. If anyone can provide any additional information, I will be very pleased to hear from them.

William, Duke of Clarence

TEDDINGTON HAS LONG CLAIMED royal connections but in this case it is absolutely true as we have given shelter to a future king of England.

William Henry, Duke of Clarence, was the third son of King George III and Queen Charlotte, born on 21st August 1765. Being the third son of the monarch, it seemed likely William would be out of the running for the succession not being 'the heir or the spare.'

After a fairly boisterous childhood, the King had William enlisted into the Navy as a midshipman at the age of 13 on the *Prince George*. He saw action against the Spanish at Cape St Vincent and also took part in relieving the siege of Gibraltar so that when he made his appearance in London Society, he was looked upon as something of a hero. Back at sea he served under Nelson in the Caribbean who was favourably impressed and the two became lifelong friends.

He left the Navy in 1783 and was sent abroad to complete his education. Here he was introduced to the pastime of gambling that was later to lead him into trouble. He also commenced on a series of liaisons with members of the opposite sex. He then returned to the Navy in 1786 and on being promoted to Captain, he was given his first command – the frigate *Pegasus*. This vessel was on duty in the West Indies, again under the command of Nelson. A couple of fairly debauched years followed, culminating with Nelson returning to London after a severe attack of 'prickly heat.' Whilst back in London, William attended Nelson's wedding and insisted on being the one to give the bride away, her own father being deceased.

In May 1789 William was created Duke of Clarence; a title that carried an allowance of £12,000 but which he claimed was insufficient to keep him out of debt. He acquired a house in Petersham which he renamed Clarence Lodge but before settling in, he was recalled to sea to deal with a spot of trouble with the Spanish.

He became a Rear Admiral the following December and shortly afterwards, retired from naval life.

At this time a young Irish actress, Dorothea Jordan, was taking the London Stage by storm. Billed as Mrs Jordan, there was always something of a mystery about her as there was no Mr Jordan. William saw one of her performances and was immediately totally captivated by her. After a pursuit of nearly a year, in October 1791 they commenced upon a liaison, which was to last for nearly twenty years. On the death of Anne Lady North in 1797, he was appointed Ranger of Bushy Park and moved into the Ranger's official residence, Bushy House, with Mrs Jordan, her two daughters from a previous affair and their son, George FitzClarence. In the following years, George was to have four brothers and five more sisters, all born at Bushy House.

Although they had an almost idyllic existence at Bushy House, William was always in debt and relied heavily on Dorothea's earnings to bail him out. He decided that he needed to marry a wealthy heiress and whilst Dorothea was touring in Cheltenham, he wrote to her requesting that she should proceed to Maidenhead to meet him and discuss terms for a separation. This was to be their last meeting and despite William's assurances of a generous settlement, Dorothea died in Paris five years later, in wretched poverty.

Meanwhile the wealthy heiress rejected his advances, as did five other eligible ladies, much to the bemusement of London Society. To re-establish the dynasty of the House of Brunswick, William's brother the Prince Regent was making enquiries of the daughters of the royalty of Europe. An introduction was made to Princess Adelaide of Sax-Meiningen and William and Adelaide were married at Kew Palace on 13th July 1818. The pairing turned out to be a complete love match with Adelaide taking on the upbringing of the young FitzClarences and coaching William in the social graces.

The following year, Adelaide gave premature birth to a girl, Charlotte Augusta, who died a day later. The next year William's brother, the Duke of Kent (father to Victoria) died and within a matter of days 'mad' King George III also passed on. The Prince Regent duly became George IV but reigned only ten years before he also expired.

William became William IV at a time when the monarchy was at low ebb and he did much to restore it to public affection despite a relatively short reign between 1830 to 1837. On his death, Adelaide quietly retired to Bushy House where she remained until her death in 1849.

During his time at Bushy House, William felled nearly all of the trees in Bushy Park to sell the timber to pay off his gambling debts. He also became involved in many aspects of village life and was commander of the Teddington Volunteers, a cross between the Territorial Army and the Home Guard, who were formed to combat the threat of a French invasion.

When asked for permission to excavate the Bronze Age Barrow in Sandy Lane, William positively forbade this, thinking it to be a plague burial mound.

He was very upset at the death of his friend Nelson at Trafalgar and acquired a section of the mainmast of the *Victory*, which he had installed in a temple in the grounds of Bushy House. Adelaide was pleased to see that a pair of robins nested in a hole made by a French cannon ball.

William was patron of Hampton's first cricket club The Clarence – who had their pitch on Molesey Hurst. It ceased to exist in the 1870s but was reformed in 1881, this time playing in Bushy Park.

William is said to have told the following anecdote at a dinner party at a cottage in Windsor Park in 1827.

'I was riding in the park the other day,' said His Majesty, 'on the road between Teddington and Hampton Wick, when I was overtaken by a butcher's boy on horseback, with a tray of meat under his arm.'

"Nice pony that of yours, old gentleman!" said he.

'Pretty fair,' was my reply.

"Mine's a good 'un too" rejoined he 'and I'll trot you to Hampton Wick for a pot o' beer."

'I declined the match; and the butcher's boy, as he struck his single spur into his horse's side, exclaimed with a look of contempt,

"I thought you were only a muff!"

Another story is recorded in *Old Kingston – Recollections of An Octogenarian* by George William Ayliffe. The story goes that George Ayliffe was living in Hampton Wick as a boy and was presented with his first kite, which he took to Bushy Park to fly. No sport of any kind was then allowed to the public. He had not been flying his kite for very long before a gentleman came up to him and said,'You must not fly your kite here.' The gentleman asked him his name, age and where he lived and whether he went to school, and on receiving satisfactory replies he said, 'Well you are a good boy, George; you may fly your kite here whenever you like. If Sawyer (the

park keeper) says anything to you, tell him the gentleman who owns the park says you are to fly your kite here.' The gentleman then shook hands and went away and young George afterwards learnt that he had spoken to the future King William IV. On several occasions afterwards, young Ayliff met William in the park he always stopped, shook hands and asked after George's welfare.

Perhaps the most believable story is this :
He was roused from slumber in the ducal bedchamber in Bushy House one morning at 5am to be informed by His Ministers that they ridden in all haste to inform him that his brother 'Prinnie' was dead and that he, William, was therefore King. He thanked them graciously and bid them rise from their knees. After refreshment for the bearers of such good tidings, he begged to be excused as he said he must return to his bed because he had always wished to
sleep with a Queen.

Ablain St Nazaire
- Part 1

THIS MONTH, WE ARE GOING A LITTLE further afield than usual – in fact over the water to France and to a small village called Ablain St Nazaire.

The reason for this was a brief radio broadcast I heard a few weeks ago saying that Canada was commemorating the 100th anniversary of the Battle of Vimy Ridge, which many people regard as the modern 'coming of age of Canada.'

Ablain St Nazaire is a small village about 120 kms from Calais, south-west of Lens and north-west of Arras, nestling at the foot of the Notre-Dame-de-Lorette spur, population – about 1,800. It possessed a 12th Century castle and a church dating from 1524. The railway station of Allain-Souchez is half a mile to the west.

The nearby town of Lens fell to the Germans in October 1914 and from then until the end of the war, this area was the scene of much activity. Vermelles was taken by the allies in December 1914. The following spring the allies went on the offensive to retake the whole of Notre-Dame-de Lorette. After heavy artillery fire, General Joffre's armies advanced on Carency, the village next to Ablain. The Evening Despatch reported on 14 May 1915 that when they reached Hill 125, the French found the bodies of three German companies.

Carency has often been referred to in the reports of the last few months as a village. It is really nothing but a heap of ruins, but ruins very strongly fortified by the enemy.

In the meantime the Western Mail reported that the French had occupied the greater part of Ablain St Nazaire on 12 May. This followed eight hours of street fighting, going from house to house. On the night of 28 May the French launched a bayonet charge on the German positions in the town cemetery with devastating results – about 100 Germans were killed and 400 more rushed into French hands under cover of white flags whilst being shelled by their own side. Fighting continued into the next day and by evening the remaining Germans retreated, setting fire to half the village. On 4 June the Manchester Evening News reported that overall there were 600 Germans dead with total losses exceeding 2,000. Every house in the village had been either completely destroyed or seriously damaged and 83 inhabitants had been killed.

The Birmingham Daily Gazette reported the Allied High Command as saying 'The capture of the village of Carency, together with nearly 2,000 prisoners and much food and equipment, the progress of our troops to the north and their occupation of the village of Ablain St Nazaire must be reckoned amongst the finest successes achieved by our troops in Artois.'

The Germans had a different slant on the French victory stating "Without the enemy perceiving it we have withdrawn from the eastern part of Ablain St Nazaire the small garrison we had there, and the maintenance of which in this advanced position would have cost us useless losses." The number of Germans killed in Ablain and the prisoners taken there gave a decisive reply to this disingenuous announcement.

This is all very interesting I hear you say, but what does it have to do with Teddington?

To jump forward to 1998, one of my brothers-in-law showed me a book he had just acquired – 'A Blue Guide to Northern France' of 1919 which carried a curious entry which read 'In the aftermath of the Great War, a number of French towns in devastated areas were adopted by British towns for sympathetic assistance. This was done at the insistence of The British League of Help of Scala House, Tottenham Street, London W1.' Teddington, it seems, adopted Ablain St Nazaire.

I had never heard of the British League of Help (or to give it its full title : The British League of Help for the Devastated Areas of France – hereafter the League of Help) and in 1998 I was completely unable to trace any kind of reference to this organisation. I tried various libraries, the internet and any other public reference I could think but the League seemed to have vanished without trace. The chance find of an article entitled 'Forgotten Philanthropy' in the History Today edition of July 2013 finally changed all that. The writer, Dr Sally White, came from another town that had supported the League and she had unearthed an interesting story.

She wrote 'A few statistics give a hint of what the French had to cope with. At the end of the war the population of the main battle zone had been reduced by 57%. Barbed wire covered nearly 400 million square metres to a depth of over one metre. Over 330 cubic metres of trenches needed to be filled in. Almost 2,000 settlements had been obliterated or badly damaged. The war zone was a virtually treeless landscape of trenches, barbed-wire, shell holes, concrete bunkers, unexploded ordnance and the smell of the dead whose bodies had been buried and disinterred in the continuation of war. Some villages were never rebuilt and were designated as having "died for France."'

With this backdrop, a group of British people led by Lilias, Countess Bathurst, who believed Britain owed France an enormous debt of gratitude, went out to France and viewed the landscape for themselves. On their return, they formed the League of Help and publicised their aims in every town in Britain. They were formally inaugurated at the Mansion House in London on June 30 1920 with Lloyd George and Winston Churchill as patrons. Response to their appeals was extremely varied with some towns flatly refusing to become involved and others offering money, labour and equipment.

The next reference I have traced was a report in the Surrey Comet of September 17 1921 to say that Teddington's newly elected Chairman of the District Council, Mr C W W Burge JP was one of a party of sixty mayors and chairmen who left Victoria Station for a tour of the devastated areas of Northern France. Earlier in the year Mr Burge had been awarded the 'King Albert Medal'
for his work with Belgian refugees. The edition of the following week carried an account of his comments to the paper:
'The destruction is terrible. I have heard of cases where labourers ploughing the land had touched buried shells and been blown

to pieces and stacks of shells could be seen collected by the workers besides tons of barbed-wire and other materials of war. There seemed to be no unemployment in the areas we visited and one Mayor told me he could start 6,000 men in work, if he could get them.' The article finished by saying that in view of the needs of the devastated areas, Mr Burge desires that the locality in which he lives, should make its contribution and he would welcome donations, which may be addressed to the District Council Offices, Teddington.

And now the trail has gone cold again. There is no mention of this in the Council Minutes and no further newspaper statement that I can find has been made. So what did Teddington contribute to the recovery of Ablain St Nazaire? I intend to find out but if anyone has any information which might throw some light on this, I will be extremely pleased to hear it.

Where We Worshipped

IN COMMON WITH MOST OF ENGLAND, since the days of the English Reformation, the predominant religion in Teddington was that of the Church of England.

Pre-Conquest, Teddington was a berewick (an outlying estate) of Staines and was included in Edward the Confessor's grant of 1065 to Westminster Abbey. What had happened before then is open to debate but it is fairly certain that when the monks of Westminster were in control, some kind of chapel, if not already in existence, would have been established. Teddington had been a chapelry of Staines but by the end of the Middle Ages, it had become independent. As we know from *Teddington 800*, in 1217 the Bishop of London asked the Abbot of Westminster 'to present a suitable chaplain, with maintenance, for Tudinton' and this marked the beginning of the Parish of Teddington at St Mary's Church.

This arrangement seems to have worked well until Henry VIII declared himself head of the Church of England and the Roman Catholic faith lost its predominant status. Ownership of the Manor of Teddington passed from Westminster Abbey to Henry VIII in 1536 in exchange for Hurley Priory and after this date, the clergy were appointed by the Bishop of London, a practice that remains to this day.

St Mary's produced some remarkable clergymen in its time; Robert Fern or Feron who in 1535 was convicted of high treason and then probably turned King's evidence and was pardoned; Ephraim Udall in 1615 who was a Puritan, Thomas Gouge (1637-8) a Non-conformist and Matthew Randal who was suspended by Archbishop Laud in 1634 for preaching a sermon over 1 hour long. Thomas Treherne also preached here although he was the chaplain to Sir Orlando Bridgeman and not the parish. Then there was Rev Dr Stephen Hales, our most famous vicar/scientist. He was followed about 100 years later by Daniel Trinder who was too 'progressive' for his own good. He had the old pews taken down, introduced 'Hymns Ancient and Modern' and preached in a surplice, all of which led to accusations of Popery. It was rumoured that children threw mud at his back when he walked down the High Street.

His ministry ran from 1857 to 1878 and before it had ended a group of parishioners had broken away in 1864 to follow the historic 'low-church' and Protestant position of the Church of England. They originally set up their premises in an iron building in Church Road (from where the road takes its name). In 1869 it moved to the newly built church in Station Road. Unfortunately the structure has now been declared unsafe and the shell of the building has been sold for domestic accommodation with all Church services being held in the Meeting Hall.

One of the most important events in Teddington history was the arrival of the London & South Western Railway and very soon it became clear that some provision needed to be made for the people moving into West Teddington. Accordingly in 1865, a 'chapel of ease' – SS Peter and Paul - was built and opened in the Broad Street. This did provide some ease on St Mary's and it became a parish church in its own right in 1880. The expansion of Teddington continued to the west and in 1913 the parish of St Michael and St George was created at Fulwell. Both churches have had mixed futures. SS Peter and Paul was knocked down in 1979 and moved over the road to be rebuilt on the site of the old Public School. SS Michael and George closed in the late 1990s and the parish was combined with SS Peter and Paul. However this was not the end of the story and in 2014, the old church was reopened as St Michael's.

St Mary's parish church in 1884 saw the arrival of Rev Francis Leith Boyd, a young priest with high ambitions. He saw how the coming of the railway in 1863 had increased the population from 1,200 to 6,500 in a matter of 25 years. His church was now full to bursting and it was plain to see that a simple extension would not serve the purpose.

Boyd therefore sought the support of some of the most influential parishioners and announced his plans to build a new church – 'the cathedral of the Thames Valley.' William Niven was persuaded to draw up the plans and the fund-raising began in earnest. The plans were for a 'French style' cathedral with work soon starting, it was opened prior to its completion in 1889 when St Mary's closed as the parish church.

John Wesley is known to have preached a sermon at Teddington in 1753 and the Methodists have always had a presence in the town since that time. The first Methodist Church was in Craig Hall, Clarence Road. This was built in 1859 and served the community well until its resources

were outgrown and the church moved to a new building in Stanley Road in 1879. All went well until a flying bomb demolished the church in 1944. It was rebuilt in 1952 and still flourishes.

Following the Methodists came the Baptists. Their beginning was in rented rooms over a parade of shops on Bridge Approach (now part of British Marine Technology) in 1877. In 1879 they moved to a larger room over the London & Provincial Bank (now Barclays Bank) and the following year they moved into Craig Hall which had recently become empty. They stayed here only a short time until they purchased a site at the junction of Walpole Crescent and Church Road and erected the 'Tin Tabernacle.' Further growth in the congregation persuaded the Church to build a permanent building which they did and the new Church opened on 23 January 1895. The Second World War interrupted things and a bombing raid in 1940 destroyed the 1895 building. Once again the Church was re-built, reopened in 1956 and is still functioning strongly today.

In the late 18th Century, the oldest Teddington industry of linen bleaching was being carried out by John Goodchild in Broom Road, all along the sites of the old film studios, the Lensbury Club and Teddington School. A few Catholic families were involved with these processes. Consequently a temporary Roman Catholic chapel was opened in Hampton Wick in 1882. This moved into Fairfax Road in 1884 with the ground floor operating as a school and the upper floor as a chapel. The Church of the Sacred Heart of Jesus was then built on the Kingston Road and this opened on 1st January 1893, the old church remaining as the school and parish hall.

The London City Mission set up in 1835 to minister to the poor and destitute, found its way into Teddington and had established a Mission Hall in Park Street by 1894. It shut up shop in 1919 stating that the population was not the type of people that the Mission had set out to minister.

Last but not least we must not forget the Salvation Army who has quietly gone about their worthy work from their Hall in Church Road for over 100 years.

Time has moved on. Craig Hall was sold by the Council and is now two private dwellings. St Alban's is no longer the Parish Church – this has reverted to St Mary's. Happily all churches are still open to their congregations and providing the spiritual support for which they were established.

Ablain St Nazaire
- Part 2

SINCE WRITING IN ISSUE NO. 83 about the Teddington connection with Ablain St Nazaire, several things have happened.

Firstly the power of the internet connected me with Yves Durin, who is the archivist of the Ablain Local History Group, the Ablain-Memoire Association. He said that he had been unable to trace any reference of help from Teddington in his archive and requested further information.

Secondly our requests to the Mayor of Ablain for any information had been passed to the President of the Ablain History Group and she was very interested in this story and wondered if we had any plans to visit Ablain. By coincidence my wife and I were actually due to see her sister and husband in the Dordogne. They already knew of our connection and were very keen to follow this up and visit Ablain. More correspondence followed and we were all invited to lunch with the President and her husband.

Monique Huchette is the President of Alain-Memoire Association and they have been very active in reviewing the history of Ablain during WW1 and recording as many oral interviews with older townsfolk as possible. Her husband, Claude, is the Honorary Leader of the Ablain Guides which provides guards of honour at the Cemetery of Notre Dame de Lorette. They usually supply ten guards per session morning and afternoon, every day of the week. The cemetery was the scene of fierce hand-to-hand fighting during the war and subsequently has become one of the biggest war cemeteries in France with forty thousand graves. The role of the Guides is largely that of an informative one, assisting visitors and relatives to find specific graves for tributes to be placed etc.

Also within the cemetery is a new panoramic series of copper plates arranged in a circular design on which are engraved the names of every French, German, British and Commonwealth soldier who fell in the conflict in the Pas de Calais region. It was opened by Francois Hollande in 2016 and contains 585,000 – a most formidable record by any stretch of the imagination.

We had previously sent out a list of questions relevant to our quest and fixed a date of the weekend of 15th-17th September. Back home in Great Britain, this is of course Open House weekend where many historic buildings are let open to the public for the only time of the year. To my surprise the French also celebrate their own Open House system and several historic buildings were open that weekend.

We met Monique and Claude on the appointed day and they were joined by the Mayor of Ablain, Dominique, who was keen to meet us. He confirmed that no sooner had the town been rebuilt than WW11 commenced and although the town was not completely flattened as before, there was considerable damage and once again, all municipal records were destroyed. A thorough search of all remaining records has not borne fruit for our cause. Dominique was very sorry but could not offer us any alternative route for research. Unfortunately he was officiating at a town wedding later and had to leave but not before presenting us with a souvenir vase of the new cemetery.

Over lunch Claude told us that a local historian had written a book on the restoration and rebuilding of the town but unfortunately he died in 2016. Even more unfortunately, nobody had

thought to obtain a copy of his book which must throw some light on the Teddington connection. Something to be left for another day.

We then paid a visit to the ruins of the old church. It was a busy place with several parties exploring the remains. Whilst it is generally accepted that churches should be left alone in warfare, in this case it was not possible. As the church occupied a commanding position in the area, the German army fortified the church and used several buildings as an ammunition dump. This was not realised until the French retook the town, albeit temporarily. The Germans counter attacked and to prevent the Germans from occupying the church again, the French were forced to blow up the church and deny the Germans the former strategic positions.

At the church, we met Yves Durin, the Ablain archivist, who confirmed to us that he had been unable to find any kind of connection that Teddington had made a formal or informal adoption of Ablain. This was not going to be as easy as I had hoped.

We also met a young historian called Machin Patrice who had set himself an interesting research project. As you may imagine and as with nearly all ruins everywhere, the old church is covered in graffiti. Some of this is the usual mindless scrawl that one finds everywhere but some of the messages are more poignant and lasting. Machin has recorded all of the brief messages from soldiers who have left their names (sometimes rank and sometimes regiments). Machin has then followed this by seeking the soldiers' full military records and details of their families. He has now published this in a short booklet which is unique in picking the graffiti artists of the church, both French and German of the First World War. He has contacted the surviving families in as many cases as possible for permission to publish the comments found. In most cases he has been given the go-ahead but there are one or two entries he would have liked to have included but was unable to do so.

Whilst it was very pleasant meeting our French counterparts and being shown over the scene of the heavy fighting that occurred during the war, it was nevertheless very frustrating to find that no record seems to exist in France of the efforts of Teddingtonians in about 1922 to offer some help to the people of Ablain in rebuilding their town.

On our return to Britain, I looked again at the papers I had collected. The League of Help wound up for 'unseemly financial dealings.' That must have been a blow to Countess Bathurst and I wondered how she might have coped with this. I then found that her papers have been left to Leeds University and on looking at lists of the various documents concerned, there were copies of the first and second years accounts of the League of Help. Will this throw any light on the mysterious Teddington connection? Well I certainly hope so and will be pursuing this.

The Normansfield Bills

ONE OF MY PASTIMES WHEN I'M NOT being chased for some deadline or other is to trawl the e-bay pages for items of Teddington ephemera. These trawls can produce some surprising results or can be a complete waste of time.

Some years ago I spotted an invoice from a firm of hospital supplies which had a very attractive letterhead. On scrutinising the bill more closely, I noticed that it was made out to Normansfield Hospital. I put in a bid and waited. On this occasion I was pipped at the last minute and lost out on that sale. Feeling slightly bitter about missing out, I looked at the same dealer the next day and sure enough, there was another invoice made out to Normansfield from a totally different supplier. I made sure of getting this lot by putting in a high bid but the item went for the original asking price and I was the happy winner. A couple of days later, two similar items appeared and I set out to win these also. Everything did not quite go to plan – I won one and lost one. There was obviously another Teddington collector in the market!

Over the course of the next week more items appeared and I think I won seven out of eight of them. It was becoming a bit wearing having to check closely on every bid submitted, so I decided to speak to the seller who was an extremely helpful chap. I explained that I was a local historian and that Normansfield Hospital was right in my patch, so to speak, and that there was a story to be had from reviewing all of the invoices together. He agreed with me and said that he had a substantial bundle of invoices left that he was feeding into ebay one or two at a time. I asked him if he would be prepared to sell the remainder outside of ebay in one batch and he said that he would. I then made an offer which was accepted and waited for the postman to deliver...

Two days later a parcel arrived containing the invoices. I spent some time going through them all and adding the ones I had already acquired. There were 137 in all covering the period from March 1921 to July 1930. Each bill was made out to either Dr Langdon Down or Mrs Langdon Down at Normansfield and was written or typed on the most attractive personalised letter heads of the day. Some were for local firms e.g. Job's Dairy had a milk book, W G Bishop of Kingston Road supplied gallons of oil and others were national retailers. All in all it was a working synopsis of how a private hospital was run.

By far and away the biggest supplier was W B Fordham & Sons Ltd, Wholesale Hardware Merchants of 36/40 York Road, King's Cross, London N1 who had 29 invoices. These supplied : 1 sack of ferlo (?) fibre, 1½ doz pulp bowls, 2 x 4 gallon tea urns, 3 x black tea trays, 1 cast iron saucepan, 6 egg whisks, 1 x 3 gallon fish kettle, 18 rolls of 'Clevedon' toilet paper, 1 doz mop heads, 1 gross of coat hangers, 6 flat irons, 3 clothes buckets, 6 kneeling mats, 3 large bottles of Cedar Oil, 4 Pioneer fire extinguishers, assorted cleaning materials, 1 No 22 Enterprise mincer, 6 more fire extinguishers, 3 doz broom handles, 3 doz chamois leathers, and so on. Almost everything one could imagine in the efficient running of a hospital kitchen.

Electricity was supplied by the St Marylebone Borough Council Electricity Department at the rate of 2/6d per quarter. How on earth did that work? A couple of interesting items appeared from Joshua Margerison & Co Ltd, Soap Works of Preston. They supplied 5 cwt of White Windsor soap and 5 cwt of Golden Windsor soap at £27.0.0d. in 5 cases and 20 boxes, carriage paid to Kingston Station. They also supplied 2 gross of Buttermilk at £3.4.6d.

Next on the list was Jones & Homersham, Wholesale Ironmongers of Clarence Street, Kingston-on-Thames. They had 16 invoices which were for the supply of : 4 doz brass hooks, 7 lbs of cut nails, 2 lbs galvanised binding wire, 1 set of castors, 1 tool bag, 6 x 6" barrel bolts, 6 x 2" cast bulbs, 1 set of fire bricks, 2 steel shovels, 1 gross gutter screws and bolts, 6 x 5" striking plates, 7 lbs wall nails, miscellaneous screws, 20 feet of lead piping, 12 bib-cocks, 1 6" mortise lock and 1 gross of curt on hooks

J C & J Field of Lambeth provided 5 cwt of Pure Oil Soap.

Two interesting items appeared from Gosling & Sons Ltd of George Street, Richmond, which seemed more suited to the Langdon Downs themselves rather than the actual hospital. The larger of the two was for £48.9.4d. and covered lace wool petticoats, navy knickers, white knickers, nightdresses, frocks, dresses, coats and a child's Jersey frock.

An account from Garhard & Hay Ltd, Shipping Agents was in connection with the delivery of a consignment of machine parts from Malmo. What could these have been for ?

The firm of George Bettle & Co Ltd, Manufacturers of Hosiery, Underwear, Ties, Shirts and Pyjamas, were a busy supplier with 12 bills to their account. These all covered items such as Dutch tape, pure linen floss, Lombard ties, linen buttons, collar studs, various pins, black bone buttons and so on etc, rather than any finished goods. Were these items for running repairs or were some of the patient's clothes made at Normansfield ?

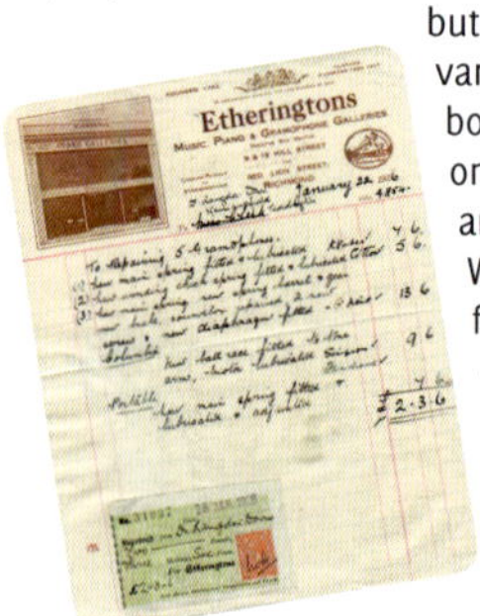
Etheringtons

A solitary invoice from Genatosan Ltd of Regent Street, Loughborough was for 3 phials of anti-influenza vaccine.

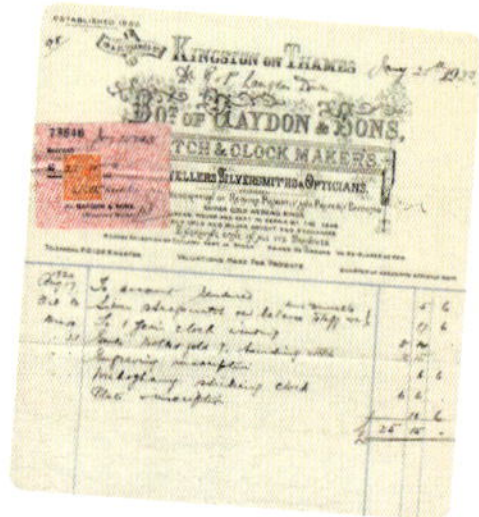
Kingston on Thames
Gaydon & Sons

There also appeared eight bills from Gaydon & Sons, Watchmakers and Jewellers of Thames Street, Kingston. These were slightly different from the others in that they were made out to Drs R(eginald) and P(ercival) Langdon Down. All bills were for clocks and watches of some sort and some even had the names of the ultimate receipient in brackets. Were these in respect of long service awards to some of the staff ? Perhaps we will never know.

A small batch of 'one-offs' were also included – Gaze's of Kingston had an indecipherable account for 5/6d, Gauntlett's Carding Machine Co produced a bill for 150 steel spikes for Carding Machine No 183, Frederick George carried out repairs to the welding operating table for 4/6d, the Formalin Hygienic Co Ltd supplied 2 x 1 ld cartons of Formalin Disinfecting Tablets, Fassett & Johnson of the Clerkenwell Road supplied 1 doz large size Angiers Emulsion, whatever that may be!

Entertainments were catered for by Messrs Etherington's of Richmond who serviced and repaired the hospital gramophones and also supplied new records. One of their invoices was for the repair of no less than five separate gramophones.

The well known firm of Eastman & Son, Cleaners kept the hospital in order with five invoices covering their services.

A lone account from Eagle Star Insurance was in respect of Normansfield's livestock.

The firm of D Wilkin & Co Ltd provided a monthly supply of 'En Avent' yeast as is evidenced by their accounts.

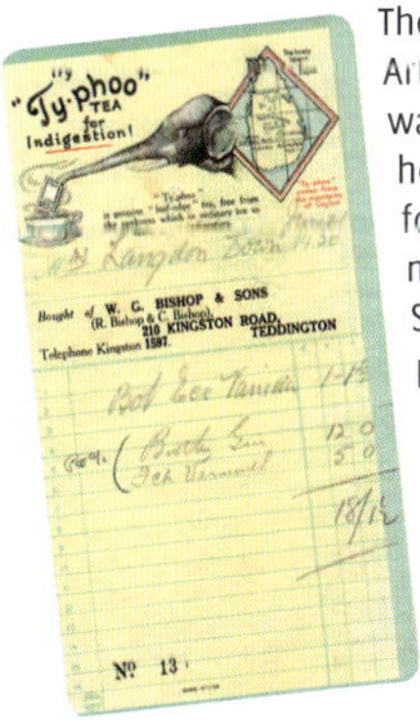
Try "Ty-phoo" TEA for Indigestion!

Bought of W. G. BISHOP & SONS (R. Bishop & C. Bishop) 210 KINGSTON ROAD, TEDDINGTON

Telephone Kingston 1187.

No 13

The still trading company of Arthur Sanderson & Sons Ltd was a regular supplier to the hospital with 16 invoices for the supply of decorating materials. Arthur Beale, Specialist Upholsterers, provided various products.

Local grocers, W G Bishop & Sons of 210 Kingston Road were regular suppliers of gallons of oil, black Meltonian, soap flakes, sugar, Ideal sauce and a variety of cakes.

A delivery book from Job's Dairy shows that there was a liking for cream at the hospital.

Lastly a couple of items of delicacy from the well-known and still trading firm of Wilkin & Sons Ltd of Tiptree, Essex. Addressed to Mrs R Langdon Down, these invoices were for various jams, conserves, chutneys and jellies. Clearly someone had a sweet tooth.

Having reviewed all of the items to my satisfaction, there was one thing that still puzzled me and I needed to go back to my seller in Dorset for this. My question was "From where did you acquire this collection in the first place?" The answer was that they came from a council rubbish tip in Reading. Rather than settle the matter, it now begs the question of how a series of settled invoices from a private hospital in Hampton Wick from 1921 to 1930 could end up in a council tip in Reading in 2009? Should any readers have any answers or suggestions, I would be delighted to hear from them.

TW11 Review Notes 2018

ANOTHER CHRISTMAS AND NEW YEAR, some new resolutions to be broken, a time for reflection and a time to look ahead. TW11 has become such a part of Teddington life that it is hard to believe that it was only in September 2010 that Dawn launched the magazine. That it was something that Teddington was looking for is borne out by the fact that it is still around and has grown from strength to strength.

Sometime in August 2012, Dawn contacted me to see if I would give her a local history article about Teddington. We met for a coffee, started talking and hit it off with the upshot that I ended up with a monthly column. In that October I broke my duck and introduced myself to the readership, giving details of my history background and how I became interested in history in the first place. I said then that 'over the next few months, I hope to bring you some interesting facts and stories about Teddington people and places.' That was five and a bit years ago and much to my surprise, I'm still blathering on nearly every month with something I think you should know about, from the Bronze Age Barrow to Teddington's connection with a first world war devastated town in Northern France.

History Focus

HELLO, MY NAME IS KEN HOWE and over the next few months, I hope to bring you some interesting facts and stories about Teddington people and places.

I can't remember what exactly set me on an historical path as history has always been a strong interest since childhood. I clearly remember the excitement of a friend discovering the skeleton of a small animal in his garden. From then on, every rusty nail and odd shaped stone went into a box at the bottom of my wardrobe. I think my mother discreetly disposed of my collection which deprived Teddington of having its own museum.

There was a gap in time when history took a back seat, and it was not until I stopped playing rugby and we had moved into our present house in Cedar Road that the interest was completely revived. My wife and I joined the History Section of The Teddington Society, and The Borough of Twickenham Local History Society. Strangely, one complemented the other with the Teddington Society group being smaller and more sociable whereas BOTLHS was more highbrow and academic.

We did a lot of listening at first until we felt confident to try and research the history of our own house. You might think that such a project could not be too onerous but even looking into a house built in 1929 had its problems. This started us working in the Local Studies Library, then at Twickenham and now in Richmond. There you will find most of the information that you need to find out the history of your own house by way of their collection of Kelly's Directories and the Road Files that are being constantly added to.

At a local history talk, I met an archaeologist from the Museum of London and asked him if he had heard of a Bronze Age Barrow in Sandy Lane. He had not but promised to look into it and a week later, a large parcel came to the door containing copies of all the main cuttings relating to this site. When I enquired if anyone had actually written a report of this, I was told 'No – why don't you do it yourself?' This started me on a quest in 1985 to find out as much as I could about the barrow and it was not until 2005 that my paper was published. There are no short cuts in history.

During the in-between years, I was part of a team to produce a 'then and now' series of pictures of Teddington for the Teddington Society. Unfortunately they ran out of money and we ended up publishing it ourselves as *Teddington Past and Present*. Fortunately it sold reasonably well and we covered our costs after about 18 months. That led to being asked to write *Hampton and Teddington Past* with my friend John Sheaf from Hampton, in 1995. This was the first full history of both towns for over 100 years and the book is due for a reprint shortly. Other picture books have followed and all seem to have been well received.

It is difficult to start the ball rolling and put something into print. Invariably as soon as this has been done, someone will come forward with irrefutable evidence that what I have just published, after months of deliberation and research, is wrong. But it is comparatively easy to challenge something written and to do so means that someone else has had to prepare that written article in the first place.

More recently I have been working with the Twickenham Museum. Although tiny and only open one day a week and weekends, this museum receives a phenomenal number of hits on the internet including many enquiries from abroad and the Teddington enquiries end up with me.

So that's how it started; please bear with me and watch this space.

34 | TW11 – October 2012

I must say that this has brought some recognition and at various gatherings and meetings, someone will invariably say "Aren't you the bloke who writes the history articles in TW11 ?" and a quick conversation usually follows with something like 'I liked your article on so-and-so' or 'I didn't know about such-and such thing.' It is always very gratifying to know that one's articles are well received and that they go down well. It is sometimes difficult to decide what will be of interest and what to avoid. Sometimes a reader will correct what I have written or better still, add to what I have said.

The series on Teddington pubs seemed to strike a chord with many readers, some of whom set out to discover the delights of these establishments for themselves. However that was an exceptional set of articles. Most of the time I have no idea how well or not the articles have been accepted or whether the subjects are of interest. My usual contact is via a reader in the street or in a pub and is then only a passing remark.

What I would like is a bit more from my readers. Are there any topics that they would like to hear about? Are there any old niggling facts that have puzzled them for years? Are there any people that they have heard of but know nothing about? I don't guarantee to be able to solve these enquiries with chapter and verse but I will certainly give it my best shot.

This brings me on to a case in point. A gentleman I have bumped into in the High Street a couple of times has asked me about the history of Railway Road. Coincidently Penny Lyndon had a query about her daughter's house – 61 Railway Road – distinguished by a Teddington Ales sign hanging outside.

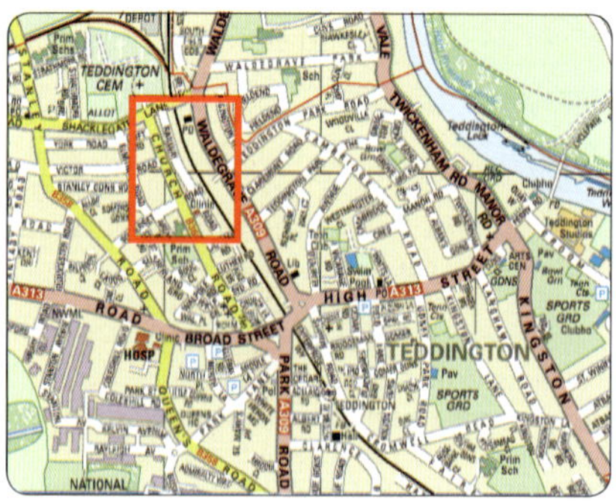

To take the age of the road first, the railway arrived at Teddington in 1863. Prior to that, the railway had been buying parcels of land through which to lay their tracks. On completion of the railway there was a surplus amount of land, particularly at trackside and the rail company was quickly seeking to recover some of its outlay by selling off these pieces of land, mainly for the building of private dwellings. Railway Road was one such piece of land. It runs from Shacklegate Lane along the railway line until it comes to an end as a cul-de-sac. It was developed in pockets of three small terraced houses. The earliest property is dated 1867 and it is said that the properties were acquired by the railway navigators, building the lines.

Turning to No 51 Railway Road, Penny's questions were : 'The house was obviously an off-licence at some time and benefits from a very nicely decorated basement, once the cellar. We are often asked by passersby when the off-licence became a house and what happened to Teddington Ales." Unfortunately I have been somewhat incapacitated by illness and unable to follow my normal research and so I asked my good friends, Dick & Gilly Hughes, to investigate.

Their enquiries read 'So far as we can judge, your daughter's property began life as No 1 Ivy Cottages (despite the board on No 52 which is the house in the middle of the terrace of three) and may have been occupied in the 1880s by William Plumbridge, Gardener. He is noted at No 1 Ivy Cottages in the 1891 census, with William Messenger, Bricklayer at No 2 and Albert Harvey, Dairyman at No 3. In 1895 the occupier is again listed as W Plumbridge with no reference to any off-licence use. We cannot confirm that No 1 Ivy Cottages is No 51 Railway Road as numbers were not introduced by the Post Office until the beginning of the 20th century. However the next reference we can trace is in 1925 when the house is first named as No 51 and the occupier is Henry Holt listed as Public Beer Retailer. In 1929 the occupancy had changed to Edward Thomas, Beer Retailer and in 1931 it changed again to William Given, Beer Retailer.'

'From 1895 to 1937 Teddington was an Urban District Council after which date Teddington became part of the Borough of Richmond. In 1963 the Borough of Twickenham then became absorbed into the Greater London Borough of Richmond upon Thames, Information in the Council records is very sketchy in matters relating to alcohol licensing and we do not know how firmly "off licensing" was policed in those days. Any surviving records may be held at the Richmond Local Studies Library of the London Borough of Richmond upon Thames, Town Hall, Richmond."

I am able to add that William Alex. Given was still in residence in 1932 and also in 1939 but after that I have no record. Still more records waiting to be discovered.

Do drop me a line with any topics you'd like me to look into, email me on howe64@btinternet.com, I'd be happy to hear from you.

Crossing the River Thames

SINCE THE LAST ICE AGE, THE RIVER Thames has flowed on a more or less continuous path through London, creating a geographical barrier between North and South London.

This has given rise to numerous debates over the years, several of which have never been entirely resolved. For instance it is widely held that Caesar crossed the Thames in pursuit of his conquest of Britain but where? Brentford and Sunbury both lay claim to that famous crossing but it seems more likely that Kingston was the most fordable location. Nevertheless the exact spot has never been clearly proven and the towns continue to stake their claims.

Rudyard Kipling famously wrote *The River's Tale* in 1911 saying 'Twenty bridges from Tower to Kew wanted to know what the River knew.' That may have been so then but we now have over two hundred different crossings. To go back to Kipling's original number, it was still a very difficult job to be able to cross the Thames from north to south or vice-versa. The further back in time one goes, the more difficult the problem was. Teddingtonians take for granted the journey into Kingston, crossing the Thames at Kingston Bridge to go to the Surrey bank, but it was not always so easy. Although the concept of the bridge was as old as pre-Conquest, very few were constructed before the 17th Century and a toll was often applied.

We must also bear in mind that road building is a fairly modern service and wherever possible, transportation by river was preferable. This produced the two livery companies of Lightermen (carrying cargoes) and Watermen (carrying passengers). Unfortunately road transport is now the predominant mode of transport in this country but there is a limited amount of river freight. The Watermen's and Lightermen's companies have now merged their resources.

In Roman times there were no bridges across the Thames. Crossing was either made at a ford in

the river or by ferry. Ferries have sprung up along the Thames at various points, signifying some means of communication between towns on either side of the river banks. This was probably trade orientated but there would also have been some military considerations as these valuable points on the river became more important in the control of lands.

Our particular wider area gave rise to several ferries, some of which are still operating today. The Ferry at Kingston claims an Anglo-Saxon origin, Hampton and Hampton Court ferries have early Tudor connections, the Twickenham or Dysart's ferry ran from 1692 to 1970. Teddington Ferry which operated from the Middlesex bank at Teddington to the Surrey bank at Ham, is of indeterminate age but in probably also Tudor in origin. The Richmond ferry has produced evidence of its operation in 1439 and finally Hammerton's Ferry at Twickenham which started in 1908 and is still running. Crossing by ferry was virtually the only way of getting from one side of the Thames to the other and this led to the lightermen and watermen running the ferries and creating monopolies in the charging of fees.

At Kingston, a bridge had existed since Anglo-Saxon times and this, a flimsy wooden structure, had been rebuilt in 1190 and again in 1318. Extensive repairs were carried out in 1567 and in 1710 it was described as 'the great wooden bridge hath 20 interstices. Two in the middle wide enough for barges ... it had 22 piers of wood and had in the middle two fair Seates for Passengers to avoid Carts and to sit and enjoy the delightful Prospect.' A further rebuild took place in 1828 and it was not until 1870 that it was declared free of toll. So from all times earlier, a toll had been levied on all cargoes passing over the bridge. Unfortunately we do not know how these tolls compared with the fees charged by the ferrymen.

Hampton Court Palace was responsible for the development of many of the local ferries and their continued occupation clearly evolved as the Palace assumed more importance in the government of England and became one of the houses of power in the country. The ferries at Hampton, Hampton Court and Teddington would have been required to transport palace staff, supplies of food and drink and the continual flow of royal guests, ambassadors and all other government officials.

There must have been considerable pressure on the palace to produce a permanent bridge over the Thames but the first one was not constructed until 1753, having been built by James Clarke. It was replaced in 1778 by a more sturdy wooden bridge but by 1840 this had become dilapidated and was in urgent need of replacement. This finally took place in 1865 when an iron bridge was introduced. It was unpopular in design but nevertheless very lucrative for its owner, Thomas Allen, bringing him £3,000 annually in tolls. He was bought out for £48,048 in 1876 by the local boards of Hampton and Molesey and the Corporation of London. The modern bridge was completed in 1933 and is still going strong. The building of the various bridges at Hampton Court clearly ended the trade of the Hampton Court ferries.

Downriver a couple of miles is Hampton Ferry which has been operating since 1514 and its incorporation makes it one of the 10 oldest established companies in the United Kingdom, placing it amongst the 150 oldest companies in Europe. It has always had a strong leisure connection, taking members of the public across to Moulsey Hurst for boxing bouts and horse racing events. Happily it is still in operation today.

Richmond followed Hampton Court in replacing its ferry with a bridge to support Richmond Palace although the first bridge was not constructed until 1777. Tolls were charged until 1859. Various tribulations were encountered in trying to find the right land for the crossing before it was set on the site of the old ferry. Once again the introduction of the bridge had killed off the ferry.

Returning to Teddington, the ferrymen were having their own way and continuing to charge what they pleased for their trouble. A lock had been constructed in 1811 and part of the construction involved creating a lock cut on the Surrey side of the bank as a navigational improvement, digging out tons of soil and creating the lock island we have today.

A bridge from the island to the Teddington bank was petitioned for in June 1873 but the Thames Commissioners declined the request. Henry Taunt, the Oxford based photographer and raconteur of the Thames, in supporting the petition noted that "a footbridge is sadly needed as the watermen on the ferry here demand the extortionate sum of three pence as their fee from passengers crossing the ferry and give as a reason the fact that being below Teddington Weir they come under the control of the Watermen's Company, and their rules allow them."

The authorities finally caved in to public pressure and agreed to the building of a footbridge. This was done on a design by George Pooley and was built by Messrs Goddard & Massey of Nottingham. The cost was £2,700 and part of this was borne by the residents of Ham. It consisted of a single span suspension bridge from the Teddington bank to the island and a girder footbridge from the island to the Ham bank. Surprisingly the ferry continued from Teddington to the island until the 1950s and the last ferryman was Harry Bishop.

There was further speculation in the 1950s about a road bridge being built over the Thames at Teddington but that is another story...

The Teddington Hospital War Memorial - Part 1

IN THIS PARTICULAR YEAR WHEN WE are commemorating the 100th anniversary of the Great War, it seems appropriate to make mention of Teddington's own memorial and how it came to be.

In order to do this, we need to go back to May 1914, prior to the start of the conflict. At that time, discussions were ongoing to build a new hospital in the town to replace the hospital in Elfin Grove, which had now outgrown its size. Matters were suspended during the war years and when war ended, the Hospital Committee met to resume their talks. Wallace Elmslie, a Trustee who had been on the 1914 committee and whose son, Lieutenant Elmslie, had been killed in action, suggested that the town's most fitting memorial to its dead would be to build a new hospital. This was endorsed by the whole committee without dissent. Two leading lights came forward to start the fund raising, Dr Percival Langdon-Down of Normansfield and son of John Langdon-Down and F Hugh Munby, Secretary of the Cottage Hospital Committee.

The new committee commenced the lengthy job of raising the money required and decided that their first duty was to provide a symbolic memorial to the dead. The job was put out to tender and it was awarded to C H Moss, Monumental Mason of Church Road. He had tendered a price of £76,000 for the supply, engraving and erection of a four sided block of Portland stone 18 ft high on two steps. It was erected in 1920 and dedicated in January 1921, eight years ahead of the Memorial Hospital itself, which still required extensive funding. Names are engraved on all sides with 279 names on the original presentation with 58 further names added later. The front panel also inscribes the 1939-45 war.

This memorial is of course, still standing and serves the town well every Remembrance Sunday. The only problem is that it only shows

337 names. This fact was first spotted by Valerie Sullivan, a long time member of The Teddington Society. Valerie was a retired civil servant and her interest began when her family asked her help in establishing what had happened to her uncle, a casualty of that war. Despite being stonewalled at nearly every point of enquiry, she persevered with her investigations until she had discovered the full story of her uncle's death.

Having achieved this, she reasoned that if she was having trouble in tracking down what happened to her uncle with all her resources and tenacity, what would it be like for someone less able to conduct such a search? Valerie then decided to simplify the process and research the names of all Teddington war dead and make this available to everyone. Firstly, she checked on the other war memorials in the town, of which there were several – the NPL, the Post Office, NatWest Bank (Parr's Bank), St Alban's Church, Christ Church, the Baptist Church, the Methodist Church, the Catholic Church, SS Peter and Paul's Church, Fulwell Bus Depot, Fulwell Golf Club and the Council School at Stanley Road. There may be others.

The problem then arose that a name might appear on more than one memorial. For example, a former pupil of Stanley Road School would certainly be on the school memorial in addition to the main hospital one. If he worked at Fulwell Depot, he would probably be on the Fulwell Memorial also. It became clear that not every soldier killed in the war was included on the memorial.

Valerie wrote to the Commonwealth War Graves Commission and obtained a full list of casualties with a Teddington connection. This showed about 550 names but from this must be deducted the names from other 'Teddingtons' and there are surprisingly quite a few. This brought the total number down to about 500. This begs the obvious question of why all of these names were not included on the Hospital War Memorial originally.

The explanation for this is that the Memorial Committee rushed the job and bungled it. They placed the following advertisement in the local papers – the Surrey Comet and the Richmond & Twickenham Times : 'Relatives are desired to send full particulars of the above who (Names of the Fallen) were residents of Teddington, in order that prompt inscription may be made on the Monument to be erected by public subscription.' The advertisement went on to list the requirement of full names, address, rank, regiment and date of death to be sent to the Honorary General Secretary. Such an advertisement took no account of relatives who had moved away since the war, those who had died of their wounds some time later and casualties who had no relatives or some relatives who did not wish to be reminded of the war. The result was that there were substantially fewer names than there should have been.

TEDDINGTON WAR MEMORIAL
(MONUMENT)

NAMES OF THE FALLEN

Relatives are desired to send full particulars of the above who were residents of Teddington, in order that prompt inscription may be made on the Monument to be erected by public subscription.

Full names, address, rank, regiment and date of death to be sent to :

The Honorary General Secretary
BERTRAM MOORE
Ivy Dale, St Winifred's Road
TEDDINGTON

This represented a good challenge for Valerie and she began the arduous process of wading through various archives and newspapers to establish a full list of names and give a brief biography of the person concerned. Unfortunately on 3rd March 2013, Valerie died suddenly and unexpectedly.

Her family were not sure what to do with her research papers and thought of giving them to the Imperial War Museum. Fortunately I was able to persuade her family to pass her papers over to The Teddington Society first and a group from the History Group was established to look at them. I think the family were relieved to find a good home for them and they promised to deliver nine crates of files of paperwork to us!

When we actually received the consignment, we were relieved to see that it amounted to less than the promised nine crates but nevertheless a very substantial archive. On looking through it we discovered that Valerie had trawled through the Surrey Comet for the war years and extracted every reference to Teddington or a Teddington serviceman. These gave a broad account of what was happening in the town during those years. Added to them were extracts from regimental histories giving details of the major engagements that were involved. It was obvious that Valerie had made several visits to France to see the massive war cemeteries and photograph the war graves where possible. This had all been done by hand, visiting public libraries and record offices and foreign destinations – the internet had not yet advanced to make the task easier.

I decided that this was too important an archive to hand over to the Imperial War Museum as they were preparing for the centenary of the start of the Great War and would very probably consign the archive to some basement storage. It was far more important for Teddington to try and wade through this and form some sort of account to commemorate the fallen. This we have done and are still doing. It is not a job that can be rushed and David Neller and Colin Hicks have done sterling work in updating the recorded names.

The list of the known dead of Teddington now stands in the 470s which is a truer picture than on the original monument. It is unlikely that there will be any further additions unless anyone knows of any memorials unknown to us and our next task will be to arrange for additional panels to be added to the Memorial to complete the monument to our war dead.

Teddington, Hampton Wick and District Memorial Hospital
Front view

The Teddington Hospital War Memorial - Part 2

LAST MONTH I TOLD YOU HOW THE memorial came into being and I mentioned some of the people who had been researching the names of some of the fallen, particularly the work of Valerie Sullivan. For this edition I will bring you a particularly poignant story that she unearthed.

PRIVATE CHARLES ARTHUR MOLE

From the Surrey Comet : August 24 1918.
Mr and Mrs Mole of 82 York Road, last week received the sad news that their younger son, Private Charles Arthur Mole, Royal Fusiliers, previously reported missing, had died whilst a prisoner of war in Germany. He was wounded in action on March 26, and his death, as reported through the Geneva Red Cross, occurred a few days later, the burial taking place at Cambrai in the military cemetery.

Charles Mole, whose age was 19, attended the Teddington Council School under Mr Orton and won a four years' scholarship at Hampton Grammar School. He devoted himself with much thoroughness to church work at the church of SS Michael and George, Fulwell, where he was an altar server, and acted as assistant scoutmaster to the local troop. His early death will be regretted by many comrades and friends.

From the Surrey Comet : September 4 1918
The following letter, 'written in a shell funnel on Good Friday March 29 1918' was recently received by Mrs Mole of 82 York Road. It was written by a German soldier and sent to a missionary in Birmingham, who translated it and sent it on to Mrs Mole.

'Dear Family Mole,
Love and a sense of duty compel me to communicate to you what will be the greatest interest to you. I am a German soldier, whose name is H. Weingartner. When our forces were moving onwards over the battlefields, which had been evacuated by the English, some of my comrades hit upon three English soldiers, of whom two were dead already and one still alive. When they returned from their reconnaissance trip they told me about it. I asked them together with some other comrades to follow and see what we could do for our fellow soldier. We took with us also a man of our ambulance staff and some warm tea. When arriving on the spot, we freshly dressed our English comrade, who evidently had made himself some provisional dressing before we came. Both his legs were badly wounded. His left leg had two big holes above the knee and three holes lower down on the foot. I severed his shoe with a knife as gently as possibly. In order to dress him properly I had to cut off the upper part of his trousers. His right leg was wounded on the shank. His hands were also wounded. After we had bandaged him up and refreshed him a little with a cup of tea, we carried him on a tent bed to the main road, lest he should succumb on the spot. We attached a little flag to his bed to direct our sanitary soldiers' attention to him when passing by. He had two letters with him, which he handed to me. These letters I am sending you with this. Whether they ever will reach you I do not know; I will try at least and send them on to a friend of mine, a missionary, Mr I Genahr, who is married to an English lady. He will know how to deal with these letters, which I presume are written by your son. Near the place where we found your son, I picked up two photos of which for the present I keep one for myself and send you the other. Maybe that it shows his own likeness, though I am not quite sure of it. Maybe

that it shows one of his friends. I could not make it out, as we could not make ourselves understood, he talking English and me German.'

'All this happened on the 26th in the afternoon. He tried also to speak some French, from what I understood that he had been lying there for two days. As the place was within some distance from the main road, no one had noticed him. Happily our column did not march the same evening. So I went again to see my poor friend late at night, when the others had taken to rest and found him still lying there, no doubt only because everything had to be done in the greatest hurry in those days. I was glad to find him still alive, and felt very happy that I was enabled once more to do him some small service of love. I had some tea and water with me and allowed him to choose what he preferred. In some other things I could also give him some relief and tucked him up as well and as warm as I could. Before I left him I knelt down at his side and prayed with him. Though he may not have understood me he well knew that I was praying with him and for him. I was moved to tears to see how grateful your son looked at my little service, and I took such a fancy to him and shall continue to remember him in my prayers. Among other things he told me that he was only 19 years old. With a sore heart I bade farewell to him late in the night. I should have liked to have stayed with him all the night, but of course this was impossible. The next morning I went again to see him and to bring him some refreshment in case he still should be there. However, he had been removed to some field hospital by an officer who had passed by, and ordered him to be driven off in a carriage to a place of safety, where he could be properly looked after.'

'This is all I can tell you about your son. I have asked God to keep and safeguard his young life and grant him a meeting again with you all. And my sincere and fervent wish is that this letter will safely reach you, especially in case your son should succumb to his wounds, and no news about him should ever reach you. If there is any possibility to write me a line and tell me whether you had any other news about your son and what has become of him, Mr G will be pleased to forward. Should your son survive, which I hope and pray for, I hope to hear from him later on. May the Lord soon grant us peace according to His everlasting mercy and grace, Yours sincerely, H Weingartner'

Information from the Commonwealth War Graves Commission :
Pte. Charles Mole died of his wounds 28th March 1918 aged 19 and is buried at Cambrai East Military Cemetery.

I wonder whatever happened to H Weingartner. Did he survive the conflict? Did the Mole family ever establish contact with him? Perhaps we shall never know.

I am sorry that this story has been so long but it is probably the first time in a hundred years that the Weingartner letter has been published. I will bring more stories to the next edition.

The Teddington Hospital War Memorial - Part 3

LAST MONTH'S STORY PROVOKED a lot of interest and if anyone has any further information on the families involved, I would be most interested to hear from them.

This month I will run through a few names on the memorial and some interesting stories arising about them.

MAJOR THOMAS JOHN MOSS MC
Thomas Moss was born in 1879 and was a career soldier. He joined the Army in 1895 and served overseas in India for seven years. His brother, David, was a Major in the Garrison Artillery in France and his father had fought in the Zulu wars. He was the son of Thomas Moss of 145 Waldegrave Rd and was married to Emily Mary Moss of 10 Claremont Road. His uncle was Councillor C H Moss, the monumental mason of Church Rd who designed and built the war memorial.

He went over to France with the 2nd Division of the Royal Field Artillery in August 1914 although it is unclear what rank he held at that time. In October 1915 he was awarded the Military Cross from King George, the first man, it is believed, to receive this honour in this war. Rapid promotion followed and at the end of October, he was given a commission as Lieutenant. The following January saw him promoted to Captain and in March 1917 he was made a Major in the 61st Division. He had seen much severe fighting and had been at each of the great battles of the Western Front since the beginning of the war. In addition to his Military Cross, he was twice mentioned in Dispatches.

He was killed in action whilst Acting Lieutenant Colonel, at St Quentin, France on 21st March 1918. He was 39. He has no known grave and is commemorated on the Pozieres Memorial at the Somme, which records some 14,690 names. He is also remembered on the headstone of the grave of his baby son in Teddington Cemetery as well as the Hospital War Memorial and the Methodist Church Memorial.

SERGEANT JAMES EDWARD NEEDS
One lady who got in touch with us had been doing a lot of work on her grandfather's life but had not been able to pinpoint his death. This was Sergeant James Needs MM. We were lucky enough to uncover a clip in the Surrey Comet of 27th January 1920 which solved the mystery.

SON RECEIVES FATHER'S MEDAL
Gallant Sergeant who was shot by German Officer after Capture
'Before a special parade of Troops at the Depot, East Surrey Regiment on Monday morning, Major J C May, DSO, Commanding Officer, presented the Military Medal awarded to the late Sgt J E Needs, Middlesex Regiment, to his son, Scout James Needs, 1st Teddington (Baptist) Troop BP. The medal was granted for gallantry and devotion to duty in a raid near Passchendaele on 3 March 1918. The deceased , who was 37 years of age when he met his death on 24 April 1918, was the husband of Mrs Needs of 37 Argyle Road, Teddington. He had served in France for over two years before his death, and had won the confidence of all the men in his platoon by his good leadership and cheery disposition. Writing to his widow some ten months after the death of his platoon sergeant, a comrade, after repatriation, stated that on the day Sgt Needs met his death the Germans broke through

on a flank. The English were ordered to retire from the trench they held, but the enemy surrounded them. They continued fighting until they ran out of ammunition and they had to surrender "and a cowardly Hun officer deliberately shot your husband, after we had surrendered," added the writer.'

PRIVATE WILLIAM ARTHUR STRINGER

A very sad case was reported in the name of Will Stringer. Private Stringer – a handsome young fellow of 6 ft. and yet less than 17 years old, lived, at the time of his joining the 13th London Fusiliers at the outbreak of war, with his parents at 80 Broad Street. He was a pupil of Tiffin School and was remembered by his schoolmates as a fine healthy minded lad of energy, vivacity and courage.

When the Nation's call was heard, Will was enthusiastic in his response, and readily joined the Territorials, though but 16 years old. 'He had the bearing of older years; and his tall, well knit figure and healthy countenance did credit to his khaki. One may be sure he comported himself well before the enemy. It was in the lad's nature.'

He was one of the victims of Neuve Chapelle and he died the death of a soldier marked by fortitude and pathos, thoughtful to the last of his home and his parents. The story of his death is told in a letter marked by deep feeling and true sentiment from the French nurse who tended him at the Base Hospital :

"Dear Mr Stringer, I am terribly grieved to have to tell you of the death of your son, William Arthur Stringer, 13th London. He came into the hospital exactly a week ago with a broken arm and a pierced lung, also with bad concussion of the head. That night he was conscious, and with his well right hand he clasped mine very tightly, and I said a prayer for him. Then he got much better. He was very comfortable in bed, with doctors and nurses to attend him, and he improved greatly. I was very fond of him, and used to help him with his meals and write cards for him and do all I could; while every night I made a practice of saying his prayers with him. He sometimes would talk to me as much as ten minutes at a time. Last night, however, he seemed much weaker. Very late when I was in the ward he beckoned to me and whispered that he was not feeling so well; would I send his love to you all if he did not get better? I tried to cheer him up and prayed again, and he fell asleep with a smile on his face. He was not conscious next morning, and passed away very peacefully at 12.00 noon. We buried him today in the little cemetery of this place, in a special spot reserved for soldiers fallen in the war. A wooden cross, with his name upon it in metal, marks the exact spot where he is, within sound of the guns.

I pray that God may help you in your great sorrow, and remember that, like our beloved Lord himself, he gave his life for others.
I am, yours in deepest sympathy,
C.M. Chavim'
Will died on 17 March 1915, aged 16. Possibly the first Teddington casualty of the war.

Thanks to the many hours of hard work by Colin Hicks and David Neller, we now have all memorial records online and anyone may look up any distant friend or relation. Go to the Teddington Society Wiki page, then the Online WW1 War Memorial for Teddington, alphabetical Index, then select a letter. All names with that letter will be drawn up, then select a name. The chosen name will appear with a brief biography.

The Women's Suffrage Movement in the Borough - Part 1

1918 WILL PRIMARILY REMEMBERED as the year that the Great War ended but there was also another long standing dispute that was resolved to some extent with the passing of the Representation of the People Act, enabling 8.5 million women over the age of 30 who met a property qualification to vote.

This was the culmination of a series of protests and deputations first started by Mrs S Hebditch of Jamaica Terrace, Commercial Road in 1832 in the Middlesex Registration Court. Various reforms were put forward over the next 80 years to give parity for women with men in the election of all matters political. In Hampton and Teddington women demonstrated their intentions by joining the Primrose League and holding offices within it. Apart from this, progress was very slow although by the end of the 19th century women's suffrage was a national issue.

In 1897 Mrs Millicent Fawcett combined several of the smaller women's societies into the National Union of Women's Suffrage Societies (NUWSS) and later in 1903 Mrs Emmeline Pankhurst formed the Women's Social and Political Union (WSPU). Still none of the major national parties would include a section on women's suffrage in their manifestos. Several attempts were made to introduce private members' bills into the House of Commons but on each occasion, they were 'talked out'. Prime Minister Asquith doggedly refused to receive any deputation on the issue of women's suffrage and he absolutely refused to grant it any parliamentary time. This precipitated a campaign of window-breaking and the arrest of Mrs Emmeline and Miss Christabel Pankhurst for inciting the public 'to rush' the House of Commons.

April 1908 saw a packed Richmond Theatre audience of the London Society for Women's Suffrage receive Miss Christabel Pankhurst, who launched an hour long scathing attack on Mr

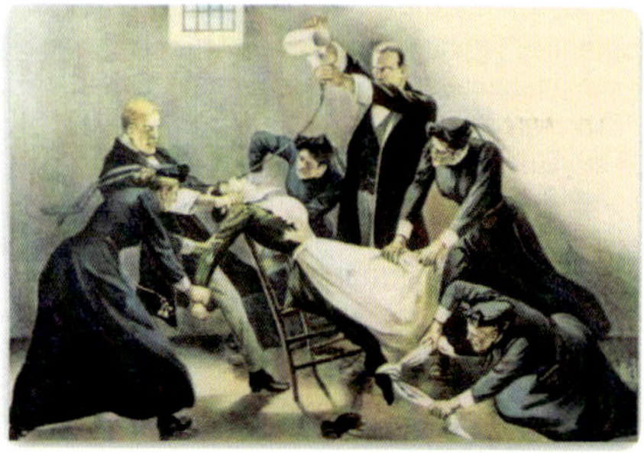

Asquith and Mr Churchill. This was greeted with loud applause and few interruptions (apart from a youth who let off a squib) but on the whole the meeting was remarkably orderly. However the continued denial of the government to discuss the issue resulted in more militant actions by some suffragettes in order to more forcefully publicise their aims.

On 8 February 1913, staff at Kew Gardens were astounded to find that two of the orchid houses had been broken into, the plants taken out of their pots and smashed to the ground – 'an outrage of a peculiarly wanton character' the Times reported. A scrap of paper was found bearing the inscription 'Orchids can be destroyed, but not a woman's honour.' Mrs Pankhurst confirmed that it was the work of suffragettes. The police had no success in finding the guilty party.

On 21 February 1913, in the early hours of the morning, the fire brigade were called to attend

a fire at the Tea House in Kew Gardens. The pavilion which was a timber building was burnt to the ground in 22 minutes, before the brigade arrived. On this occasion however two women were arrested nearby shortly after the blaze. They were seen running across Old Deer Park playing fields at 3.15am and both threw away bags they had been carrying on realising that they were being pursued. The bags were found to contain a small saw, a hammer, a bundle of tow (a hemp or flax fibre) and three pieces of paper smothered with tar – not exactly the normal contents of a ladies handbag. Cards were found at the scene, 'hysterically printed' with the words 'Peace on Earth, good will to men – when women get the vote.' They were arrested and charged at Richmond Police Court. They had given their names as Lillian Lenton, aged 22, and Joyce Locke, an art student, aged 23.

When charged, Miss Locke picked up a directory and threw it at the head of the Chairman of Magistrates. Luckily it missed. They were refused bail, but Miss Lenton was later released as she had pleurisy and pneumonia. When the hearing resumed a week later Miss Locke was released on bail and was hissed at by a large crowd as she was driven away. The case was committed to the Old Bailey, and at the hearing on 9 March 1913, Miss Locke,(whose real name proved to be Olive Wharry), was sentenced to eighteen months' imprisonment with costs. Miss Lenton was also found 'Guilty' but her sentence is not clear. Miss Locke/Wharry regarded the proceedings as a 'Good joke' and she stated that they had both checked that the pavilion was empty before setting fire to it.

The damage caused amounted to £900 and the building which was privately owned by two ladies, was only insured for £500. Miss Locke/Wharry said that they believed that the building belonged to the Crown and regretted the damage but 'she wished for the two women to understand that she was fighting a war, and that in a war even non combatants had to suffer.'

Olive Wharry

When sentenced, she cried out 'I will refuse to pay. You may send me to prison, but I will never pay costs.' They were both sent to Holloway Prison. Both women went on hunger strike with different results. Lillian Lenton, who was already ill, was force-fed by the prison staff. It took two doctors and seven wardens to restrain her and in the end food entered her lungs which caused her to become seriously ill with pleurisy. This caused a public outcry, made worse by the fact that the Home Secretary of the day, Reginald McKenna denied that she had been force-fed and that her illness was actually caused by her hunger strike.

A leading surgeon of the day claimed in a letter to The Times 'The Home Secretary's attempted denial that Miss Lenton was nearly killed by the forcible feeding is worthless... she was tied into a chair and her head dragged backward across the back of the chair by her hair. The tube was forced through her nose twice... after the second introduction when the food was poured in, it caused violent choking.'

To get themselves out of trouble, the Government hastily convened the Cat and Mouse Act whereby suffragettes on hunger-strike in prison could be released on licence when they were too weak to cause any further damage, only for them to be re-arrested in the future, on the original sentences.

Olive Wharry did not broadcast her hunger-strike, passing her food to other prisoners. This went on for 32 days during which time her weight had dropped from 7st 11lb to 5st 9lb (50 kg to

13107 The Refreshment Pavilion, Kew Gardens.

36 kg). How the warders failed to notice that anything was wrong beggars belief but Wharry was released into the care of Dr Flora Murray, a WSPU member who cared for hunger strikers after their release from prison.

Both Lenton and Wharry avoided re-arrest by a series of clever evasive moves and both went on to re-offend at different locations throughout the UK. Both women received the WSPU hunger strike force-feeding medal, which reads 'For Valour' across the top and 'Hunger Strike' on the bottom.

To be continued...

I am indebted to Gerald & Joan Heath's work The Women's Suffrage Movement in and around Richmond and Twickenham' and to The National Archives.

The Women's Suffrage Movement in the Borough - Part 2

THIS MONTH we will be looking at matters a little closer to home and a little livelier also.

On 11th March 1913 the Hampton & Teddington branch of the NUWSS held a meeting at Elleray Hall, Teddington. Long before the meeting began, a large number of youths entered the hall and took up positions at the back. The hall was soon filled to overflowing and the band of youths commenced their programme of disruption. Despite appeals for a fair hearing, the interrupters created such havoc that the meeting had to be abandoned.

On 15th March 1013 a meeting of the Kingston & District branch of the WSPU was held at Ive's Restaurant at Hampton Court under the chairmanship of Princess Sophia Duleep Singh. She was living in Faraday House (the one time home of Toby Jessel MP) which was then a grace and favour house opposite Hampton Court Green. Her father had been the last Maharajah of the Sikh Raj and her mother was Bamba Muller, the daughter of a German banker. Her godmother was Queen Victoria.

Princess Sophia held very strong principles and demonstrated these by taking an active role in the Women's Tax Resistance League. She refused to take out licences for her five dogs, her male servant and for a carriage with armorial bearings, and she then refused to pay the fines for not taking out the licences. 'When the women of England are enfranchised, I shall pay my taxes willingly. If I am not a person for the purpose of representation. Why should I be a fit person for taxation?' she insisted. A few weeks later a diamond ring of hers was seized and was put up for auction at Ashford. It was purchased by a member of the Women's Tax Resistance League and returned to her. On another occasion bailiffs seized her 131 pearl necklace and a gold bangle studded with pearls and diamonds in lieu of payment. These jewels were put up for auction at Twickenham Town Hall, bought by fellow suffragettes and handed back to her. Princess Sophia was regularly seen at her pitch outside Hampton Court Palace selling 'The Suffragette.'

At about the same time, a Mrs Rawles of Hampton Wick took similar action and a diamond pendant of hers was seized and put up for auction at the Clarence Hotel, Teddington. Once again the jewel was purchased by a sympathiser and returned to its former owner. After the sale at the Clarence Hotel, a protest meeting on behalf of the WTRL was held and was well attended. A motion calling upon the Government to pass legislation to extend the franchise to women was passed with one dissentient.

On 25th April 1913 the eight carriage 9.15pm train from Waterloo to Teddington had been shunted into the railway sidings between Hampton Wick and Teddington stations according to 'The South Western Gazette'. The next part of the story tells that a policeman cycling home about 3am along Fairfax Road spotted flames issuing from the

CARRIAGE SEVERELY DAMAGED BY SUFFRAGETTES AT TEDDINGTON.

train and coaches and duly summonsed the fire brigade. The Gazette tells us 'Three second-class compartments were entirely burnt out, and others damaged. The flames were fortunately extinguished by the local fire brigade before further damage could have been committed but there is no doubt that the total destruction of the entire train was the ambition of the ghouls who perpetrate these senseless crimes. The train, which consisted of eight coaches, had been set on fire in several places and was burning furiously.'

'Among the articles on the train were a large number of partially burnt candles, four cans of petroleum, three of which had been emptied of their contents, a lady's dressing basket containing a quantity of cotton wool, and packages of literature dealing with the women's suffrage movement. The cushions were first saturated with petroleum, and then small pieces of candle were lighted immediately under the seats. It was evident that if the fire had raged undetected for a few minutes longer, it would have been impossible to have saved the train from complete destruction.'

Kitty Marion

Women's footprints were found on the ground from Fairfax Road where intruders had entered the siding and gained access to the line by removing a paling from the fence nearly 6ft high. It was evident that there was more than one person involved. Despite strenuous enquiries by both the Railway Police and the Metropolitan Police, no arrests were made.

The most outrageous incident followed on 4 June 1913 at the Epsom Derby when Emily Wilding Davison, a long time campaigner for women's rights, stepped in front of the King's horse in an attempt to pin a 'Votes for Women' badge to the horse. She died four days later from her injuries after the horses trampled over her. However the news cameras captured the event and the pictures were transmitted around the world.

Five days later on 9th June the racing world was rocked again by another incident. In the early hours of the morning, Kitty Marion and Clara (Betty) Giveen dragged a large carpetbag filled with paraffin soaked wood chips through the streets of Kew towards Hurst Park racecourse near Hampton Court. On reaching their destination at about 2am they decided that the racecourse's bandstand was the best target and set about scattering 'Votes for Women' leaflets around the area so that there could be no doubt as to who was responsible for the outrage.

Kitty Marion later stated 'We turned off the road, towards the river between which and the course was a cricket field with a tool shed near the 'unclimdable fence' as the Press later called it, where we had decided to climb over with a foot hold on the tool shed. How we got over and back again beggers description. We both regretted that there was no movie camera to immortalise the comedy of it. We carried our 'baggage' through the long grass, to the Grand Stand at the other end of the course. We spread our munitions ... and left a piece of candle burning which should have lasted at least an hour to give us time to get away before igniting its oil-soaked base.'

The fire started quicker than anticipated and the two were forced to make their escape and head back to Kew. No sooner had they reached home when they were arrested, for they had been spotted at various points of their journey and the sight of two young(ish) women walking unaccompanied through the night had not gone unremarked. Both were charged with arson, found guilty and jailed.

Further incidents took place. The picture galleries at Hampton Court were closed. Special watches were put on places like Tagg's Island. In October letters in the letter box at Twickenham Post Office were burnt. On 6th October 'The Elms' in Hampton High Street and Rachel Peace and Mary Richardson were arrested in Teddington carrying cans of paraffin.

1914 saw a continuation of events but by now the public at large were becoming more and more incensed at the damage caused by the militants. The outbreak of war brought a truce between the suffrage societies and the Government and fortunately such incidents did not resume after wartime.

Once again I am indebted to Gerard & Joan Heath, Richard Nye and the National Archives.

A Story of Dunkirk

Local history enquiries come in all shapes and sizes and from all corners of the globe. Most of these are of a family history nature and relate to distant relatives or ancestors, who once lived in Teddington, or to the very road(s) that they may have occupied.

Last September, Father Joe, at St Mary's Church, received a most unusual request from the USA. This came from Steve DeBoer, in Colorado, who was researching a story told to him by his very dear neighbour and friend, Stanley Holcomb, a one time resident of Teddington, now in his 80s.

The story is that Stanley, a schoolmate of his and the schoolmate's father were on a boat trip along the River Thames, when they were told that the boat would be confiscated. Here the story becomes a little confused, and Stanley's next recollection is awaking in Dunkirk harbour to find the boat filling with troops. By some amazing quirk, when the boat was moored at Gravesend, the boys were not disturbed and the boat set sail for Dunkirk with the rest of the 120 vessel Teddington flotilla. When the boys were discovered, the boat was directed to immediately turn home with the first load of their passengers, the task of Stanley and his friend being to make and serve tea for the soldiers aboard. The boat returned to Teddington with the friend's father taking both boys to school, resulting in Stanley being in the "worst trouble of his life", when he finally went home, as his mother had no idea where he had been.

Interest in the story had been revived with the new film version of "Dunkirk" being screened in the USA, and Steve and Stanley watched this together. The film clearly stirred some memories within Stanley, but a 77 year lapse makes for a challenging experience when recalling every detail. Stanley and his family went to the USA in 1952/3 and he made America his home, becoming a highly decorated Colonel in the U.S. Army and a successful businessman thereafter.

However, one of the biggest disappointments he has ever encountered is that he cannot remember the name of his schoolfriend, who had accompanied him to Dunkirk in 1940. Steve decided to take up researching the name of this friend, on behalf of Stanley, but without telling him what he was doing, hence his letter/email to Fr. Joe at St Mary's. Fr. Joe duly passed this on to St Mary's archivist, Dr Chris French, a retired history lecturer from Kingston University.

A request for fuller and further information followed and, surreptitiously, Steve tried to talk to Stanley in greater detail. Stanley has repeated that there were 50 or more soldiers involved and that his friend's father was the owner, with the name of Rixson or Rexson. He concedes that waking up to find soldiers wading through the water and clambering aboard was a lot to take in for an eight year old, and the actual number might have been over 50 or simply a dozen. He is not so sure of the ownership of the boat but is certain that the father was an employee of Tough Brothers. A further complication arose with Stanley's recollection that his friend's mother had possibly been married before, thus making his friend the "father's" stepson and not necessarily carrying the same name. By this time, the cat was out of the bag and Steve had to confess to taking on his researches. Fortunately, Stanley was not at all upset, as he is planning to visit his sister in Teddington in September.

Chris French had asked for my help in trying to uncover any references to the Holtom family. By coincidence, Chris is a governor of St Mary's and St Peter's School, the replacement for the old Teddington Public School, which Stanley attended. Chris was able to check the school logbooks and found Stanley named, in 1942, as being awarded a place at secondary school and again, in 1939, on the list of Bridgman prize winners. He established that the Holcomb family was at 19, St Mary's Avenue, in 1939. Moving on, Stanley be a complete listing of every vessel that took part in the Dunkirk evacuation, even taking off a single soldier, but has never been published. It was compiled very soon after the event. This may be of some interest. emigrated to America in 1952/3 and commenced a new life. Chris related several names from the logbook to Stanley as being of the same era, because the class registers for this time no longer exist. Unfortunately, none of the names rang any bells with Stanley.

John Tough, of Tough Brothers, was approached to see if he could identify the boat or seaman in question. John was able to confirm that none of the boats taken up river from Teddington were big enough to have carried 50 soldiers, so we must definitely be looking at a smaller number. Mike Pemberton had sent copies of pictures from Tough's boatyard at the time, and Stanley immediately recalled being towed in a group to Ramsgate. He also recalled "a roof" over the back end of the boat and having to walk down several stairs from the back deck to a lower level, where the stove/burner was and where they made tea for the soldiers. Peter is the name that comes strongly to mind when thinking of his friend.

The boat sailed from the main yard at Teddington. The original plan was for Stanley to stay overnight at Peter's house after school. When they jumped on the boat, it was on the understanding that they would enjoy a short ride downriver prior to the boat being taken away for special use. Having reflected on the voyage for a couple of months, Stanley recalls that a naval rating needed to be aboard each craft. He now thinks that 6 – 8 men were brought back on the deck above and two additional soldiers, who were wounded, were brought below and were tended by the sailor who had come aboard at Ramsgate. Stanley remembers the navy man pulling a blanket completely up and over the face of one of the wounded soldiers and now realises that that soldier was dead.

Steve has discovered that there is an E-2 Research Guide at Greenwich which purports to complete listing of every vessel that took part in the Dunkirk evacuation, even taking off a single soldier, but has never been published. It was compiled very soon after the event. This may be of some interest.

All obvious avenues of enquiry have now been explored and, whilst Stanley has been pleased to recall items and faces of his earlier life in Teddington, it is frustrating that neither the elusive surnames of Peter and his father nor the name of the boat have come to light. It would be amazing if Peter were to read this article and come forward to meet Stanley on his return visit.

In the meantime, we will have to content ourselves with Teddington having provided the youngest crewman of Operation Dynamo.

The Churches of Teddington - Part 1

In issue no. 84 I wrote a piece entitled "Where We Worshipped", at the suggestion of a vicar friend of mine, and the intention of the article was to show the houses of worship that had been used at different times in the 19th century and were no longer churches. Because of my clumsy title, many of you were rightly offended that your churches were not included and berated me for not recognising how beautiful some of them were. I certainly won't make that mistake again, and hopefully I will now put things right and talk about all of the churches that are still with us.

For the purposes of these articles, I will deal with the churches in their chronological order:

St Mary's 1217
Methodist Church
Craig Hall 1859
Stanley Road 1879
Christ Church 1864
St Peter & St Paul 1865
Baptist Church
Craig Hall 1879
Church Road 1881
St Alban 1889
Sacred Heart 1893
St Michael & St George 1913
St Mark 1939

Last year, we celebrated the festival of Teddington 800 when we acknowledged the long 800 year history of the Church of St Mary (now St Mary with St Alban), founded in 1217. It is commonly held that there was probably some sort of chapel at Teddington before that time, but 1217 is the first clearly defined year that the Parish of Teddington is recorded. I have already given an account of the church and churchyard in No. 42, but as this concentrated on the memorials within and outside of the church, I should say something about the building and its priests.

We are told that in A.D. 971 the Manor of Teddington was gifted to the monks at Westminster by King Edgar. This would have included all buildings and whatever chapel existed at that time. There was probably no resident priest and the village was under the ecclesiastical control of Staines Abbey.
1217/8 saw the control passed to the Abbott of Westminster who then appointed and paid a vicar to administer the village. This arrangement seems to have worked well enough until 1539, when Henry VIII carried out the Dissolution of the Monasteries and any other church lands that took his fancy. The Manor of Teddington was ideally placed to become part of the Honor of Hampton Court (a term to signify the hunting area of the district), and so Abbott Boston of Westminster Abbey surrendered the advowson or patronage of Teddington to Henry.

This patronage was to confirm who appointed the parish priest and, in 1547, it passed from the Crown to the Lord of the Manor, George Gates, who was granted a lease from Edward VI. The stipend that went with the advowson was £6 per annum plus 4s for "sacramentals", that is to say candles, bread and wine. It should come as no surprise that not many clergymen could afford to stay on for very long in such a lowly paid parish.

At this point, it is worth mentioning some of the priests that were in office at those times. I have already mentioned Robert Feron, or Fern, in No. 30. He was the vicar who was arrested and charged with maliciously speaking out against Henry VIII's divorce from Katherine of Aragon, and his subsequent marriage to Anne Boleyn. He, along with six others, was found guilty and sentenced to death by hanging, drawing and quartering. On 4th May 1535, five of the prisoners were taken out and executed but of Robert Feron there was no trace. It is recorded that he was pardoned on account of his youth, but this is generally held to be a euphemism for turning King's evidence.

In 1603, the Hill family were Lords of the Manor and also strict Puritans. One of them appointed Ephraim Udall, also a strict Puritan, in 1615 and they seem to have worked together quite successfully. In 1631, we hear of Matthew Randall, or Randoll, who was suspended by Archbishop Laud for having preached a sermon of over one hour long. Many's the time I have wished for some similar sentence when I have been chained to a pew on a sunny Sunday morning. A most unusual case was that of Rev Robert Mossom, parish priest from 1647 to 1650. He was a Royalist and had served in the King's army. "By administering Holy Communion monthly and using the Book of Common Prayer he offended against the new laws established by the Puritan government. For this he was sequestrated in 1650." He was not replaced and Teddington had no priest for several years thereafter. Mossom, however, later became Bishop of Derry so the experience cannot have affected him too badly.

After the Restoration, when the Puritan values had been displaced, Sir Orlando Bridgeman, former Lord Keeper of the Great Seal, retired to his country seat in Teddington and set about supporting the neglected church. He purchased some "Farm Fee Rents" to the value of £80 to augment the living of the priest, in addition to many other benefactions. Although he was not the Lord of the Manor (as this was William Hill), Bridgeman took on the responsibility of the advowson and came to an arrangement with Hill for them to share the presentation of the living of the parish in alternative years, an arrangement which did not always prove satisfactory. Years later, the Earl of Bradford,

successor to Sir Orlando, acquired the whole advowson and this prevailed until 1913 when it passed to the Bishop of London.

Sir Orlando died in 1674, leaving the church in a much better state than he found it. His widow and his son continued the good work and supported the church and its liabilities, e.g. almshouses and school. However, the church must have fallen into disrepair as almost the first thing that the Rev Dr Stephen Hales did when he was appointed was to authorise some building repairs. In 1716, the church was repaired and an extension to the south aisle, with a south west gallery, added. In 1734, he negotiated the enlargement of the churchyard and replaced the shingled spire with a lantern containing a loud bell. 1748 saw the modification of the tower windows, and in 1753 a new north aisle was built. The following year the wooden tower was replaced by the present brick one. Many of these alterations were paid for by Hales himself.

Rev Dr John Cozens succeeded Hales and matters proceeded without much disruption, although there was a change in the village. In 1857, the other religions were springing up and Rev Daniel Trinder was being considered too "popish" by his congregation. The sale of the manor, in 1861, and the coming of the railway, in 1863, brought about a population explosion in the village. The population had been 699 in 1801, going up to 1,183 in 1861, and 4,063 in 1871. This was to bring about many changes, as we will see in the next issue.

I am indebted to George and Katherine Worth for their excellent "The Parish Church of Teddington", still available from the Church.

The Churches of Teddington - Part 2

Last month, we left on a note of population explosion with the sale of the manor lands in 1861 and the coming of the railway in 1863. Rev Trinder was still the vicar of St Mary's and he was becoming very unpopular with some of his parishioners on account of his "popish" ways. He was preaching in a surplice, which was a sure indication of Roman Catholicism. He introduced the singing of "Hymns Ancient and Modern" - another Roman practice. It is said that he was so unpopular that children in the street used to throw mud at his back as he walked along the High Street.

The feeling against him was so strong that a proportion of the congregation broke away and formed Christ Church, the Free Church of England Congregation, in 1864 and erected an iron church building in what is now Church Road. Quite how many people defected to the new church is not known, but it would have been a significant number.

With the increase in population and new houses being built on manor lands, the congregation of St Mary's was growing rapidly and Rev Trinder had already started to plan for additional premises to take the strain. In 1865, SS Peter and Paul opened in Broad Street as a chapel of ease to St Mary's, once again supporting "high church practices". In 1869, Christ Church opened a new church on its present site in Station Road. This gave Teddington two new churches in the space of five years.

Despite these measures, the population continued to grow. Rev Trinder left the parish in 1878 and it was not until 1884, when Rev Francis Leith Boyd was appointed vicar at age 28, that any significant changes were made. Boyd was a very ambitious man and saw the opportunity of creating "the Cathedral of the Thames Valley", in Teddington. In this he was fortunate in having the support of many wealthy parishioners,

including architect William Niven. Boyd persuaded Niven to design the new church and set about raising the funding to build it. Building began in 1888, a mere four years after Boyd's appointment, and by the summer of 1889 the new Church of St Alban the Martyr opened for services, although not yet completed.

At the start, the new church flourished. Boyd was a gifted orator and his fire and brimstone sermons packed the church. The Surrey Comet reported that the crowd of the congregation was so dense that it was not possible to close the doors. However, the influx of newcomers to Teddington did not sit well with the wealthy established parishioners, particularly as the trams were running right past their houses and invading their privacy. Many moved to the quieter suburbs, like Esher, and Boyd lost a source of income for the completion of St Alban.

Fortunately, it had been decided to retain St Mary's and although it had been allowed to fall into decay, it was redeemed as an important surviving old building. It was rededicated in 1939 and used as a chapel of ease, providing occasional services.

By 1977, the spectrum had gone full circle and the falling attendances at St Alban's meant that it was no longer economically viable to keep it open. St Alban's was therefore declared redundant, and the rearranged church of St Mary with St Alban was again the parish church, although with a smaller area following the establishment of the other new churches. Under the guidance of a new and enthusiastic vicar, St Mary's is again a vibrant centre at the heart of Teddington.

Teddington Methodist Church

Teddington has a very early connection with the Methodist Church, recorded by the founder of the movement himself, no less, John Wesley. The entry in his journal for Tuesday July 3rd, 1753, reads: "I rode over to Mr K's at Teddington, an Israelite indeed. Dr Hales sent after dinner to desire our company and showed us several experiments. How well do philosophy and religion agree in a man of sound understanding." The following Sunday, Wesley preached both the morning and evening service from St Mary's, before moving on to Kingston.

Very little seems to have happened in the village for the next one hundred years. It is thought that students from the Wesleyan Theological College at Richmond set out to evangelise the surrounding villages in the 1850s, and that is probably how Methodism came to Teddington. Their efforts were clearly successful as in 1859 they built a chapel in Clarence Road, named Craig Hall, which became attached to the Richmond Circuit. In 1866, it was recorded that they had a membership of 28.

Mr Bennett's guidebook of 1939 mentions two early incidents in the history of the chapel:
1) A meeting of the leaders is recorded for the purpose of dealing with a quarrel that had arisen between two ladies of the Society (congregation). The Superintendent was in the chair and both women were present. Mrs C abruptly left the meeting and Mrs D was requested to leave. After careful deliberation it was resolved that Mrs D had laid herself open to the charge of Indiscretion thereby endangering the peace of the Society.
2) It was recorded that the Teddington stewards raised strong objection at the Quarterly Meeting to the use of the Liturgy in the services and after a petition had been presented to the Trustees it was abandoned."

By 1870, the chapel was becoming outgrown and a move was made towards building a new one. In 1876, a member of the church, Walter Taylor, residing at the old Manor House, offered to subscribe a quarter of the cost of the new building provided that it was completed within two years. Work began in 1877 on a chapel to accommodate 385, at a cost of £3,000. Despite some minor setbacks, the foundation stone was laid on October 14th, 1878, and the old chapel (Craig Hall) was sold (to the Baptist Church) for £350. The chapel opened July 1st, 1879.

Writing in June 1880, Walter Taylor said, "I am grieved to see so few attending the new place. The morning attendance is less than that in the old chapel." Mr Bennett deduced that the new building had been erected more to secure the generous offer of the donor (Taylor donated £655) than to fulfil a demand for a larger place of worship. Bennett also mentioned the names of other influential members of the church – Mr C H Moss will be remembered not only as a loyal officer of the church for a generation but as the mason responsible for the stonework of the new chapel (Moss was later to build the War Memorial at Teddington Hospital); and Mr T J W Buckley, who acted as treasurer of the Building Fund, as well as being a liberal donor, had held all the offices of the church open to a layman, at various times.

By 1884, the debt had reduced to £370 but vestries were added to the chapel at a cost of £230. Two years later, an organ was purchased at £157.10s.0d., although this was covered by raised subscriptions. 1887 saw the church join the newly formed Hampton Court Circuit.

The Churches of Teddington - Part 3

Following on from last month, matters progressed slowly into the next century. Additions were made to the Methodist Church, "The Chapel", as it was known, with a pair of wrought iron gates fronting a paved path which, in turn, led to a flight of stone stairs which brought the visitor to the chapel entrance itself. I should have mentioned that The Chapel was built on a first floor position, with a hall immediately beneath it, where the Sunday School was conducted.

Mr Bennett mentioned "The coming of the electric tramways to Teddington in 1902 caused great consternation to the Trustees owing to the danger of these vehicles running near to the footpath in Stanley Road. After negotiation with the Tramway Company a strip of land was sold for £500 and the boundary wall rebuilt with the main entrance and iron gates as they are today (1939)." The opportunity was taken to renovate the chapel, repair the roof and windows, and add seat cushions and umbrella stands.

In 1907, Bedford Villa, 6 Hampton Road, was purchased for £575 and the property proved to be a valuable investment. 1914 saw the purchase of the properties known as Cobden House and Huntingdon House, Nos 8 & 10 Hampton Road, for £1,015. Cobden House was renamed "Le Chateau" and was let as an investment. Huntingdon House later became the Methodist Church House and was put to use as the graded Junior and Senior Departments of the Sunday School.

1914 saw the outbreak of the Great War and some of the upper rooms of Church House were put at the disposal of some Belgian refugees. The war took its toll on the congregation and a brass memorial plaque was erected in the lower part of Church Hall, which was then named Memorial Hall in the 1920s. After the war, a troop of Boy Scouts was formed under the ministry of Rev George Forde. Forde had been a missionary in the Transvaal, South Africa, and spread his zeal to supporting overseas missions, something that carries on to this day. 1922 saw extensive renovations carried out; the side screens were removed, as was the rostrum, the organ was moved to the left from the centre and the choir pews on the right were removed also. In 1932, deaf aids were installed, although it is not known how effective they were.

By 1939, at the start of WWII, church membership stood at 145, and the Sunday School had 160 scholars and 40 teachers. War came, and the church escaped the early bombing of Teddington. However, on the morning of 24th August 1944 a flying bomb demolished the church. Whether the target was the National Physical Laboratories or General Eisenhower's base in Bushy Park we will never know, but the bomb struck the north side of the church and school hall, damaging it so badly that the building had to be demolished. For the next seven years all services were held at the Memorial Hall in Church House, No 8 Hampton Road.

The foundation stone for the new church was laid on 6th October 1951, and the church was opened on 25th October 1952. The Youth Hall was added later and in 1976, the Main Hall. Many modifications have taken place since then and the church proudly stands as a modern multi-purpose building, in addition to being a religious centre.

Christ Church Teddington

In last month's edition, I mentioned that Rev Trinder of St Mary's was becoming very unpopular with some members of his parish on account of his "popish" habits. Nevertheless, Trinder had recognised that the local population had outgrown the building of St Mary's Church and that some form of expansion was necessary.

Trinder issued a statement on 26th November 1864 to say "that in 1861 the population fell just short of 1,200, that 600 acres of land had been sold for building and that by 1864 the population would have risen to 1,600. The existing church holds about 500 and all the pews are allotted, except about 60, the worst in the church, which are free for the poor and newcomers." Several influential members of the congregation supported the idea of a new church which they saw as additional to the existing St Mary's. Trinder suggested that the new church should be a "Chapel of Ease" rather than a second ministry, so as to avoid there being "a house divided against itself."

A committee was appointed to look into the building of a new Chapel of Ease in Upper Teddington, to seat 600 at a cost not exceeding £2,200. The committee were charged with "the appointment of a Minister or Clergyman, whose name shall be submitted to the Bishop of the Diocese for his approval and, should the Bishop refuse to license the Church, the Committee shall take such steps as they deem desirable to have public worship duly carried on in the Church by Evangelical Ministers until the Bishop shall be induced to license the building." On 10th June 1864, J M Strachan and others of the committee issued a statement to say that they had failed on both objects and they were now relieved of their obligations. In the autumn of that year, a further statement was issued by Thomas Luxmoor Wilson and others, former members of the St Mary's Committee, deeply regretting the lack of an Evangelical Ministry in the Parish and advising of the erection of an iron church, called Christ Church, in what is now Church Road.

"On completion of the building, application was made to the Lord Bishop of London for a license. The reply pointed out that the first step was to communicate with the Incumbent (Rev Trinder) without whose consent the Law did not allow a Bishop to license a clergyman for any new place of worship in connection with the Church of England." Not surprisingly, Rev Trinder declined to give his consent but on Sunday 20th November 1864, and without the Bishop's license, Christ Church opened for Divine Service with Rev T Dugard and the Rev J Sugden officiating.

On 31st December, the church was licensed according to an Act of Parliament as a place of meeting for religious worship by a congregation or assembly of persons calling themselves "Free Church of England Congregation." In January 1865, Rev J Sugden was invited to become the Minister on condition that the services were to be in accordance with the Liturgy of the Church of England. This invitation came from thirty-three seatholders, amongst whom appear the names of Anthony Spurr, Mary Collis, James Arthur Messenger, G N Lemon and Charles Allison. Rev Sugden accepted the position and commenced his work on 5th February.

The first annual meeting of the seatholders took place on 30th November 1865. Top of the agenda was a proposal for a new school, closely followed by the desirability of enlarging the church as more accommodation was urgently required. It was agreed that both proposals were passed for suitable action. This seems to have encompassed the now time-honoured nineteenth century practice of fundraising.

History Focus Review

About this time last year, I decided to have a review of the articles I'd written for TW11 and seek the advice of readers as to what they enjoyed and what they'd like to see in future issues. I was certainly not disappointed with your responses! By and large, I am glad to say readers seemed happy with the articles. In particular, the series on the pubs of Teddington struck a chord with many of you, and a full publication will be forthcoming at some later stage. Stories connected to the War Memorial were also popular, and one reader even went to the trouble of translating H Weingartner's letter back into German to send to his German pen pal. There are many more WW1 stories to be told. In fact, a friend of mine in the Rugby Club has challenged me to compare the names in the team photos of Upper Teddington Cricket Club (now Teddington Town Cricket Club), from 1914 and 1919, and discuss the missing names from the 1914 picture.

Whilst the story of our churches is perhaps not quite as popular, I found it fascinating to think that even as late as 1850, the only Parish Church was St Mary's. There are still a few more places of worship to write about before I move on to other subjects.

Many people have asked for pictures of some of the older properties of Teddington. One reader, Nuala Orton, compiled a comprehensive list of buildings but, as is often the case, pictures of many of these properties remain elusive, despite much searching. Anyone having such pictures or photographs would be doing me a huge favour if they would loan (or donate!) them to me for copying. If they don't need to be returned, Twickenham Museum is building up a fine collection of old photographs, postcards and pictures of what formed the old Borough of Twickenham (i.e. Teddington, Twickenham, the Hamptons, Strawberry Hill, St Margaret's and Whitton) and would be delighted to receive more.

Reader John Brady enjoys the history of specific roads, many of which were developed at the coming of the railway, in 1863. He also referred to the connection that Thames TV made with Teddington, it being the location for 'Love Thy Neighbour', in Wick Road/Bushy Park Road, and 'George and Mildred', in Birch Close/Manor Road. Many other programmes featured Teddington roads as their permanent base, and it was not uncommon for various "cops and robbers" series to show car chases around our streets. I used to watch out for the whacky chase scenes at the end of the Benny Hill Show (Benny was a resident of Mallard Place) to see what part of Teddington would feature that week. It was a great shame that Thames TV lost its franchise, and many ex-employees will tell you that it was the government of the day that brought the company down. With a plethora of luxury flats now being built on the site, we will never see its like again.

Two sisters, who once lived in Bolton Gardens, (Gene now living in Shoreham and Gillian living in Stroud) have been receiving TW11 for some while and have been pleased to read about events in Teddington. They both have fond memories of their childhood here and Gillian wrote me a lovely letter with some of her adventures as a youngster. She wrote, *"I was born at 15 Udney Park Road and we moved to Bolton Gardens when I was 3 years old. My mother moved from Teddington to Brighton while I was at Stroud, so I lost all local news. My brother decided to write to our old address but did not expect to receive a reply. He was surprised to receive a letter a few days later, inviting us to all go and meet the family. A few months later we all went and they have been keeping us up to date with Teddington news ever since. We really enjoyed the history news you have found out."*

"We girls went to St Catherine's convent in Twickenham and my brother went to boarding school. We were sent to South Wales on and off during the war, I was then 4 years old. On one of my visits to Teddington, I decided to see 15 Udney Park Road. I knocked on the

*door and a young man came and asked what I wanted. I told him I was born there and would love to see the house at some convenient time to them. However he just shouted, 'No and B***** off!' So I never got to see my old house."*

"I had an aunt who lived in Railway Road (Ed. Railway Road again!) and I remember going there quite a lot. One day I was asked to take a jug and get uncle's beer from the pub at the end of the road. I was very young at the time." (This may have been the Abercorn Arms in Church Road or the Waldegrave Arms at the other end of Railway Road but as the family lived at 42 Railway Road, it's more likely to have been the off licence at No 51). "My aunt's house only had gas lighting and outside the street lights were also gas. I remember the gas lighter coming in the evenings to light the street lights. I remember

the trains thundering past."

I'll leave Gillian there for a moment and return to Railway Road. The last time I left you there, William Alex Given was still the proprietor of No 51, in 1939. There are still a few blanks, but Alan and Jean Leadbetter moved to 42 Railway Road in 1957 and Ethel Steven ran the off licence then. At some later stage, Mrs Hastings took over the business. Her son David and his wife Mary lived at No 40, with their three sons. David was the Twickenham ferryman, operating from the White Swan to the Ham bank in competition with the Hammertons. He also kept calves in the back garden, which occasionally got loose.

Mrs Hastings was still in business in 1967, when Margaret and Dick Beasley moved into No 57. The shop was still open when Mary Scurlock moved into Railway Road, in 1984, but carried little stock then. Was this because the road was too narrow for heavy delivery lorries? Cllr Martin Elengorn recalls the shop when he was first elected, in 1982. Planning permission for change of use (to a full dwelling house) was never approved but this became an established use through the passage of time. As to what happened to Teddington Ales, I am still investigating......

Another pleasant outcome of my review was meeting so many readers of TW11, and I can honestly say I have met scores of people who want to discuss my articles or suggest other topics. Readers also pop up everywhere: in pubs, restaurants, bars, on buses, in the street, on bridges, at the recycling centre and even once when I was on a hospital trolley in Kingston, as I was being wheeled off for an unpleasant procedure. It has been a pleasure to meet you!

The Churches of Teddington - Part 4

The year is 1866. Christ Church had been operating for just over 12 months and the future was looking bright, plans for expanding the church had been approved and a proposal to open a church school had been accepted. The previous December, Mr Wilson had reported to the committee that he had purchased a small plot of land "opposite the Church" and this was intended for "a room to contain at least 100 children and for facilities for enlargement." On 26th January 1866, it was decided to open a fund for "a permanent church" but in the meantime, the Iron Church was enlarged by the addition of a north side, at the cost of Mr Thomas Luxmoor Wilson.

The next reference to the new permanent church was made on 4th November 1868, as to be "in the Grove Field". Foremost amongst the contributors of the building costs were Mr Wilson with £500 and Mr Higgs with £300. Soon after, the plans of architect Mr Goodchild were approved. A view of the proposed church, printed for money raising purposes, shows a similar structure to the present church with a spire, to seat 651 persons and at a cost of £4,000. On the 30th January 1869, it was decided to instruct the architect to prepare working plans for the construction.

At this time, a letter was received from the Rev Trinder asking that a meeting be arranged between the Building Committee and himself and some friends, that "the welfare of the Parish might be served to remove all needs for grounds of difference between neighbours in the most sacred of all matters, that of religion." He was asked in reply to state "precisely the matters he wished to discuss and that the building of the new Church could not be discussed." It seems that no agreement could be reached on a format for a meeting, and it was not proceeded with.

On 30th March, it was decided to modify the plans so as to provide a church to hold 500 sittings, at a cost of £3,000. The architect reported that contractors Messrs Rogers and Manley were prepared to do the work for £3,189. However, by May some difficulties arose on the supply of funds as one of the largest contributors failed to fulfil his promise, and whilst work did proceed, it would be forced to cease when the funds in hand had been spent. The foundation stone was laid on 14th July, and surprisingly all of the opening speeches seemed to be aimed at keeping the Rev Trinder and his "Romish practices" out, rather than urging a mighty push towards solvency. October showed an amount of £1,480 outstanding and this increased to £1,579 the following year. However, fervent drives by the committee served to reduce this to £85 by March 1872. It was later noted by Bishop Sugden, the original minister, that the church had been built mostly at the expense of Mr T L Wilson and Mr C B Ker.

The years rolled by and the church flourished. There were always matters of maintenance and improvement and later the support of overseas missionary work was added to the church's expenditure. There were the usual peaks and troughs that any organisation faces and two world wars made their mark on the community, but the church came through undamaged. In the late 1970s, there was a major disagreement within the community which resulted in the departure of the followers of the "Charismatic movement", and this virtually halved the congregation. More recently, a problem has been found with the electrical system and this has rendered the church unsafe for services. A rough estimate to cover the cost of renovations and repairs was put at £900.000 plus, which was way beyond the means of the diminished congregation. The church has been sold to be developed as flats and all services have been moved to the church hall, where they are held to this day.

Christ Church

St Peter and St Paul's Church

Despite several of the St Mary's congregation having decamped to form Christ Church, there were very many newcomers to the village and it was deemed necessary to find increased space for the new worshippers. Whilst the dispute between the churches was raging, plans had already been agreed for a new church to be built and St Peter and St Paul's appeared on the corner of Broad Street and Church Road. It was built as a chapel of ease to St Mary's, to take the overflow of new residents. It had been designed by G E Street and was completed in 1873, except for the tower and spire which were never built. The Victoria County History of Middlesex describes it as "of red and yellow brick with stone piers in the nave. It consists of a chancel, a nave of five bays, and north and south aisles with chapels."

Because of the growth of Teddington, it became a parish in its own right in 1880 and there were 116 names on the electoral roll, which does not seem that many for a new parish. The area was bounded by the railway on the eastern side and covered much of the areas of new development to the west.
The village school stood opposite the new church, in Church Road, and was renamed St Mary's and St Peter's School in 1906 to reflect the influence of both churches on the school. The first three quarters of the twentieth century moved ahead without any really memorable event but in the 1970s, it was deemed that the school, which had been built in 1832, was now a little tired and not fit for purpose. The numbers attending SS Peter and Paul had also fallen somewhat and it was decided to replace both buildings. Starting with the school in 1974, this was moved further down Church Road and built partly on the site of Argyle Road, which had been completely erased by enemy action in World War II.

The old church was sold for a joint housing/ commercial venture and the old school was demolished. The church was then built on the old school site and is still in its rebuilt form. In Church Road itself, the gate posts and a section of wall are still visible as a reminder of the old church.

Teddington Baptist Church

The London Baptist Association movement was expanding in London in 1865 but the nearest it came to Teddington was at Kingston and, in the days of limited transport, this meant a two and a half mile walk, each way twice a day, on Sundays to attend a place of worship. The enthusiastic congregation felt their time would be better served worshiping somewhere nearer to home than on the tedious travelling to and from Kingston. In 1877, these dedicated followers rented a room above Ethel's Cafe on Bridge Approach, in Waldegrave Road. They quickly outgrew this room and moved to another on the site, now occupied by Barclays Bank.

Once again, the ever growing numbers meant that larger premises were required. At this time, the Wesleyans (Methodists) had outgrown their chapel at Clarence Road and were moving to their new iron church in Church Road. This left Craig Hall free and the Baptists prepared to move in.

The Churches of Teddington - Part 5

Last month, we left the Baptists about to move into Craig Hall but it was discovered that the rent was £20 per annum, a little beyond the means of a little company. However, the owner, John Cornelius Park, was sympathetic to their cause and agreed on two years' tenancy for that sum.

The church continued to grow, and in April 1881 they declared themselves "independent and self-supporting." Matters moved quickly and an iron building was found and purchased. This was erected on the site of the present church and its opening service was on Sunday 30th March 1884. By 1888, yet again the accommodation was found to be too small and serious consideration had to be given to a larger building. The membership now stood at 90 with some 130 at Sunday school. More land was purchased and the building commenced on a tender of £2918. The new church was completed, with seating for 560, on 21 November 1894.

Times moved on and, by 1903, the church was free from debt and had acquired two houses which were demolished to create the Sunday School Buildings. The First World War saw the inclusion of many young men of the church in the armed forces. Three of them were lost in the conflict. The late 1920s and early 1930s was marked as a time of "evangelistic zeal and outreach", which saw success in all activities and the start of missionary work which is still ongoing. A new minister came to the church shortly after the start of the Second World War, and three weeks into his ministry, the church was completely destroyed by enemy action. The night of 29 November 1940 saw the heaviest bombing raid ever on Teddington, with 43 fatal casualties. Eight members of the church were to lose their lives before this war was over. Services were held in the church hall until hostilities ceased and rebuilding commenced.

A foundation stone for the new church was laid on 29 January 1955, and the opening ceremony took place on 15 September 1956. During this period, the church had become involved in the Billy Graham Crusades of 1954, 1955 and later in 1961 and 1966. Various church activities have been and gone and the church has kept pace with all national and international developments.

St Alban

I have already written about St Alban's Church in TW11 No 60 and I don't think I can add anything to that.

Sacred Heart R C Church

The Roman Catholic faith was outlawed for many years in England; in fact since Henry VIII declared himself head of the Church in England. Over the years a degree of tolerance was creeping into English politics and in 1778, Sir George Savile introduced a Catholic Relief Act. This upset many staunch and extreme Protestants and one of them, Lord George Gordon, demanded the repeal of this act. A mob of 60,000 then took to the streets, occupied London for 6 days and destroyed as much Catholic property as they could find. This action had many consequences and in general brought about a more sympathetic attitude towards the Catholics.

Moving forward 70 years, the railway system was engulfing England and the massive job of building the railway tracks was given to the navigators or "navvies", as they were nicknamed. Their jobs had started with the building of the canal system and waterways and then moved on to the railways. In 1845 there were about 200,000 navvies working in England and about 35% of these were Irish. Ireland was still predominantly Catholic and so when the Irish came to this country, they understandably wanted to continue to worship their faith. Catholic chapels started to appear all over the country and the first one in this area opened at Ivy Cottage in Hampton Wick in 1882, probably the dwelling of the priest.

Shortly afterwards, a "catholic school was built in Fairfax Road, South Teddington, in 1884. The ground floor served as a school and the upper floor as a chapel until the present Church of the Sacred Heart of Jesus was opened in 1893." In 1920, the priest, Fr Philip Foley, kept a most enlightened log-book of parish affairs and the first item was an outstanding mortgage of £833. This seems to have been a common factor in all of the new churches in Teddington since 1860. Fr Foley managed to clear the debt in four years. His log-book shows some interesting ideas on fundraising: "Arranged a bazaar to raise money to pay off debt. After much wrangling it was held Easter Monday and Tuesday. Not well attended but raised £170." Another entry in February 1922 reads, "Tried a dance for debt – turned out a failure." Despite this setback and later being without heating for over a year, the church has survived and is moving comfortably into the 21st century.

St Michael and St George

The expansion of Teddington continued well into the end of the 19th century and despite the opening of SS Peter and Paul, there was still a need for new accommodation. St Michael and St George opened in 1913. It was designed by J S Adkins. Its parish, formed out of that of SS Peter and Paul, was assigned to it in 1914. It was barely established before having to survive both world wars and followed the fate of so many British churches post war, of suffering a falling congregation.

Unfortunately, the fluctuating fortunes of SS Michael and George and SS Peter and Paul in the last quarter of the twentieth century led to them being rejoined as one parish, on the grounds of cost and upkeep. This did not please everyone and in the 1990s SS Michael and George closed its doors. However, the church reopened in late 2014 as St Michael's Fulwell and flourishes.

St Mark

South Teddington was boosted by the gas works opening in Sandy Lane in 1851, and this gave rise to new housing which again increased with the coming of the London and South Western Railway. This expansion caused Rev Daniel Trinder to open a new school in School House Lane, Teddington Wick, in 1875. Also, at this time Rev Robert Spencer Borland came back to Teddington (the third son of Dr James Borland, Inspector General of Army Hospitals, had been born in Bridgeman House in Teddington High Street).

Using his own money, in 1880 Rev Borland had built a corrugated iron church on fields at the border of Fairfax and Bushy Park Roads. Rev Borland continued to serve the Church until his death in 1910. The first step to St Mark's being created a separate parish was in 1929, when it was declared an independent Conventional District. Extensive fundraising saw the purchase of land for the new Church of St Mark which was built at a cost of £10,000 and opened on Wednesday 28 June 1939, despite the theft of the church silver and records in 1937. Happily, the church has gone from strength to strength and continues to offer a wide range of social as well as spiritual services to its community.

I am indebted to Rev Dominic Stockford for information regarding Christ Church, to Dr Christopher French for SS Peter and Paul and SS Michael and George, to Dr Colin Hicks for the History of Teddington Baptist Church and to the Churchwardens of St Mark's Church.

TW11 Review Notes 2019

One of the good things about carrying out a review of one's work is that it puts you in touch with some old friends and makes you some new ones.

Firstly, hello **Chris Jarvis.** I hope the next time we meet I won't be being wheeled off to have a camera stuffed down my throat. As you said – not a pleasant procedure but it has to be done.

Next, hello to **Trixie Dolores of Queens Road**. Trixie wants to know what has happened to all the bats that she used to see when she first moved here 30 years ago. Well, I must confess to being a bit stumped here – bats aren't my usual subject. I know that they eat hundreds of little flies every day, so I suppose they have gone further into Bushy Park where the supply might be more plentiful. I do know that they are alive and well at Udney Park Playing Fields, probably to the developers' annoyance.

Talking of Bushy Park, that wonderful green space is always good for a story or two, and Douglas Craik has come up with a remarkable one which has lain hidden for 75 years as a result of being misattributed to Osterley Park in a book entitled, "Bomb Disposal and British Casualties of WW2" by Chris Ransted.

An Unexploded Bomb in Bushy Park in WW2

The night of 29th November 1940 was the night of the heaviest bombing over Teddington, and it is probable that the NPL was the principle target. 257 bombs were recorded with 150 houses destroyed and 43 killed, 31 in and around Church Road where the Willoughby Hotel and the Baptist Church were hit. The NPL escaped damage but an air raid shelter on site took a direct hit, with six women and children from nearby houses killed.

Unexploded bombs were categorised as needing immediate disposal (Cat A), delayed disposal (Cat B) or blow up on site or move it to safety (Cat C). In early 1940, time delay bombs had two fuses. The first was a clockwork one that ran for up to 80 hours but could jam and restart when moved. The second was an anti-movement fuse that went off if the bomb was moved; this was powered by a capacitor which lasted 60 hours and then went dead. A Cat B bomb was left for 96 hours and could then be tackled as the timeclock would have run down and the capacitor would be dead. This fits the timeline of the bomb dropped on 29 November, with disposal attempted on 10 December.

A Bomb Disposal Squad consisted of an officer, a sergeant and 14 men. Normally the sergeant and most of the section would dig a hole to reveal the bomb, and then most of the men would move on to the next bomb. The officer alone would then disarm the bomb. For a time fuse bomb this involved fitting a very strong electro-magnet around the fuse to "freeze" the clock working mechanism. By December 1940, this was a well established process. The officer and the remainder of the squad would then lift the bomb out of its hole for removal (in the case of West London – to a quarantine area in Richmond Park).

The incident occurred on 10th December 1940 when 725 Section of No 2 Bomb Disposal Company of the Royal Engineers, based in Balham, attended upon a site near the Diana Fountain where an enemy bomb had landed but failed to detonate. The squad consisted of Lieutenant K G Hope, Sapper J Darsley aged 19, Driver Arthur Hartland, Driver F Horton RASC, Lance Corporal

Cyril Lebbon aged 43, and Sapper Jimmy Hulme and another ten men. It was a bitterly cold day and the hole was dug as quickly as possible; the sergeant and most of the men then moved on to the next bomb. The squad followed the standard practice of setting up camp a little way from the bomb. Sapper Jimmie Hulme had done this, lighting a fire and setting up a large dixie of tea. Hulme was going back to the camp to check on the progress of the tea when the bomb detonated. He was thrown forward by the blast and a piece of shrapnel hit him in the neck. The rest of the squad were killed outright. After a spell in hospital, Hulme rejoined his unit although he was left with a slight stammer.

In late 1940, the Germans had introduced a new version of the anti-movement fuse, which had a long-life battery rather than a capacitor so that it did not become "dead" after 60 hours, or even several months. By early December, this had not yet been discovered by the British. In the first two weeks of December 1940, more bomb disposal soldiers were killed than in the preceding six months. This is probably the cause of this particular explosion. All but absolutely vital bomb disposal was suspended in late December, until a solution was found in January 1941. Alas, too late for the men of 725 Section.

This story did not ring quite true with Douglas, as he was the Vice-Chairman of the Friends of Osterley Park and had not heard of an explosion on 10 December 1940, in the Park. Douglas then contacted Chris Ransted, the author of the piece about the bomb in the first place. Chris explained that the unit records had been destroyed (ironically) by enemy bombing in May 1941, and the sole source of the information for the article had been in an interview with a friend of the sole survivor, Sapper Jimmy Hulme. This took place in the 1990s, and the friend remembered that the team had attended bombs at Syon House, Bushy Park and Osterley Park in the same week as the explosion and he assumed that it occurred at Osterley. After publication of his book, Chris was contacted by a relative of one of the unit that was killed, who had the Death Certificate of the soldier which gave Place of Death very clearly as "Lime Walk Bushy Park". He was also contacted by the great grand-daughter of Jimmy Hulme, who lived on the south edge of Bushy Park, and she verified that the explosion had taken place in Bushy Park.

Douglas now had the correct details and the correct location. The site of the explosion is shown in the broken red circle on photograph no. 1, and the likely site is obvious and can still be clearly seen in photograph no.2. As if to enforce the story, two of the soldiers, Lance-Corporal Cyril Lebbon and Driver Arthur Hartland, are buried side by side in Teddington Cemetery.

Thank you, Douglas, for bringing this story out into the light and telling of the bravery and dedication of the bomb disposal soldiers all over the country. I wonder how many such stories were lost to paperwork being destroyed by enemy bombing or to simple misattribution of a particular site in the general wartime confusion.

A Close Call in 1944

We have had a significant year so far. No sooner have we commemorated the anniversary of the signing of the treaty for the end of The Great War (the war to end all wars), than it is time to remember the 75th anniversary of D-Day in World War II. Although mercifully with fewer fatalities than the First World War, there were nevertheless very large numbers of soldiers, sailors and airmen lost. Even more poignant was the number of civilian casualties in this war – 50 to 55 million worldwide and 67,200 in Great Britain.

There were heavy losses in the early years of the war, with the Blitz of London in particular. The Blitz affected this area on 24 August 1940, when an enemy bomb destroyed a house in Tudor Road, Hampton. It resulted in no casualties but caused heavy damage. The intensity of the bombing increased, and on 7 November, two houses in Hampton suffered hits, with 5 fatalities. The worst night was, however, 29 November and is still remembered by some older residents. The raid began at 7.20 pm, and altogether 257 separate incidents are recorded in the Borough Incident Book for that night.

A particular tragedy occurred when the Willoughby pub, situated in Church Road, suffered a direct hit. A larger than usual number of people, including some children, had assembled for the Christmas Club pay-out. 17 people lost their lives. The Baltic timber yard and the Baptist Church were set alight; more people died in Railway and Tranmere Roads; and in Shacklegate Lane, 14 people were killed. Some residents from the Walpole Road area were evacuated to the supposed safety of the NPL shelters, but unfortunately one took a direct hit, with 6 fatalities. In all, 45 people perished that night and 10 more were detained in hospital.

Despite losing the Battle of Britain, the Luftwaffe continued their night raids on Britain until May 1941, but they concentrated their terror attacks on larger cities with heavy civilian populations. Teddington thankfully did not suffer much from any more bombing, apart from the odd lone enemy bomber following his route home along the Thames and jettisoning his bomb load over what seemed to be a good target.

By 1944, the tide of the war changed and the allied forces launched their invading forces on D-Day, 6 June. However, the German scientists had not been idle, and since 1939 they had been working to perfect the first of their range of "Vengeance Weapons" – the buzz bomb, the doodlebug or, as it was more commonly known, the V1.

This was a bomb with wings. It resembled a small aircraft but had no pilot, was powered by a simple jet engine, and carried a 1,870 lb warhead. It could travel at 400 mph with a range of 150 miles. It contained a device that counted the revolutions in a tiny propeller in its nose, and when it reached the number calculated to have brought it over its target, the engine cut out and the missile fell to earth, detonating on impact. It carried a distinctive sound of the putt-putting of a two stroke motorcycle engine.

The first one was launched on 13 June from the French coast, and it exploded in the East End of London. Witness statements tell of a noise that was thought to be a low-flying aircraft on fire, with flames belching from its tail. *"Whenever we heard a doodlebug everyone looked up and*

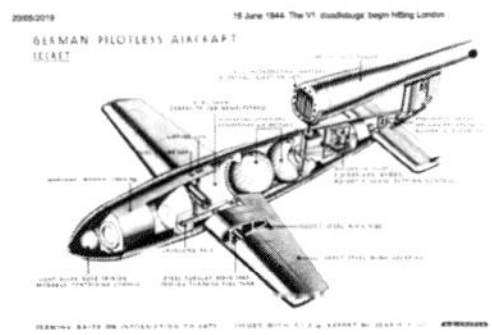

followed it with their eyes until it had gone over past where we were standing. If the engine stopped before it got to us first, that was the time to worry!" Most of these bombs dropped to earth immediately, but some would continue to glide, gradually losing height. In all, 9,521 V1s were launched at London, until the last launching sites were overrun by allied ground forces.

To come back to our story, Doug Jerome and a school friend were walking home from school along Cambridge Road one day, when the air-raid siren sounded. They then heard the tell-tale sound of a V1 engine. "Hit the deck!" yelled Doug to his friend, and both of them flattened themselves on the pavement. The doodlebug was travelling low and they saw flames spitting out from the back of the engine. It passed overhead and hit the ground with its engine still running, before coming to a halt at Church Road/Argyle Road. There was a massive explosion which completely obliterated Argyle Road, killing 9 persons in the process. Borough records show that this took place at 16.50 hrs, on 24 July 1944.

Doug had another escape after attending a wedding ceremony at the Wesleyan Chapel, in Stanley Road. It was later so badly destroyed by a flying bomb, on 24 August, that it had to be demolished for safety reasons. I am pleased to say that Doug survived these attacks, to be able to tell the tale.
An earlier doodlebug had hit Warner Bros Film Studios in Broom Road, on 5 July, killing the Head of Production Doc Soloman, his secretary Elizabeth Roe and his driver Henry Brayfield.

There were to be no other major bombing raids on Teddington until the end of the war.

It is hard for those of us who have never experienced the horror of war to imagine what people throughout Britain and the rest of Europe suffered. We can only hope and pray that this never happens again.

I have come across another story from one of my friends:

The Corner Shop
Gillian remembered the old shops from her time in Teddington, around the early 1950s –
"I remember the swimming pool off the High Street which was always freezing! The cycle shop, Lemons the bakers PS my husband was a baker, we had our own business ! Mervilles the Chemists, a Cinema, a Toy Shop near the bridge, a paper shop which sold sweets, A pub at the end of the High Street, I think it was 'The Plough' (Ed I think it was 'The Royal Oak'). Mr Roper's Green Grocer on the corner of Field Lane. Mrs Wiltshire's corner sweet shop. I have a sorry confession to make. I once put silver paper round a farthing and put it on the counter and asked for 6d worth of sweets which in those days would have been a lot !! However she must have twigged it but she weighed some amount I didn't see and gave me my sweets. I have never forgotten ! A kind lady! Mr Roper the Green Grocer was inclined to be grumpy. We didn't dare pinch a tomato or anything. I think he sold sliced bread as well. His shop was on the corner of Field Lane and Gomer Place."

How things have changed so much in a short space of time.

Memories of Teddington

I have found that there is no better way of jogging peoples' memories than by either showing them pictures of the past or relating stories that other people have kindly provided. Therefore I am pleased to present new stories that have been inspired by the previous issues of TW11.

Memories of Teddington
Jeanne and Tony Gask came to Teddington in 1964 into a house in Blackmore's Grove and Jeanne recalls "and had to sell our much-loved Morris Traveller and borrow £200 from Tony's brother to pay for the deposit."

I remember Roper's the grocer on the corner of Gomer Gardens and Field Lane. He and his French wife were a silent couple, no communication at all.
(Ed note : it has been reported that Mr Roper was a grumpy individual but the reality was that he had been deafened in the First World War and most of the time could not hear his customers.)
He kept a large leather pouch at his front bulging with notes and change. If you ordered cheese, a large piece was brought out of the fridge and your quarter was cut accurately. Also you went into the back of the shop for paraffin, had it measured up into your empty can and brought home to fill the sitting room stove. (No Health and Safety then!)
Collis Primary School was in Cedar Road, where the pre-school play group is now; school fetes were held on the patch of ground opposite, now the public car park. Bridgeman Infants School was where Collis is now.
Two old ladies used to lean over their fence in one of the old cottages in Blackmore's Grove and chat. They remembered R D Blackmore's fruit and veg wagons trundling off to Covent Garden very early in the mornings.
When I became pregnant with our third child, we decided it was time to buy a washing machine. We went to a white goods shop on the bridge (I don't recall the name – Ed neither do I), between Broad Street and High Street. We bought a Hoover twin-tub (remember them?) and received 6 LP records as a bonus.

One evening our gay friend Terry came to see us : he'd heard on the grapevine that there were 'Tranny' evenings in Teddington. What on earth were they?
We followed him along the High Street and came to a dilapidated old pub, the Royal Oak (where the new houses now are, behind the Cotes Brasserie). It was well set back from the High Street as there were plans at the time to build a road going over the river (it never happened thank goodness). (Ed note – this site was for one of the oldest pubs in Teddington, going back 300 years. As Jeanne says it was set back in 1935, having been demolished, to make way for a road bridge across the Thames which never happened).
In the back room (Ed note - known as The Blue Room) was a small stage and a most extraordinary sight, a transvestite in a long dress, a huge bouffant hair-do and heavy make-up, singing songs like 'I am what I am' from 'La Cage aux Follies' and a favourite with the audience, 'Lola' by the Kinks.
Looking around the audience, most of them were similarly dressed, shouting constant abuse at the compere and similarly abused from the stage, they all seemed to be acquainted.
During the evening, taxis were drawing up outside and the small room was filling up. It was obvious the word had gone round the area. They turned up, dressed up for the party in silks and furs, perfumed, some as high as seven feet in their high heels, looking extremely exotic. I had never seen anything like it.
Tony and I returned a couple of times; then there was a police raid and the Transvestite evenings were closed down. Homosexuality was legalised the next year, 1967.
There was a change of management which revived the pub until 2005 when it was again demolished and rebuilt roadside and became Cotes Brasserie in 2014.

Jeanne remembers another pub: in the1960s the Builders Arms on Field Lane had three entrances and was split into four separate areas : bar, smoke room, lounge and off-licence. In the comfortable lounge where drinks cost more, there were often three old people : Barclay, his brother and brother's wife. Barclay always had a beaming smile on his face for everyone and would happily talk to his brother's wife while the sour-faced brother kept his distance at the other end of the bar. Ménage a trios? It appeared to be an arrangement that suited them all."

Jeanne went on to recall some of the shops and traders in Teddington at that time. "We eventually installed coal fires, one in the sitting room and one with a boiler which heated the water in the kitchen/diner. The coal merchant, H Comfort & Son, was where the Cheese Shop is now on Station Road and the coal yard was behind it. There was a further sales shop on the bridge. When the coal was delivered, a sackful was carried by the coalman on his back, down the entry at the side of the house, along to our garden gate, up to the garden and into the coal bunker."

"Every Friday I went to the bank to draw out £11 for the week's shopping. (In those days the banking system still supported Teddington and we had three of the main clearing banks in the High Street, the Midland, Lloyds and the Westminster with Barclays on the other side of the bridge.) "I went to Barclays on the junction of The Causeway and Broad Street, the entrance was right on the very corner. (Sometime later this moved into The Causeway itself, presumably for reasons of safety ?). My 60 year-old daughter tells me that there was a greengrocer opposite which had a Myna bird who talked!

I then took my two little girls to Woolworths (now Superdrug) and bought them a treat. On the way on the bridge was The Model Shop (now the closed Sony Repair Shop) which had a small model railway circuit. There was a slot in the glass by the end of the window and by rolling a 1d coin through the slot and down the ramp inside, a model train would come out from a hole in the back, chugging along a little way and complete a circuit before disappearing through another hole at the back of the display – the girls loved it. (On the opposite side of the bridge going into Waldegrave Road was The Toy Shop run by the Misses Watson).

"Coming back into the High Street there was a great variety of independent shops. I particularly remember 1966 and the Football World Cup when I took the girls shopping so that Tony could watch the match in peace. We went down to the Westminster Bank passing Gilberts the Furriers (now Hamptons), crossed the road and went to Jarvis the Fishmongers (now Cavan the Bakers), passed Keith Luxford's Saddlers (now Jenny Blanc), Charlie Dobny's Grocers (where Waterston's now stands), the Kings Arms (now The Clockhouse), The Thames Valley Stamp Shop (now Jude the Obscure) and finally Charlie Dobny's Greengrocers (now an Estate Agent). This was before supermarkets came to the High Street. (Ed note – and England beat Germany 4 – 2 in the final).

Thank you Jeanne for a nostalgic trip down Memory Lane. Readers might also be interested to read Jeanne's account of the war years – "Nell and the Girls": the true story of a British girl and her family in occupied France in 1940-44.

R D Blackmore and Lorna Doone

Was his greatest success a fluke?

In 1857 a young schoolmaster from Hampton Wick came into an inheritance which enabled him to change his circumstances and embark on a third career. The young man in question was Richard Doddridge Blackmore, a Classics Master at Wellesley House Grammar School; he was 32 and had married Lucy Maguire four years earlier. Initially he embarked on a career in law and joined the Middle Temple in London where he practised conveyancing. However he moved from the law for medical reasons and later told a friend *"My once excellent health became impaired. My medical advisor said I would have to give up my profession, seek an outdoor employment, or die young."* He was suffering from epileptic fits, a legacy of the bullying he endured from his days at Blundell's School.

R. D. BLACKMORE.

Blackmore took a house in Hampton Wick, the first Gomer House, and walked daily to and from Wellesley House to take in the outdoor exercise his doctor had recommended. Although not as stressful as the law, his pupils were not as committed to the Classics as he would have liked. However the job allowed him time to write poetry and short prose items which were encouraged by the headmaster, Thomas J Scale, who shared Blackmore's love of the Classics and became a lifelong friend.

The bequest had come from his uncle, the Rev Henry Hey Knight and helped achieve an ambition that he had quietly nursed to become a horticulturist. This would give him all of the outdoor life he needed. He set about purchasing a 16 acre piece of land in neighbouring Teddington, designing his own house and planning out the plot as a market garden. Little did he know of the problems that lay ahead with the fickleness of the climate, the tricky side of human nature and the intransigence of the London and South Western Railway.

In 1860 Blackmore set off on his new venture. The "Victorian Web" best sums up his attitude – *"He did so with the express purpose of setting up a market garden. It is not clear that he had any exact plan for the project. The enterprise caught hold of him, and seems to have grown on him. By temperament he was a romantic rather than a commercial person .It was always of greater interest to him to grow a new or different species than to optimise and capitalise on a lucrative line. He was typical of the English attitude that somehow it was unseemly to make money, yet at the same time it was proper to complain how badly off he was and would become. In fact his horticulture was almost never profitable. He indicated that in 40 years, he only made a profit in two years."*

Even in the early days, it became clear that it would be difficult for the market gardening business to support itself unaided. His main crops were fruits – strawberries, pears, peaches and grapes and it is fair to say that he became expert in them, and by the 1880s he was nationally renowned and was a figure on the Royal Horticultural Society Committees. However to continue to live life to a reasonable standard, he needed another source of income. He decided then to move from his poetry to writing novels as this appeared to pay well. In addition to this, he also translated Virgil's *"Georics"*. He wrote to a friend *"All I make with the pen, I cast away with the spade."*

"Clara Vaughan" was his first published novel in 1864 although the first draft of this had been completed in 1853. As was the accepted practice this appeared in the literary weeklies of the day. In 1866 the second novel, *"Cradock Nowell"*, was published by a different publisher, again in the weeklies. Neither story set the world on fire and when they had run their course in the weeklies, both books were published in three volume sets, as was usual at the time. The reception of both works was poor and Blackmore was disappointed.

Blackmore and Lucy used to holiday in Devon and in the mid 1860s they were in North Devon where he researched his next book. He was able to recall his own childhood and that of his relatives' memories to catch the mood of the book. Although he normally reserved his writings for the winter months, from spring 1867 until April 1868 he drove himself on to complete his latest work. This was to be *"Lorna Doone"* or to give it its full title *"Lorna Doone – A Romance of Exmoor"*, the book that was to introduce a new Christian name – "Lorna" - to the English language. Blackmore then set about seeing it published but this proved to be more difficult than anticipated. All of his previous publishers turned it down but eventually Samson Low, Son & Marston accepted *"Lorna Doone"* for publication in January 1869. There was to be no serialisation and the book was hastily printed in three volumes. Incredible as it may seem now, the book failed to sell. Of 500 copies printed, only 300 were sold. The remainder were shipped to Australia and there the matter may have ended – *"Lorna Doone"* was a flop.

Mr Sampson Low was then in a quandary. Should he forget the book altogether or gamble on a single volume edition? Perhaps he took pity on Blackmore who wrote subsequently *"It is the merest fluke that Lorna Doone was ever heard of any more."* The single volume issue went ahead.

In October1870, by coincidence, the announcement was made of the engagement of the Queen's daughter, Princess Louise to the Marquis of Larne. The single volume version of *"Lorna Doone"* was published the very same month. This time followed by two favourable reviews , one in *The Saturday Review* in November and another in Blackwood's Magazine by the most respected Mrs Margaret Oliphant in January 1871. Blackmore was later heard to say *"people confused Lorna with the Marquis of Larne, and thought it might show them the fashions."* The marriage of the Princess and the Marquis duly took place in March 1871, and by then sales of *"Lorna Doone"* had taken off. In a letter 0f 1876, Blackmore referred to sales of 16,000 which was phenomenal.

After the amazing success of *"Lorna Doone"*, Blackmore wrote several more novels but never came close to capturing the popularity of his most famous book.

It is very interesting to think that but for the wrong throw of the dice by Mr Samson Low, *"Lorna Doone"* might have disappeared into obscurity.

More Teddington Memories

There is nothing like reading someone's memories of life in Teddington to trigger off one's own recollections of earlier times. Many of you have read Jeanne Gask's and Gillian Harding's memories with interest and today I am including some of the additional reminiscences I have received.

Firstly is Anne Spragg (nee MacCullough) who has been a resident in County Mayo for the last twenty years but still regards herself as Teddington 'born and bred.' She has vivid memories of WW2 and has started to write these down for her family.

The MacCulloughs lived at 7 Sydney Road and their father died in 1940, leaving her mother as a single parent to bring up four children, of whom Anne (now 81) was the youngest. *"I remember things like searchlights and the sirens' ghastly noise and huddling under the kitchen table because mum didn't like going to the air raid shelter at the bottom of the road. There were days when we couldn't get to school. My older sister recounted what happened on the night the Willoughby (Hotel) was bombed.(Ed. Note : This was the night of the 29th November 1940 when the Christmas Loan Club was paying out. The pub took a direct hit and seventeen people were killed. The pub was never rebuilt.) Shelagh remembers the flames when the (Baptist) Church took a hit. Mr Ballard who had the corner shop opposite the Church brought his horse to the Sapworth's back garden at the bottom of Sydney Road to keep him safe. Our windows were blown in. My brother and his friends used to play amongst the rubble of the church before a new church was built.*

In 1944 we were evacuated to Cardiff. This was late in the war but our school (Sacred Heart School in Fairfax Road) was requisitioned. I was 6 the youngest of the 4. I remember the noise and smells of Paddington Station. We were the last family to be picked out on Cardiff Station, too many to be kept together ! My eldest sister went off with my brother and my other sister and I went to a family in Talbot Street. It took a while to settle but then I was happy. When the war ended we had a street party and all the children were given a ride on Mr Ballard's horse up and down the road."

"Like Gillian I remember the old Teddington, Broad Street rather than the High Street. On Saturdays my brother and I would carry the accumulator for our wireless round to get it recharged so we could listen to the afternoon football results. With our ration books we bought sweets for a farthing in Barton's in Church Road and crusty rolls from White's Bakers. And Oh what heavenly fish and chips for sixpence in Walpole Road. Again like Gillian I have a confession. I once got rolls without my coupons and I promised I would be back with them – and never did. That still comes back to haunt me ! Our weekends were spent in Bushy Park. At the round pond we used to wonder aloud if Diana really did kill her children (Ed. A popular myth at the time). Hampton Court Palace was completely open to us – we could go through all the rooms (I remember sliding along the floors) no charge – and the Maze cost one penny! Men would be home from

the war and many a sailor was chased so we could "Touch collar, never swallow, never catch the fever!"
Ah what larks!"

Thanks for that Anne. I'm sure many of you have similar recollections of those troubled years. Sue Pruen (nee Evans) also contacted me as a result of being given a copy of "Teddington As It Was" on her 70th birthday.

"I found it immensely interesting, recognised so much and brought back so many memories.
I lived at 89 Queens Road for the first 22 or so years of my life, opposite the NPL. I remember the air raid alarm going off every Friday morning. My family moved there in 1946, three years before I was born. I was born at Bearsted, Hampton Court. I went to Stanley Road School for the first part of my schooling, then I went to St Marks School Hampton for 2 years but unfortunately it was closed so then I had to go to Whitton Secondary School – which I often walked to and from – till I was 15. I worked at Kelly's Directories in Hampton for a couple of years, I then left and went to work at Teddington Technical Services (TTS) for a Mr Ron Duck and Mr David Roberts (both now deceased). Their premises was in the Old Dairy a few doors down from the laundrette and the fish and chip shop. Mr Duck also had a transport business, he stored Marks and Spencer counters. Mr Roberts also had the antiques shop towards the top of Queens Road, opposite where Honey's stood.

Looking through your (Teddington Society) website I noticed that the Park Lane Stables are still there, I started riding there when I was 9 (my father couldn't put up with my crying any longer – I could see the horses going out from my bedroom window!). Peter Churchill, an ex jockey, took over the stables a year or so later. He used to have an equestrian shop in the High Street, he later wrote in "The Horse and Hounds." I learnt so much from him but my father wouldn't let me make riding as an instructor my future. I know I have a video (made from my father's film camera) of mine and my brother's first riding lesson when I was about 9 ...so 1958ish. This was in the paddock opposite the stabling (now occupied by a block of flats) – is it still there and used ? It would be ideal to make a ménage for the Riding for the Disabled."

The Park Lane Stables has had an interesting history in itself. At some time in the 18th century, the village pound was established in Park Lane, next to the Parish Cage or lock-up. It is hard to imagine stray animals roaming the streets of Teddington at that time when the estimated population was slightly less than 700 living in about 120 houses but nevertheless an animal pound was established. In about 1830 this had fallen into decline and was taken over by the village fire brigade as the home for its horse drawn fire engine. This lasted until the new Fire Station next to the Library in Waldegrave Road was opened. Park Lane Stables was then established and despite some glips in the years, it is still going strong today.

Growing Up in Teddington
- Part 1

Many people express surprise when I tell them I am a born and bred Teddingtonian. I don't know why, after all it's not that long ago that people moved into their forbears' homes and continued a tradition of living in the same place for a century or two. I can't quite claim that but certainly my life has been spent in Teddington. I was the Allied Forces' secret weapon, when I Popped out in February 1945, Hitler decided he had had enough and started to wind down the war. That February was the only time, apart from holidays that I was away from Teddington. As my mother was a nurse, she was accorded the privilege on giving birth in Chiswick Maternity Hospital and for 2 days I was in alien territory.

I had better start by talking about my parents. My father's family were all agricultural labourers in Pavenham, Bedfordshire. At age 8 my grandfather James and his elder brother Charles, moved to Wolverton, Buckinghamshire where the London and Birmingham Railway had opened up a major repair depot. The reason is obvious, railways paid about 4 times the pay of a farm labourer and more and more land workers were moved into industrialised towns and cities. Thus my father and his brothers joined my father and his uncle in working for the railways. My father was apprenticed to Vauxhalls in Bedford as a coach builder and his brothers were in various railway trades. My grandfather was an upholsterer.

L & B Railway had come to Wolverton in 1838 and became part of the London and North Western Railway in 1846. Wolverton expanded from a repair and maintenance depot to actually building locomotives and by 1865 it was the largest carriage works in the UK. It had a long tradition of providing carriages for the Royal Train and all such trains were maintained and serviced here. A special Waiting Room was built for Queen Victoria at Wolverton. Whenever the Royal Train was on a trip to Balmoral or Sandringham, a specially assembled crew of railway craftsmen accompanied the Train, each man being a specialist in his trade, so that any mishap to the train could be remedied whilst the journey was taking place. In the 1880s, James Howe as senior upholsterer, travelled on the Royal Train.

Quite what made my father come to Teddington in the first place I will never know. He did have a brother who was in business in Teddington and this must have been one of the main influences. His brother Walter was a Stationer and Confectioner at No 17 The Causeway and he took over the business of William Bibby as Newsagent and Tobacconist at No. 23. This was the situation in the late 1920s and in the 1930s Walter returned to Wolverton to be replaced by his sister and brother-in-law, Doris and Harold Hobson. They successfully traded alongside each other until the war years when No 23 The Causeway sustained some bombing damage, rendering the premises uninhabitable. They then merged the two businesses to operate out of one shop at 17 The Causeway. By 1950 this arrangement had outlived its purpose and my aunt and uncle also moved back to Wolverton to open an Off-licence, leaving my father as the sole partner.

On the other side, my mother was one of a family of ten from Midleton, Co.Cork. My grandfather there was a drayman working for Jamieson's Distillery in Cork. Job opportunities were few in Ireland at that time and my mother wanted to go into nursing. Several of the family had already come over to England and she followed them to go into a training hospital. Again the years are a bit sketchy and she seems to have been around West London, Twickenham and Portsmouth.

Mum and dad met during wartime when she was at St John's Hospital, Twickenham and he was in Twickenham Fire Brigade. Dad had been married before but his wife then died of pneumonia, leaving a daughter of two who was brought up by my grandparents. They married in 1944.

I started school when I was four and went to St Paul's Convent School at the top of Fairfax Road/ Kingston Road. There was a large wooden gate in Fairfax Road and a steep flight of concrete steps going down to a sunken playground and access to the classrooms was at this level. There was a corrugated iron building in the playground where we would go if it was raining. I remember a young French boy of about my age causing a bit of a stir by dropping his shorts. All of the teachers were nuns and I'm not sure they knew how to deal with this. No doubt there were phone calls/letters to parents etc but after that day, we never saw that boy again.

Teddington at that time was recovering from the war. There were slight bits of bomb damage in most roads and some carried temporary corrugated iron buildings in place of damaged ones. Motor cars were very few and most transport was by bus or trolley bus. The 601 was the main service. It started at Barclays Bank in Twickenham and followed the same route as the 281 today. Over Teddington Bridge it passed the Savoy Cinema and went down to Teddington Lock where it turned right and went into Kingston. It was powered by electricity from overhead wires and run on tracks set into the road. There were two long arms fixed to the top of the trolley bus which were then connected to the overhead wires. Not infrequently the arms came off and the conductor would then have to pull a long bamboo pole out from under the bus and reset the arm onto the wire. By and large the trolley buses were very reliable. The main problem with them was that they moved along so silently. Many jaywalkers had to jump back onto the pavement suddenly at the approach of one of these. There was another trolley bus, the 605 which came from Kingston and turned around at the Savoy Cinema and turned back to Kingston. This was mostly done by way of the overhead wires but there was also a turntable outside the Savoy which could be operated in an emergency.

The other bus service was the 27 or 27A on Sundays. This would go from Teddington Station where it would be parked in Adelaide Road and then to Twickenham, Richmond, Chiswick and into West London. On Sundays the 27A would continue to Hampton Court where it turned around.

My dad would take me up to St Paul's in the mornings. We would walk down the railway passage and then cross the footbridge. He would bring his bike and I would be riding on the crossbar. Coming home I would get the 601 from the Sacred Heart Church. The fare was 2d but if you walked down to the next stop at Holmesdale Road, the fare was only 1d, leaving 1d for the purchase of a Topsy ice lolly from one of the small shops in that parade.

Growing Up in Teddington
- Part 2

I am pleased to say that last month's edition has drawn a lot of comment and support from the readership. Firstly full marks to Doug Jerome who has pulled me up on a couple of points. The trolley buses did not run on tracks as I said last month; - they were free wheeling from the driver's steering wheel. The tracks in the road were left over from the trams. There was no turntable outside the Savoy Cinema. I challenged Doug on this but he was living at 32 High Street at that time and every Sunday afternoon, he and his friends would wait at the top of Station Road by the Westminster Bank (the now closed National Westminster Bank) for a 605 or a 604 from Wimbledon to come along. The conductor would then take out the long bamboo pole and transfer the trolley head from one set of overhead wires to another which was turned to face Kingston. This procedure was then repeated with the other arm. The pole was replaced under the trolley bus and the driver would then start to turn the bus around. At this point Doug or one of his friends would leap onto the open platform of the bus, hang onto the fixed pole and get a free ride as the bus turned around. The trolley buses continued running until 1962 when they were replaced by a fleet of diesel Routemasters.

When I was seven, it was time to leave St Paul's and I transferred to St James' in Twickenham. This was then in Grosvenor Road, behind the Police Station. It was a four storey building with a flat roof which was a playground. I don't think it would be allowed today! The headmaster was Mr Cole and some of the teachers were nuns from St Catherine's Convent nearby. I used to catch the 27 bus, which in those days terminated in Adelaide Road and went to Twickenham Junction. Coming home there was a choice of bus of either the 27 or the 601 as the stops for both of these were next to each other. If I caught the 601, I would get off at Broad Street and pop into dad's shop and scrounge some sweets. It's a miracle I wasn't the size of a barrel. Rationing had not been completely abolished but I think it had been lifted on confectionery.

My mum's sister worked in the shop and lived in the flat above it. We were living in Victoria Road, next to "The Railway Hotel." On the other side were the Butler family who used to run "The Duke of York" in North Lane. This closed sometime in the late 1940s/ early 1950s and Reg Butler went to work at Hawkers in Kingston. In 1953 we had new neighbours when the Carman family took over the "Railway" – Bill, Marie and young Mick who has remained a close friend ever since.

I can remember the long hot summer holidays we had which seemed to last forever. Mick and I would go off to Bushy Park after breakfast and stay there until teatime. We used to treat the Park as our personal back garden. Part of the Park was still occupied by American airmen from the USAF who had made a base there – Camp Griffiss – in wartime, home to the US Eight Army Air Force. The base was taken over by General Eisenhower who was living on Kingston Hill nearby, as HQ of SHAEF – THE Supreme Headquarters of the Allied Expeditionary Force and from here the D-Day Landings in Normandy were planned. In wartime the Park was heavily camouflaged as the Chestnut Avenue and the Diana Fountain were very distinctive landmarks and clearly visible from the air.

There was a local theory that the Americans came here in 1942 as a result of a navigational error, for which they had something of a reputation, and instead of setting up camp at Bushey Heath, Hertfordshire, they arrived here. By the time the error was spotted, the construction of the camp was well underway and it was decided to leave matters as they were. One very important proviso was written into the agreement and that was that as soon as the war was over, the camp would be dismantled and the area returned to Royal parkland. Both sides of the Chestnut Avenue were lined with rows of Nissan huts erected between the trees. On the cessation of hostilities, the number of servicemen was quickly reduced and the Nissan huts became free. Immediately there was a huge rush of homeless families, many of whom had been bombed out of the East End, to claim the empty properties. The local council was forced to re-house these families and they then demolished the huts to prevent a repeat of unauthorised occupancy.

The administrative part of the base remained open and most of the remaining servicemen were housed within the local community and merged into Teddington life. My own parents befriended an American family who were living off the Kingston Road and the four of them often went to the base theatre on a Saturday night when top line American entertainers would be present for the purpose of entertaining the troops. I went to the Saturday morning Cinema several times for the children's' programme. The facilities at the American base were quite incredible, especially to the war weary people of Teddington who had endured much in the war years and were only slowly moving into normality. Apart from the cabaret restaurant and the cinema, there was a fully fitted ten pin bowling alley, a baseball diamond and a cinder running track which was second to the White City at the time. The camp closed in October 1962 with a dinner for residents hosted by the camp colonel, ending twenty years occupation on the site. Little wonder that many people did not wish to see the camp bull-dozed with such facilities going to waste. Bill Carman mounted a petition from his pub to retain the camp as a social centre but the Ministry of Works (as it was then) dug their heels in and insisted in the full destruction of the camp. On the 50th anniversary of D-Day, a plaque was unveiled by the American ambassador to commemorate the site of Eisenhower's old HQ.

Rail transport at the time was switching from steam locomotives to electrified trains. When the steam trains were running there was always a rush of children to the small railway bridge from Station Road to the railway passage. The bridge was of fairly basic construction and consisted of a series of timber planks connecting both sides. As the train was passing under the bridge, the funnel would be churning out huge billows of smoke which would then rise up through the creaks in the timbers and engulf the children standing there. The smoke would travel up the legs of one's shorts, much to the amusement of the owners. It's hard to believe that such simple things were popular with us youngsters then but times change and things have quite definitely moved on.

Growing Up in Teddington - Part 3

At the time of the coming of the railway to Teddington in 1863, the town was literally cut in half by the building of the railway bridge over the old pond, which later re-connected Broad Street to High Street. When I was young, the High Street was a foreign land to me and it was not until later life that I got to know it apart from the Savoy Cinema in the High Street where they showed Saturday Morning Pictures. You had to join the ABC Minors and admission was 6d. There were cartoons, a serial and the main film – usually a western and as I recall, the cinema was usually pretty packed. The audience was a fairly cross-section bunch and I do remember getting into a few punch-ups because mum insisted that I wear my school cap when going out.

I have mentioned St James' School and it was here that I met Mick O'Donnell, who I am pleased to say is still a good friend. I do recall when we were both sent to Mr Cole to receive the cane for some misdemeanour or other. Mick was first in the queue and he bravely extended his hand, palm upwards. Mr Cole raised his arm to deliver a stroke of the cane but at the last minute, Mick pulled his hand away and Mr Cole hit his own foot with the cane. I could not contain myself and burst out laughing. The cane was dutifully applied to Mick and then it was my turn. "So you think that was funny do you?" said Mr Cole as he laid into me and gave me an extra stroke for my trouble. That was the first of many scrapes that Mick got me into in our school lives although more about those later.

Teddington in the late 1940s/early 1950s was a very different place to live. There was much evidence of war damage and several partly standing buildings were being occupied for small trades. In Queens Road/Little Queens Road there were a couple of panel beaters that always seemed to be busy. I don't know what happened to them when the area was redeveloped. Similarly West Road received some damage and was completely cleared when the present Tescos was opened, and provided the car park area. At one end of the Broad Street going towards Hampton, Honey's Grocers had been bombed and on the opposite side of the road, Gould's the Chemist was also damaged.

The Causeway was quite a different road from today. Starting at the Park Road end north side, there was a new block to replace the bomb damage where my dad's first shop stood. There was Jember Bros. Joiners and Carpenters with solicitors P Hart on the offices above. Then White Knight Dry Cleaners and Evelyn Cheeseman Florist, then my dad's shop S E Howe Newsagent, Confectioner and Tobacconist. Derrick Looker Gents Barber was next, followed by Mr Lewin's Camera Shop. Then an Electrical Repairs Shop before moving onto a gift shop (whose name escapes me) and part of Grundy Engineering before coming to Barclays Bank which had taken over the old National Provincial Bank. Coming back on the other side, there was a small tobacco kiosk at the start, next to Deayton's Grocers. Then Sims the Opticians with William Erik Oakley the Dentist above. This was followed by MacFisheries and the Coombe Bakery. Eastmans the Dry Cleaners and a Ladies Hairdresser. We then had Dales the Drapers and Haberdashers; they were famous for having the Lampson overhead cash carrying system where cylinders containing money were sent in a series of tubes to a cash desk out of sight of the main showroom. John Follett the butcher – he had been the "Capt Mainwaring" of Teddington's Home Guard, Cheeseman's the Greengrocers and

John Quality the Grocer. Then there was Charlie French who had what we would now call a Collector's Shop but in our day it was a Junk Shop, followed by Partridge Moss Solicitors, then Barry's Estate Agents and finally the showroom for A V Motors on the site of the burnt down Town Hall. Apologies for the lengthily list but I needed to get the shop names down whilst I still remembered them. Have I missed any?

I was recently reminded of one adventure that Mick Carman and I had in Bushy Park. We were strolling amongst the trees in the Lime Avenue to the left of Chestnut Avenue from the Teddington Gate when we spotted a young bird that seemed to be grubbing around on the ground. We approached him and he hopped away from us. We tried again and the same thing happened. It was obvious that the poor thing could not fly. After a brief consultation, we caught the bird which was a young jackdaw and he had a damaged wing. We decided that he would not be safe if we left him in the park, unable to fly, so we brought him back to Mick's. His mum was not best pleased but his dad was very sympathetic to our cause.

He constructed a cage for the bird and mounted this on the wall of the pub. Every afternoon "Jacko" as he was now called was taken into the upstairs Clubroom where Bill Carman virtually taught him to fly. Eventually he got the hang of flying and made friends of the pub regulars although he was not too popular with the lady customers. The day came when he had to be released back into the wild and Bill, Mick and I took him into Railway Station Gardens (now houses) and let him go. After looking around for a bit, he flexed his winds and off he went. We were both happy and sad to see him go but we hadn't seen the last of him. As the evening grew darker, he returned to his cage and cawed loudly for his dinner. Bill fed him and then removed the front of his cage so that he could come and go as he pleased. This arrangement seemed to be working quite well but Jacko expanded his area and used to patrol the station taking to the air when trains departed or fly parallel to them as they arrived. Bill had one or two phone calls from Waterloo Station to say that Jacko had got into a Waterloo bound train and was now looking lost on one of their platforms. Jacko and Bill had built up an amazing bond and Bill would cheerfully hop on a train to go and collect him. Jacko earned the nickname of Dr Beeching by the various station staffs. I can't remember how long this lasted, certainly longer than a year until one day he was flying in to greet a train when one of the passengers opened the slam-door of the train before it had stopped and Jacko flew straight into it, falling dead on the platform. A very sad end to a very entertaining friend. I understand that a book about the life of Jacko aka Dr Beeching is in the process of being written. Once I have more information, I will inform my readers. (To be continued)

Photographs: Broad Street, Old Town Hall, Savoy Cinema

Stanley Road

One of the frequently asked questions I receive is "Where does the Stanley in Stanley Road come from?" If fact only this week I met a gentleman and his son in York Pet Supplies who asked me the self same question. I'm afraid you're in for a long answer.

How many of you remember when Alpha Veterinary Services was Livingstone's Wine bar? I thought it a very witty name at the time – Livingstone & Stanley – and I must confess that this may have clouded my judgement somewhat. I knew that Henry Morton Stanley visited Teddington to call upon the renowned Boat builder, James Messenger, to build a boat in five sections to be capable of being carried overland for his African explorations. The boat named *"The Lady Alice"* (after Stanley's girlfriend of the time) was duly built and played a large part in his African travels and in finding Dr Livingstone in 1871. What finer way would a grateful town commemorate the works of such a man as Stanley other than by naming a road after him, a road that grown considerably since the coming of the railway to the present time of about 1872.

I had barely finished slapping myself on the back when some papers came to light which had dates that threw my theory into disarray. On 16 June 1868 there was a sale of land at Maud Cottage in Stanley Road, purchased by no other than James Messenger. Henry Morton Stanley was not commissioned by *"The New York Herald"* to find Dr Livingstone until 1869, by which time Stanley

Road in Teddington already existed. Back to the drawing board!

In 1800, the year of the Enclosure Act of Teddington, what is now Stanley Road was merely a lane connecting Teddington to Twickenham. By 1862 it was known as Webb's Lane after the name of the farmer of the Manor Farm and consisted mainly of Maud Cottage, Manor Farm and its outbuildings and a few small dwellings near the junction with Shacklegate Lane.

1868 is the first year that written records note the existence of Stanley Road although in 1871 and 1873 it was also known as Fulwell Road which is borne out by some sale catalogues. Phillipsons Directory of 1873 shows it supporting 19 houses, a considerable growth since the map indication of 1862 and largely due to the coming of the railway in 1863 although a water colour painting of the time does not give the impression of a very built up road.

What could have occurred between 1862 and 1868 to give rise to the change of name of the road to Stanley? Nothing is recorded in the local press of the day and it was necessary to look outside our local area for an explanation.
Our Local Reference Library feels that the connected name was that of **Edward Henry Stanley, 15th Earl of Derby**. Born 1826 – he entered Parliament as MP for King's Lynn in 1848. Although sitting with the Conservatives, he held very strong Liberal feelings. He travelled

extensively and his knowledge of foreign affairs was widely respected, even to the point of being offered the throne of Greece on the deposition of King Otto in 1863. He served as Foreign Secretary under Disraeli and reluctantly took Britain to the brink of war against Russia in 1878. He retired from public life in 1891 and died of a heart attack in 1893.

So there we have it. Or do we? Although a very able, respected and dedicated politician, by 1868 he would only have been 42 and was probably still learning his trade – hardly a likely candidate for having a road named.

On the other hand, his father – **Edward George Geoffrey Smith Stanley, 14th Earl of Derby** is a more likely candidate. He was born in 1799 and entered The House of Commons in 1822. He served as Prime Minister in four Parliaments and only handed over office to Disraeli in February 1868 as a result of his own ill-health, only to die the following October. In his time he had a most distinguished career and was very popular with the people. In all circumstances it would hardly be surprising for towns all over the country to name developing roads after him.

Whilst we can say that Stanley Road was named after **Edward Stanley, Earl of Derby**, but was it the 14th or 15th Earl?

Whilst looking at Stanley Road, it is interesting to go back to the origins of house numbering in the United Kingdom which is by no means straight forward and may even be considered to be haphazard. House Numbering is said to have come about as a result of the Postage Act of 1765 although the wording of the Act is sufficiently ambiguous to prevent a direct interpretation to apply to all areas of the UK. One of my hobbies is collecting postcards and watching the growth of the postcard industry. The very first postcard was sent in 1840 although the practice was not widespread. It was not impossible for a postcard to be addressed as merely:

Mr Ken Howe
Teddington

And the card would in all probability have been delivered. It was not until 1894 that the Post Office allowed for picture postcards to be sent by the Royal Mail.

At this time it was common practice to address a postcard as:

Mr Ken Howe
Cedar Road
Teddington

nd this would have been sufficient to enable the postcard to be delivered. As the roads became more built up and the number of houses in each grew rapidly, it became the practice to name each individual house, such as The Elms or Greenacres or some other such name to make identification of that house very clear. This worked well for a while but the ease at which postcards could confirm appointments both business and social brought about an avalanche of post with three deliveries a day. It was clear that a simple standard form of address was needed to allow the postal service to operate. In our area 1908 seems to be the time that house numbering became compulsory and it is something that we have all lived with ever since.

This brings me on to a puzzle that has been put to me. In 1901 there was a house named *"Holbeach"* in Stanley Road. By 1908 this house would have been given a number and gradually the name would have disappeared. Does anyone happen to know the current number of the house that was known as *"Holbeach"* ? It's tempting to say "Answers on a postcard please."

Growing Up in Teddington
- Part 4

2nd June 1953 – a most memorable date as the Coronation of Queen Elizabeth II. We had recently acquired a television set, something of a record for my dad as he was not renowned for taking the lead in new fashions. The set itself I believe was a Baird and was a rather odd shaped piece of furniture. It was rectangular and stood upright with a screen that seemed to be about 12" square. We then placed a high magnifying screen in front of the main screen to obtain a bigger picture.

I wasn't sure what to expect as my dad had told me about Coronations, having lived through two himself, but he had never actually seen one, except for some film clips on Pathe News. I was getting ready to witness the celebration from my favourite chair when a long procession of neighbours and parents' friends all trooped into our front room and positioned themselves around the TV set.

Needless to say I was relegated to the floor and I seemed to spend a good part of the set fetching and carrying cups of tea from the kitchen.

I remember the smooth silver tones of Richard Dimbleby as he followed the procession into Westminster Abbey. What a loss to broadcasting he was on his death in 1963. This was the first Coronation to be broadcast in Great Britain and the whole world was looking on. The sheer spectacle of the event was quite breathtaking and it seemed as if the world was there inside the TV screen. The weather was not particularly good with a steady rainfall from leaving the Abbey to going to the reception at Buckingham Palace. One guest in particular, Queen Salote of Tonga stood out. She refused to raise the canopy of her carriage and continued waving to the crowd of thousands as the procession made its way on the five mile journey. She must have been absolutely soaked. Definitely a day to remember!

My First Bike

I've always been under the illusion that every boy looked forward to his first bicycle. This didn't really apply to me but nevertheless I was told that I would be getting a bike for my birthday (?) I cannot recall how this came about but sure enough about the time of my birthday, a two wheeled vehicle appeared. It was not a new bike and had all the appearances of being an "industrial" bike. This was perhaps because I had to share it with my dad's shop. Let me explain, his newsagents part of the business covered a huge area of Teddington – there were 14 separate paper rounds. Not all of the paper boys/girls had bikes of their own and hence "mine" was called upon to be used by whomever. Not only that but if any one of the said paper boys/girls called in sick, then yours truly was summoned from home,(without having had a chance to eat my breakfast) to fill in the missing link. The route could have been any one of the fourteen and by the end, I had a fair working knowledge of Teddington. If it had looked a bit battered before it came to us, the bike certainly did look somewhat worn a few weeks later.

When we first got the bike, I could not ride and so I took it up to Bushy Park and muddled around on the grass until I got the hang of it. I had managed to get a clip or two around the ear from the park keepers for cycling on the grass. However with my new found confidence, I set off into the park to gain experience. When I came to the boating lake, there was a small wooden bridge crossing the stream that fed into the lake. Rather than dismount, I proceeded to ride across the bridge but for some strange reason I could not hold a straight line and steered myself off the bridge and into the water. I am sure that some people must have helped me and bike out of the water but I have no recollection of that now. All I wanted to do was get home and change into some dry clothes.

I don't fully remember what happened to the bike. It seemed to be used more and more on shop business although my dad had his own bike. I think it was stolen or not returned after a mission and that was the end of that.

My Dad's Shop

My dad's shop was a Newsagent, Confectioner, Tobacconist and Stationer and was at No 17 The Causeway. Originally this shop had been a confectioner's in the hands of my uncle, Harold Hobson and my dad had the corner shop, No 23 as a newsagents. As a result of wartime bombing, No 23 became unsafe and the block of 19-23 had to be pulled down. My dad and my uncle combined their businesses at No 17 until sometime in the 1950s when my uncle and his family decided to return to their home town of Wolverton, leaving my dad solely at No 17.

It was a very busy shop and had, as I have mentioned, 14 paper rounds around the town. On Saturday mornings I was required to help out in the shop as this was one of the busiest periods with customers coming in to settle their newspaper bills. One of my tasks then was the banking and I would have to take the last few days takings along to the other end of The Causeway to Barclays Bank. In those days the entrance to the bank was at the junction of the Broad Street and The Causeway. It was not until many years later that it moved to be from The Causeway itself. I don't know what the general public thought, seeing a young boy producing wads of money and sometimes coins from a shopping bag and passing them across the bank counter. Would Health and Safety allow that to happen today?

At first I missed not going to Saturday Morning Pictures at the Savoy but I soon settled into a routine and got used to the regular customers. As I grew older, I also had to relieve my dad for his tea and run the shop alone for about an hour. The evening trade was vastly different to the Saturday with a strong emphasis on daily horseracing. Customers would buy the evening papers; there were three of them – *The Star, The Evening News and The Evening Standard,* to find the day's results. Some of them would leave bets for the local bookmaker to collect – there were no licensed betting shops in those days. Some of the customers would wait for my dad's return, reading the papers in the shop. Others would pop in and pass a small parcel across the counter to clear their "slate." The parcel would usually be a dead rabbit and no questions were asked although it was obvious that it had come from Bushy Park and was offered in payment or part payment of their various accounts. The earliest form of barter was alive and kicking in the 1950s.

Growing Up in Teddington
- Part 5

Edmund Hillary and Tenzing Norgay

One thing I forgot to mention when talking about the Coronation was another world shattering event that took place about the same time and that was the conquest of Everest. The news was everywhere and Edmund (later Sir Edmund) Hillary and Sherpa "Tiger" Tenzing Norgay were international heroes. Anyone would think we had won the war ! Their final ascent was made on 29 May but communications being what they were at that time (no mobile 'phones), word of the success only reached London on 2 June 1953, the morning of the Coronation.

A film of this achievement was made in record quick time and I clearly remember the whole school going to the Odeon Twickenham to watch the film for free. I can think of no such similar occasion where the school/cinema combination was used again but by then the advance of television and the growing number of sets available probably made an event like this redundant.

That was probably my first visit to a cinema. My dad's shop had an advertising stand for the Odeon on the outside and for this, he received two complementary tickets a week. My mum and I were to make good use of these in the years to come. The local cinema was the Savoy which (I may have mentioned before, probably in conjunction with all other cinemas), held a Saturday morning programme for children. This consisted of a couple of cartoons - usually "Tom & Jerry", a serial – very often "Flash Gordon" the first of the super heroes and finally a full length film – usually a Western, all for the princely sum of 6d (2.5p). I became one of the ABC Minors and spent many happy hours going to the Savoy until it was time to take my turn in helping out at my dad's shop.

A lot of people have asked me what Teddington looked like just after the war. Were there bomb sites all over town ? Were areas roped off as being unsafe for people to walk ? Not that that made any difference to us kids, we would get under the ropes and explore bomb craters and ruined buildings to look for pieces of shrapnel. What must be appreciated is that whilst the town of Teddington in itself was not a strategic target of enemy action but it was the home of the National Physical Laboratory which was carrying out some top secret work. Also from 1942 the USAF base in Bushy Park was high on the list of places to be destroyed. Added to this, Teddington stands on the banks of the River Thames and enemy bombers returning home after a raid would follow the course of the Thames from the air and unload their unused bombs over the riverside towns, like Teddington. Tough Bros marine works had been given over to the production of naval vessels and German intelligence would have known about that.

In the course of the war 654 houses were either destroyed or so badly damaged that they were pulled down. A further 762 house were in such a state that they had to evacuated before they could be repaired. 161 people were killed with 275 seriously injured. Teddington certainly had its fair share of these with areas like Little Queens Road and Argyle Road being obliterated. In peacetime there was a huge shortage of building materials and the rebuilding of many parts of the town was delayed. It was probably a good 10 years after peace was declared that this was completed.

The area around Little Queens Road was occupied by a few businesses in the motor trade with panel beating being to the fore. These were gradually cleared away and Queens House was constructed. The cross roads at Broad Street/Hampton Road and Queens Road/Stanley Road were badly hit. Honeys the grocers on the corner of Queens Road/Hampton Road was completely wrecked. Goulds the chemist opposite lost its top storey. The Wesleyan/Methodist Church was so severely damaged that it had to be pulled down. Of the four corners of the crossroads, only the Queen public house remained standing. There must be a moral in there somewhere !

I was working in my dad's shop on Saturday mornings, doing the odd paper round and was at school at St James' in Twickenham until by some fluke, I passed the 11+ (I don't actually remember a specific examination) and went to Gunnersbury Grammar in Chiswick. The bus journey on the 27 went from the terminus in Adelaide Road to the flyover of the Great West Road and took 45 minutes. On the return journey, I would pop in at the shop and relieve my dad for his tea. This went on until I left school and went into full time employment.

My academic performance was not particularly brilliant and my parents toyed with the idea of me working at the shop permanently. Having watched my dad for all of my life doing long hours on a six and a half day week, I said "No thank you" pretty quickly. I then had to find something that looked like a career and I thought of teaching. An interview with the principal of Strawberry Hill Teachers College (it wasn't to become a university until many years later) followed. I can see the Rev Kevin Cronin now saying "It doesn't look if you've ever done much work at school; why should I think that you will start now?" End of teaching career. Whilst contemplating the next round, I went into the fashion world, working at a neighbour's West End store as a cashier and stock controller. Amazingly this lasted a couple of years but although the money was good, it was a five and a half day week stretching into six days over Christmas. Nearly all of my friends had cushy 9 to 5 office jobs on a 5 day week. Hence I drifted into the world of insurance.

Leisure time was a bit of a problem – not much to do – nowhere to go – I'm sure you've heard it all before. Coffee bars seemed to spring up all over the place. My favourite was L'Auberge on Richmond Bridge next to the Odeon and another in Teddington Broad Street which is a Chinese take-away now.

Youth Clubs were very popular, most being spin-offs of various churches. I went to Hampton Hill and I'm pleased to say met one of my life-long friends there. It was held on a Sunday night between 7.00pm and 10.00pm. We used to bring our latest 45 rpm records to play and sometimes dance. The clubs were mixed and ours was about 50/50 boys to girls. There were table tennis tables and everyone had a turn on these. The club leaders were Mick Martin and Nelson Sullivan and occasionally they would bring in a colleague to give us a talk – loosely career based – for half an hour. By being a member here, you could go to the main Youth Centre at Heatham House any night of the week where the activities were much more numerous. Then came the music boom with the Rolling Stones playing at Eel Pie Island – another world !

I think by now I have hit adulthood and can consider myself grown up. I hope you have enjoyed the shared experience and perhaps this might make you think about writing up your own. In the time of the present coronavirus, there could be no better time to reflect on your own lives and record the stories for your families.

Teddington TV Studios

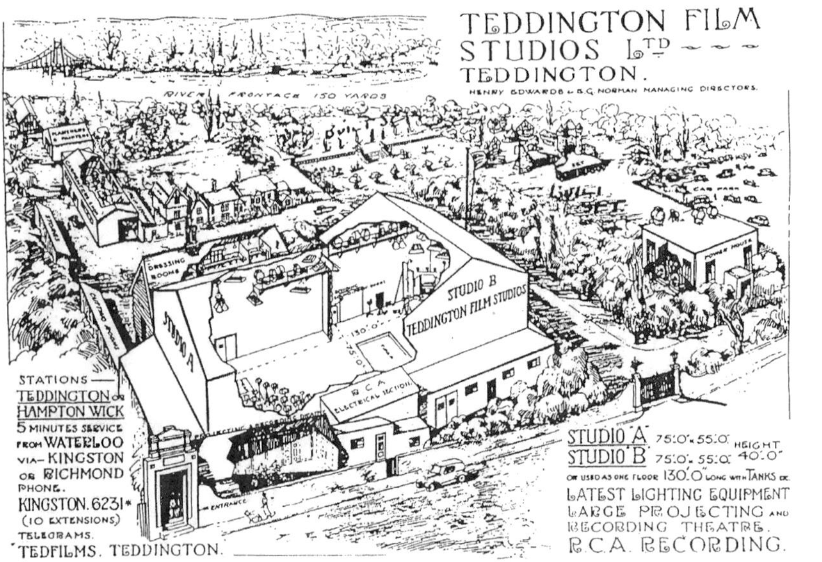

Visitors to Teddington Lock over the last couple of years cannot fail to have noticed the massive housing development going on at the site of the former Teddington Studios which closed in 2014. I have already written about the Studios in terms of the film production there (see Hollywood on Thames - Sept 2014) and now I hope to continue the story when they became television studios.

Warner Bros closed down their studios in 1952 and the premises remained dormant until 1955. 1954 had seen the birth of commercial television in the UK when the Independent Television network was established. ABC Television purchased the Teddington site and set about converting the studios for television production. The new company was responsible for many new innovations in television production such as video tape recording which put the studios at the head of Europe in such production.

A series of successful programmes were made in the late 1950s and in 1964 ABC made a remarkable signing when they enticed Eamonn Andrews from the BBC. This brought about a new kind of entertainment – the chat show, and "The Eamonn Andrews Show" commenced "live from London" but actually recorded earlier in that evening. Although there were several similar shows running in the USA, there had been nothing quite like this on UK television.

Andrews had made his name as a sports commentator and this was something of a very new adventure for him. He did not take naturally to the job and became famous for ad-lib gaffs which did not work such as "Speaking of cheese sandwiches, have you come far?" However the viewing public loved him and the show was famous for hosting well established stars as well as introducing many up and coming artists and singers. It ran for five years from 1964 to 1969, so someone was doing something right.

Whilst that show was running, many other series had commenced, including the highly successful "The Avengers" which was to make its stars Patrick McNee and his leading ladies Honor Blackman and Dianna Rigg household names. At the start of the series, McNee shared top billing with Ian Hendry who starred in many other Teddington productions.

In 1967 ABC and Rediffusion merged to form Thames Television which handled the Monday to Friday programming with London Weekend Television doing Saturday to Sunday. This gave the studios their golden 25 years when they seemed to be producing the ITV ensemble. The number of comedy hits that were churned out is amazing: "Alastair McGowan", "And Mother Makes Three", "The Benny Hill Show", "Birds of a Feather", "Bless This House", "Bremner Bird & Feather", "Bring On The Girls|", "The David Nixon Show". "The Des O'Connor Show", "Father Dear Father" – I could go on and finish this article with merely naming the other shows on the Thames comedy circuit.

There was also a steady roll of drama coming from the production line – I have mentioned "The Avengers", there were also "Callan", "Edward & Mrs Simpson", "Hazell", "Jenny Lady Randolph Churchill", "Napoleon", "The Rivals of Sherlock Holmes", "Van Der Valk" and "The World at War." The full list is not quite endless but certainly unrivalled in programme making.

The effect of the TV Studios on the town was substantial. To start with, there were no alcohol bars in the studios until the late 1970s and so all of the local pubs benefitted from the custom of the stars and their entorages. Honor Blackman and her set were in "The Kings Arms" every Friday night. Ian Hendry gave forth in "The Anglers." Jon Pertwee and his scriptwriters were to be found in "The Tide End Cottage." Every pub in Teddington had its own

celebrity(ies) and in the main this was good for business. Also every local hall in the area was hired for rehearsals which proved very lucrative. When working in Hampton Wick I happened to meet and befriend Windsor Davies in "The Old King's Head" when he was making "Never The Twain." A more charming bloke you couldn't wish to meet.

Whilst the stars of the shows used to come and go, the technicians were permanent fixtures and most of them bought houses and moved into the area. This must have had a strong effect on Teddington house prices which has lasted to today. In fact it is still possible to see many familiar faces shopping, taking their children to and from school and following all the things in Teddington life.

Probably the most memorable comedy recorded was the Benny Hill Show. Having crafted his unique style of entertainment at the BBC, he switched to ITV in 1968 and joined Thames TV. Thames began their broadcasting in 1969 with the very first edition of the show for ITV. The Show featured Benny in various short comedy sketches and was full of slapstick, burlesque and double entendre. Each show closed with a sped-up chase scene involving Hill and a crew of scantily dressed girls, to the accompaniment of the raunchy saxophone playing of Boots Randolph's great hit – "Yakety Sax."

Benny Hill moved to Teddington to be nearer to Thames Studios. He was a regular at the King's Head where he went for lunches and he willingly posed for photographs and signed autographs despite being essentially a very private person. He could be seen regularly walking around the streets of Teddington usually with a Tescos carrier bag on his arm.

In May 1989 Thames cancelled the Show's contract. Benny Hill announced that after 21 continuous years at Thames, he was taking a year off. During his time there he had made them £100 million with audiences peeking at over 21 million. He continued living normally in Teddington but on 22 April 1992 he was found dead in front of his tv set in his flat at Fairwater House. He had suffered a massive coronary thrombosis and had been dead for 4 days. Ironically in the pile of unopened post was the draft of a new contract with ITV.

Another very popular show was the Dave Allen Show which moved on to Dave Allen At Large and featured the Irish comedian. Apart from some comedy sketches, there was always Allen's signature joke – sitting on a high stool, smoking and holding a glass of whiskey in his other hand, with the lights turned low, telling a ghost story. Apart from all that he also undertook some death defying stunts on the show. One of these was escaping from a Mini car which had been immersed fully in a huge glass tank filled with water.

It looked as if the life of Thames TV would go on for ever. However there was trouble ahead and many ex-employees feel that its closure was the faulty of the Government. In 1988 Thames made a documentary called "Death On The Rock" which reconstructed the shooting a group of IRA bombers by the SAS in Gibraltar. The Thatcher government asked Thames not to broadcast the programme but they went ahead. Thames' franchise fell due for renewal in 1991 and at a silent auction, they lost their bid and their services were no longer required. Could the Government have had an influence on this decision ?

Thames tried to soldier on as an independent maker of films and also hired out the studios to other film makers. Thames was acquired by Pearson Television in 1993 and was moved on in a succession of sales and takeovers to the extent that it lost its identity completely.

Teddington Studios carried on for some years without ever approaching the success of former years, despite being sold to Pinewood Studios who pulled out on 24 December 2014. The premises were then sold to a Hong Kong developer for housing, an ignominious end to one of the most successful film studios.

Last Words

I am often asked "How old is Teddington?"

The reply is the same: "I don't know".

We know of the Bronze Age Barrow, which was about 1,500 B.C. but there are no signs of settlement around that. Saxons settled here and the place was known as "Tudincgatun" at that time, 969 A.D. The remains of a Romano-British farm were found in Udney Park. The Norman invasion passed almost unnoticed and Teddington gets no mention in the Domesday Book. The village prospered and grew and by the time the Railway came in 1863, Teddington had grown into a town.

A town full of character and full of characters. We have seen the population grow from 700 in 1801 to 14,000 in 1901 and this has continued to 30,000+ in the 21st Century. Each generation leaves its mark and many stories to tell. The problem is sometimes finding them. I enjoy digging in the past to unearth such tales and then sharing them with the readers of *Teddington TW11*. I never know from one day to the next what will come to light. That's the great thing about history, it does not have an ending...

Thank you for all of your support over the years and keep your enquiries coming. I won't guarantee to answer all of them, but I'll give it my best shot!

Ken Howe,
September 2020